EVERYTHING
CASINO POKER

EVERYTHING CASINO POKER

Get the Edge at Video Poker, Texas Hold'em, Omaha Hi-Lo, and Pai Gow Poker

Frank Scoblete
with Bill "Ace-10" Burton,
Jerry "Stickman,"
and John "Skinny"

TRIUMPH
B O O K S

Library of Congress Cataloging-in-Publication Data

Scoblete, Frank.
    Everything casino poker : get the edge at video poker, texas hold 'em, omaha hi lo and pai gow poker / by Frank Scoblete.
        p. cm.
    ISBN 978-1-60078-707-2
    1. Poker. 2. Video poker. 3. Gambling. I. Title.
    GV1251.S342 2013
    795.412—dc23
                                2012043192

This book is available in quantity at special discounts for your group or organization. For further information, contact:

Triumph Books LLC
814 North Franklin Street
Chicago, Illinois 60610
(312) 337-0747
www.triumphbooks.com

Printed in U.S.A.
ISBN: 978-1-60078-707-2
Design by Patricia Frey

Images courtesy of Frank Scoblete

From Bill "Ace-10" Burton:
Dedicated to my loving wife, Sandy

From Jerry "Stickman":
Dedicated to my loving wife, Tres

From John "Skinny":
Dedicated to my loving wife, Jean

From Frank Scoblete:
Dedicated to my loving wife, the beautiful AP

(Guys, these dedications will get us some good husband points! —Frank)

Contents

Introduction

Why Shouldn't You Have the Edge?
There are approximately 54 million casino gamblers in the United States alone, plus a few million from Canada as well. How about all those European and Asian tourists who descend on Las Vegas to the tune of several million players per year? I'd guess we are now talking about at least 63 million (plus) casino gamblers happily (or unhappily) playing their favorite games in American casinos. Those numbers would place casino gamblers, if they were a nation, approximately 21st on the population charts for all countries on earth, which number some 242 nations.

Yes, there are more casino gamblers playing in America than most countries have people! That is a staggering fact.

Now to the big question: what percentage of these gamblers are long-term winners? Almost none! In fact, the number of winners probably doesn't equal the population of the Cook Islands, which is country number 225 on the national population list with approximately 17,791 citizens. I'm guessing the long-term winners are half that much, probably closer to Gilligan's Island than the Cook Islands. If I really wanted to go nuts here, I could figure out how many gamblers are on Earth, and we'd probably have competition for the top 10 countries. Hey, move over China! But I've made my point: gamblers abound!

So who are these rare, exotic birds—these long-term winners at casino gambling? Well, occasionally some lucky—and I do mean *lucky*—player nails a monstrous slot jackpot that is so big, he or she never goes back into the red even if they continue to play stupidly. That's it for luck, as luck really doesn't spread itself too far.

Gamblers who rely solely on good luck in the casinos will discover, to their chagrin, that good luck can't help them become long-term winners except in those very, very, very, very (add more *very*s) rare occasions when the slot machine yells to the winner, "Okay, your dream has come true. You're rich," while simultaneously yelling to the other slot players, "Fat chance for you, bub! Keep dreaming."

However, there *are* long-term winners who rely on skill. They are out there right now in casinos all across America doing what all casino players should want to do, and that is get an edge for themselves. Come on, why play casino games if you can't really beat them in the long run?

There are a few thousand card counters in blackjack and even fewer dice controllers at craps. These folks are long-term winners. You also have poker players whose skills are good enough that they make more money than they lose. There are also some video-poker players who win in the long run as well. And how about those little-known Pai Gow Poker players who have figured out just how to turn that game in their favor?

Sounds like a lot of advantage players out there, doesn't it? Sadly, hardly. The numbers of advantage players—even if we combine *all* the advantage players playing all the games that can be beaten by skill—are miniscule. Sad to say, casino gamblers are losers.

If there were such a thing as a predator that hunted losers, just plop those predators in a casino, and they would be able to gorge themselves to their heart's content. Actually, the multibillion-dollar casino industry is just such a predator, even if it seems invisible to the players. The casinos feed on losers, for such folk are the casinos' life blood. Casinos hate even those decidedly few advantage players, and I hope that when you finish reading this book and start putting into play what you have learned in these pages—the casinos will hate you too! You should love to be hated.

Casinos don't want to lose money to skilled players. Sadly, all except a handful of casino players don't seem to care if they lose their money to the casinos. That's unfair, isn't it? A multibillion-dollar industry goes bonkers with the idea that some few players can beat them, while the 21st-largest nation of the world (Casinogamblia) doesn't care if it loses consistently. There is definitely something wrong with that picture and those hapless citizens of Casinogamblia.

I am guessing that since you are reading this book, you have decided to find the best path as a casino player, and that path is the one that allows you to turn the tables (and the machines) on the casinos. I am guessing that you have decided to become a part of the gambling elite—those players who can walk with confidence into casinos knowing they are not relying only on luck to win. You want to hone a skill—a winning skill. Let luck take care of itself, because in the long run it will not take care of you.

This book will show you how to win at many video-poker games, the card-room poker games of Texas Hold'em and Omaha 8 Hi-Lo, and the stepchild of advantage play, Pai Gow Poker. All these games can be beaten, and we will show you exactly how to do it in this book.

Some thoughts before you plunge ahead:

Mathematical Advantage, Monetary Advantage, and Disadvantage

There is no need to go into depth about what a true mathematical advantage is at a game. It means that, in the long run, the statistics work out in your favor. Blackjack card counters, dice controllers at craps, advantage video-poker players, advantage Pai Gow Poker players, and card-room poker players can all establish what their respective edges are and even what their long-term hourly win rate is. They have a clear mathematical edge, period.

But there is also another type of edge, something I call the "monetary edge." Here we take into consideration all the "free" stuff—meaning comps that the casino gives you—and add those to your theoretical long-term losses at the game you are playing to see if more money in the form of goods and services is coming in your direction than going in the casino's direction. Simply put, say your expected loss is $400 for a trip but the casino gives you $600 in comps. You could consider this an advantage play if you wish. You are up $200.

Some of the games in this book will work out as "monetary advantages." Pai Gow can give you a mathematical edge, but by adding in comps, that edge can soar even higher. Some, but not all, video-poker machines mathematically favor the player, but for those that don't give the player such an edge by figuring in comps, the monetary edge can be achieved.

Sadly, with card-room poker the comps are not so hot—especially for low-limit players. The monetary edge is probably not to be had. Still, in both Texas Hold'em and Omaha 8 Hi-Lo, you can get a definite edge, sometimes a *strong* edge, over the other players and win their money. Winning at poker is possible for two reasons:

1. If you know how to play, you will know which hands to play and which hands to fold.
2. Most of the other players stink.

Knowing what you are doing against players who don't know what they are doing or against players who just can't refrain from "gambling" are the keys to success at card-room poker. Play as we say to play in this book, and you are on your way.

Sadly, even on some of the video-poker machines we analyze in this book, no edge—mathematical and/or monetary—can be had. Still, since there are so many video-poker choices to be had in casinos all over the country, we felt it was proper to alert you to the best of the worst, so to speak.

Machines that do not fit into this "best of the worst" category should be avoided like the plague. You'll note that we don't discuss machines with more than a 2 percent house edge or a 98 percent return (two ways of expressing the same thing). Even though you might not have an edge on these machines and even though the comps might not put you into positive monetary realms, between the low house edge and the comps, you will not take much of a beating if you play the correct strategies.

The 401(g) and Fake Money

This concept will be mentioned again (and again) in this book, but here is your first hit with the 401(g) sledgehammer: Do not use "regular" money when you gamble. Use "fake" money. Fake money is real money in terms of playing and buying value, but it is money specifically set aside for your forays into the casinos.

You must (yes, you *must*) set aside playing money. This money is not to be used for anything—even your heart surgery—other than playing.

> **Please Note:** *I prefer in this book to use the term "playing" as opposed to "gambling" because if you have an edge, you will win in the long run.*

Open a checking or money-market account and put your playing money in there. This is your 401(g)—the G stands for *gambling*—and you will only use this money to play with. If you are well-off and can take a chunk of real money and immediately put it into a 401(g), then do so. If you are not yet rolling in the dough, then slowly add money weekly or monthly as you get your paychecks or money from your business. In a short while, you will build up the 401(g) so you can hit the tables and machines.

With an advantage over the casinos, you should find a slow and steady increase in your funds. Yes, you will have losing sessions, days, and trips—all advantage players ride the ups-and-downs roller coaster—but over time you should find your 401(g) increasing, if you are playing correctly, that is.

How much do you need in your 401(g) to begin your career as an advantage player at the games in this book? How about $1,000 for every $1 you wager? If you are playing a $3/6 Texas Hold'em game, why not have $6,000 before you begin your career? If you are a 25¢ video-poker player playing five coins ($1.25 per hand), why not have $1,250? At Pai Gow Poker playing $25 per hand and banking, let's go with $5,000 as an absolute minimum. (Banking will entail a larger short-term risk.)

Is a $1,000-to-$1 ratio a good one? You have to decide that. If you can tolerate the thought of losing your entire 401(g), then you can be somewhat more aggressive. If (like me) you can't tolerate such a catastrophe, then $1,000-to-$1 might be too aggressive; you might want $2,000-to-$1 or more.

Having once lost my entire 401(g) to overbetting in the late 1980s, I will never play with that prospect again. I have made sure that I can't drain the account, even in the worst of years or during a sustained losing streak. I need that sense of permanence in order to play a perfect game against the casino.

How much you keep in your 401(g) is up to you, but having a 401(g) is a necessity.

Keeping Records

Scratch a gambler by asking this question, "Hey, how are you doing in your gambling career?"

The gambler will respond dishonestly by saying, "Oh, I'm about even," which means he is losing. Or he will respond, "I've lost a little," which means he's lost a lot. Or he will respond, "I've lost a lot," which means he could be living in that dumpster in the shopping center. Gamblers are truly unable to see the truth of what they are doing or what is happening to them. Gamblers are—almost without exception—losers trying to pretend they know it all. Come on, they don't know what they are doing, and that's why they are losers!

You may now be thinking to yourself, *How hard are the strategies I am about to learn—or about to* try *to learn? Do I have to work hard at them?* Yes and no. In Pai Gow Poker and video poker, the strategies are fully laid out for you. Just follow what you are being taught. The learning curve is fast and easy—and when I say "easy," I mean it. You can play *advantage* Pai Gow Poker and *advantage* video poker and know almost nothing. So imagine those poor ploppies who are such poor gamblers that they know almost less than nothing.

Playing card-room poker will take more effort. It will involve more on-the-fly decisions. It is a combative environment in a casino card room. You have to beat the other players, and those other players are trying to beat you. There is far more psychology involved in card-room poker—your psychology and your opponents' psychology—so there is a slower learning curve after an initial spurt.

What is the "initial spurt"? If you follow our advice and play only the correct hands in the correct positions, you will improve your skills markedly right off the bat. Still, you then have to take those skills and pit them against other players. You don't have to become the best poker player at your table, but you have to be better than the majority you are playing against. If you follow the advice in this book, you should be better than most of your opponents. That means over time, you will win the money.

So Who Are Bill "Ace-10" Burton, John "Skinny," and Jerry "Stickman"?

The above coauthors of this book are three of the most knowledgeable gambling authorities in the country. Burton is an extremely intelligent poker writer and player. He is an advantage player in craps and video poker. John "Skinny" is known as "the King of Pai Gow Poker," and he too is an advantage player at craps. Jerry "Stickman" is an advantage player in blackjack, craps, advantage slot machines, and video poker.

All three of these fellows are excellent players and excellent researchers; each deserves full credit for their sections of this book. Their sections will be written with their voices, much as I have been the voice of many of my craps books. They are "the man" when it comes to the games they are writing about.

Please Note: *All my coauthors are long-term winning players. They know their stuff and can write about it and teach it.*

So Burton will handle Texas Hold'em and Omaha 8 Hi-Lo; Skinny will handle Pai Gow Poker, and Stickman will handle video poker. Each one of these men has major writing credits to their names. Many of you reading this book have seen their articles and columns in some of the finest gambling magazines and on many of the finest Internet gambling sites in the country.

They deserve high praise, indeed. Now, read on and learn from them!

—Frank Scoblete

PART I: Texas Hold'em

CHAPTER 1

Texas Hold'em

[The voice in this section is Bill "Ace-10" Burton.]

At the turn of the century Texas Hold'em was an obscure game. In most poker rooms around the country, Seven-Card Stud was being played by the majority of poker players. No-Limit Texas Hold'em was being played in major tournaments such as the World Series of Poker, but the average poker player playing kitchen-table poker at home had never heard of the game. Poker rooms back then also had a darker reputation for being full of sharks waiting to gobble up any amateur foolish enough to sit down at a table. The majority of casino players never thought of entering into a casino poker game. All that changed in three years.

The World Poker Tour made its debut on the Travel Channel on Sunday, March 31, 2003. Suddenly poker was taken out of the smoked-filled casino card rooms and transported into the well-lit living rooms of millions of people. The game they were playing was Texas Hold'em, and by utilizing a special hole-card camera, poker became a spectator sport that captured the fancy of the young and old alike. People who had never played a hand of poker before wanted to play Texas Hold'em.

Texas Hold'em is fast paced and easy to learn. The game can be played with more players, which means bigger pots, making it exciting and profitable for those players who make the effort to learn correct play.

The basic concepts of Hold'em are easy to learn and understand. Each player is dealt two personal cards, and then five community cards are dealt faceup in the middle of the table. Since there are five community cards, you do not have to keep track of all the dead cards that were folded by your opponents as you do in Stud. You can easily learn guidelines for which starting hands to play and which to fold.

Please Note: *Hold'em is a positional game.*

1

A dealer button rotates to the left after each hand. The player to the left of the dealer button acts first. Players will always act in the same order for the entire hand. If you have the dealer button, you will act last during each betting round. The later you act, the more information you will have to help decide whether you should enter the pot or fold your hand.

There are no antes. The player to the left of the dealer button puts up a blind bet usually equal to half of the minimum bet for the first round, and the player to his left puts in a bet equal to the minimum bet. These are called "the blinds." The rest of the players do not have to put any money in the pot unless they are calling the blind bet. This means that in a 10-handed game, you will get to see eight hands for free. If you don't have a playable starting hand, you can toss it in and wait for your next hand.

Hold'em is a faster-paced game than Seven-Card Stud. You can play a hand in about two minutes. This means you will see more hands during your playing session. This allows you to be more selective, which should lead to profitability if you capitalize on the poor play of your opponents.

Please Note: *Most poker players are, in fact, poor players.*

The use of five community cards, called "board" cards, means that more players can play. A full game will have 10 or sometimes 11 players. Since many players will enter a hand, there is a potential for bigger pots in Hold'em.

There are a wide variety of hands that can be made from the five community cards and the player's two pocket cards. All of the players are using 71 percent of the same cards to make their hands. This means that there is no way to immediately determine who has the biggest hand. When you are playing Stud, if you saw that your opponents had two aces showing, you could determine if he had you beat and then fold. Since this is not the case in Texas Hold'em, more players will stay in the hand longer, adding to the total size of the pot.

In a low-limit $3/6 game, there could be $30 in the pot before the first community cards are revealed. It is not uncommon to see pots in the $50 to $100 range. In this game, if there were five players entering the pot and staying to the end, making minimum bets with no raising, the pot would be $90. You can afford to be selective in your starting hands because it is possible that winning just one hand can cover the cost of your blind bets for the entire evening.

You always know how the strength of your hand stacks up against the best possible hand during each betting round. A pair of aces is the best two-card starting hand. This probably changes once the first three community cards are flopped and again when the fourth and then the fifth cards are turned over.

You can tell the best possible hand by looking at the board cards. Although it is not certain that one of your opponents will actually have the best hand, you can assess the strength of your hand in relation to the best *theoretical hand* and determine if you have a chance of winning the pot. This is known as "reading the board" and will be discussed in detail later in this book.

The most compelling reason to play Texas Hold'em is that you are choosing a game that can be profitable for a player who takes the time to learn how to make the correct decisions. It's that simple.

Know Your Limits

There are several variations of Texas Hold'em, and they are determined by the betting structure. Limit and no-limit games are the two most popular, but you can also find the game played with pot limits and spread limits. These betting structures are also used in Omaha, Seven-Card Stud, or any other type of poker. These can be a little confusing if you have never played them before. Here is a look at the difference between the games:

Fixed Limit

Fixed-limit games have structured betting limits for each round, with a minimum and maximum bet. You cannot vary your bet from the amount of the structure, and you must bet in multiples of the amount for the limit you are playing. The limits vary with the round of play. In Hold'em and Omaha, the amount of the blinds is based on the limit of the game. Let's look at a typical $4/8 fixed-limit game.

The $4 denotes the betting limits for the first two betting rounds. The big blind would be $4, and the small blind, which is half of the big blind, would be $2. During the betting for the pre-flop and flop betting rounds, the players must bet and raise in multiples of $4. After the flop the betting limits are increased to $8, and all bets and raises must be in multiples of $8. In most casinos the lowest-limit Texas Hold'em game you can find will be $2/4, but the limits can go up to any amount.

Limit Hold'em and Omaha games are listed with the numbers reflecting the amount of the big blind and the amount of the bet after the turn, such as $4/8, $5/10, $10/20, etc.

Spread Limit

Spread-limit games are similar to fixed-limit games, except that the players are allowed to bet within a range. Spread-limit games are most common in Stud games but have been used in Texas Hold'em. You may see a game listed as $2–$10, which means that players can bet any amount within that range at any time. The lowest number represents the amount of the big blind. Spread-Limit Texas Hold'em games are not very common these days. However in many Seven-Card Stud games, you have a spread betting structure.

No Limit

In no-limit games you can bet any amount at any time. This format is the most popular for tournaments; however with the demand for no-limit cash games, many casinos are offering more of them.

When the betting structures of no-limit games are listed, the figures usually represent the amount of the small blind and the amount of the big blind. For example a $5/10 no-limit game means the small blind is $5 and the big blind is $10.

No-Limit Texas Hold'em is, of course, the most popular no-limit game in the card room, but any other poker games can be played using this format as well.

Pot Limit

Pot-limit games are similar to no-limit games in that there is no fixed betting amount. However, the size of your bet cannot exceed the size of the pot. For example, if there is $400 in the pot, your bet cannot exceed $400.

In most games, before the flop they treat the little blind as if it were the same size as the big blind in computing pot size. A player can open for a maximum of four times the size of the big blind. For example, if the blinds are $5 and $10, a player may open with a raise to $40. (The range of options is to either open with a call of $10 or a raise in increments of $5 to any amount from $20 to $40.) Subsequent players also treat the $5 as if it were $10 in computing the pot size, until the big blind is through acting on the first betting round. The betting structures of pot-limit games are listed the same way as no-limit games, with the denomination being the amount of the small and big blinds.

No-Limit Texas Hold'em is very popular for tournaments, but Limit Texas Hold'em is the structure many players prefer to play for a cash game. When you start to play Texas Hold'em, you will want to start playing in the low-limit games, which is what will be described in this book.

As you master the game, you can move up to higher limits or even no limit if you wish, but while you are learning, you will want to limit your risk. Mastering Low-Limit Texas Hold'em can afford you the opportunity to win money on a consistent basis. If you follow these guidelines, you will know more about playing the game than most of the other players at the table. Many of your opponents in low-limit games will be at the table for the action and the entertainment of playing casino poker; you will be there to win money—*their money!*

CHAPTER 2

How to Play Texas Hold'em

The rules of the game are fairly easy to learn. Limit Hold'em has structured betting, and the lowest limit you will find in most casinos is a $2/4 or $3/6 game. Other limits you may find are $5/10, $10/20, or higher. I will be using the $3/6 game as an example in this book. That means the minimum bet is $3 during the first two rounds of betting and the minimum bet is $6 during the last two betting rounds. These same limits are used when you raise as well.

The Dealer

Since the casino supplies a dealer, one player must be the "designated dealer" who will act last during the betting rounds. A disk or "button" is used to identify the dealer, and this is rotated to the left after each hand. Unlike Stud, all the players do not ante each round. Blind bets are posted to generate a starting pot.

The Start

To start a new hand two "blind" bets are put up or "posted." The player immediately to the left of the player with the dealer button puts up or "posts" the small blind, which is approximately half the minimum bet. Since there are no 50¢ chips, the small blind for the $3/6 game is $1. The player to the left of the small blind posts the big blind, which is equal to the minimum bet—$3 for this game. The rest of the players do not put up any money to start the hand. Because the button rotates around the table, each player will eventually act as the big blind, small blind, and designated dealer. It will cost each player $4 every time the deal makes a complete rotation around the table.

The Opening

After the blinds are posted each player is dealt two cards facedown with the player on the small blind receiving the first card and the player with the dealer button getting the last card.

The first betting round begins with the player to the left of the big blind putting in $3 to "call" the blind bet, putting in $6 to "raise" the big blind, or folding his hand.

The betting goes around the table in order until it reaches the player who posted the small blind. That player can call the bet by putting in $2 since a $1 bet was already posted. The last person to act is the big blind. If no one has raised, the dealer will ask if they would like the option. This means the big blind has the option to raise or just "check."

By checking, the player does not put in any more money. A rookie mistake sometimes occurs here. Because the blind is a live bet, the player with the big blind has already put his bet in. I have seen some players throw their cards in, not realizing that they are already in the hand. Another rookie mistake is betting or folding your cards when it is not your turn. You must wait your turn before you act.

The Flop

After the first betting round is completed, the dealer will "burn" or discard the top card on the deck. This is done to make sure no one could have accidentally seen the top card. Three cards are dealt and turned faceup in the middle of the table. This is known as the "flop." These are community cards used by all the players. Another betting round begins with the first active player to the left of the designated dealer button. The minimum bet for this round is also $3.

The Turn

When the betting round after the flop is completed, the dealer burns another card and turns a fourth card faceup in the middle of the table. This is referred to as the "turn." The minimum bet after the turn is now $6 and begins again with the first active player to the left of the button.

The River

Following the betting round for the turn, the dealer will burn another card and turn a fifth and final card faceup. This is called the "river," and the final betting round begins with $6 being the minimum bet. There is usually a three- or four-raise maximum during all betting rounds, except if the play becomes heads-up with two players. Then the raises are unlimited.

The Showdown

To determine the winner, the players may use any combination of their two hole cards (either one or both) and the five cards on the board to form the highest five-card hand. In some rare cases, the best hand will be the five cards on board. In that case the active players will split the pot. A sixth card is never used to break a tie.

Additional Information

The five community cards are referred to as the "board." Unlike Seven-Card Stud, all the players use the same board cards. Because of this you don't have to remember cards that were folded by other players.

Although the game looks deceptively simple, there is a lot of strategy involved. Your position in relation to the designated dealer button is important in deciding which beginning hands you play. It is also important to learn how to read the board to determine the best possible hand.

> **Please Note:** *In Texas Hold'em you must learn the three Ps—Position, Power, and Patience.*

You need to be aware of your position when deciding which starting hands to play. You want to play powerful starting hands for that position, and you need the patience to wait for these hands. These will all be covered in the following chapters.

But first let's look at the hierarchy of poker hands:

Hierarchy of Poker Hands

Royal Flush: This is the best poker hand. Ten (T), Jack (J), Queen (Q), King (K), and Ace (A) of the same suit.

Straight Flush: Five cards of the same suit that are in sequence.

Four of a Kind: Four cards of equal rank, such as Qc, Qh, Qd, Qs.

Full House: Three cards of equal rank and two other cards of equal rank (three of a kind and a pair), such as 8, 8, 8, 5, 5.

Flush: Any five cards of the same suit, such as As, Ts, 9s, 7s, 5s.

Straight: Five cards of mixed suits in sequence.

Three of a Kind: Any three cards of equal rank.

Two Pair: Two cards of equal rank and two other cards of equal rank.

One Pair: Two cards of equal rank.

CHAPTER 3

Position

One of the most vital aspects of Texas Hold'em is position, and one of the biggest mistakes that novice players make is ignoring their position at the start of each hand. Position ranks second only to starting cards in deciding whether or not to play your hand. Understanding position is an important concept if you want to be a winning player.

Your position is determined by where you are sitting in relation to the designated dealer's button. Unlike games such as Stud, where the betting order changes with each betting round, the order is fixed in Texas Hold'em. Before the flop the person to the left of the big blind bets first. After the flop the first active player to the left of the dealer button acts first. If you are in early position, you will remain there for all betting rounds.

If you play a weak or marginal hand in early position before the flop, you are at risk of getting raised by those acting after you. There is also a possibility of multiple raises. If you decide to fold, you have cost yourself a bet without ever seeing any other cards.

Before you make a bet in early position, you have to ask yourself if the hand is strong enough to call a raise from a player in a later position. If you would not call a raise with your starting hand, you should throw it away. Some hands are drawing hands that play better with many opponents calling the pot. If you have to act first, you have no idea how many players will call or fold.

When you are in the late position you will have an idea of the strength of your opponents' hands by how they bet. If there have been no raises, you can play weaker starting hands and hope that the flop will fit your hand. If there have been no callers and you are last to act, you can sometimes steal the blind merely by raising with a marginal hand because of your position. You will hear players refer to this play as a "positional raise."

In late position after the flop, you have more information to help you decide how to play. You can raise if your opponents bet, or you can bet if everyone has checked. You may decide to check to gain a free card. If there have been bets or raises before you, and your hand was not helped by the flop, you can fold without it costing you an additional bet.

In early position you do not have this luxury after the flop. If you bet, there is the chance that you will be raised. If you check in the hopes of "check-raising," there is a chance that everyone else will check and you will lose some potential money that would have gone into the pot.

The chart below shows a quick reference to the positions in a 10-person game. If there were fewer players in the game, you would adjust this.

Table Position in a 10-Player Game

1	Small Blind	Early Position. Under the gun after the flop
2	Big Blind	Early Position. Has the option of checking on first round before the flop
3	Under the Gun	Early Position. Acts first before the flop
4	Early	Second person to act before the flop
5	Early/Middle	Third person to act before the flop. Middle after the flop
6	Middle	Can play a few more starting hands if no raises
7	Middle	Can play a few more starting hands if no raises
8	Middle/Late	May be considered middle in aggressive game
9	Late/ Cut off	Second-to-last after the flop
10	Dealer	"On the button." Acts last after the flop

The person on the button gets to act last, except during the first betting round, which starts with the first player to the left of the big blind. A player acting first is referred to as being "under the gun." After the flop, the player posting the small blind is under the gun if they are still in the hand. The dealer button rotates after each hand, so your position changes after each hand is completed.

As a player it is important to be conscious of your position for each hand. Players are making a big mistake if they play weak or marginal hands without giving consideration to their position.

Please Note: *There are only about 20 hands that are strong enough to play from an early position.*

CHAPTER 4

Starting Hands

The most important decision a player will make in Texas Hold'em is which starting hands to play. There are 169 possible two-card starting hands. Hands of equal rank but different suits are counted as one because they have the same value before the flop. For instance an ace and king of hearts has the same value as the ace and king of spades, clubs, or diamonds.

Out of these 169 hands there are only about 75 that are playable. Which of these 75 you play will be determined by your position relative to the dealer button. Not all of these hands can be played from every position. Cards of the same suit are more powerful than unsuited cards because of their flush potential. Strong starting hands, such as big pairs, have a better chance of holding up to make the winning hand than smaller cards.

Please Note: *Most players lose because they play too many hands.*

The combination of starting hands will fall into four categories. Actually you could further simplify this by noting that there are two categories: big-card hands that will win in a small field without improvement and drawing hands that need help

Pocket Pairs
Big pairs are powerful starting hands. A pair of aces is the best starting hand, but a pair of deuces is a weak hand that can only be played in late position in an unraised pot. Some medium pairs can win the pot, but with the smaller pairs, you will be looking to make a set or possibly a straight draw.

Connectors
Cards that are next to each other are called "connectors." They can be suited or unsuited. These are hands such as K-Q, J-10, or 9-8. Connectors are used in making straights. Suited connectors can make straight flushes, straights, or flushes.

Gapped Cards

Gappers are cards that have one or more gaps between them. These are cards such as Q-10, J-9 or T-8. The smaller the gap, the easier it is to make a straight. With a hand that has a gap, you are looking to fill an inside straight or possibly a flush, if they are suited. As with the connectors, the suited cards have more potential.

Big Cards

Cards of higher value than 10 are considered big cards. Suited cards are more valuable than unsuited cards. These hands still fall into the categories of connectors or gapped hands; however, because of their higher value, they can sometimes stand on their own if you pair them up on the flop. You should tighten your starting requirements if your cards are not suited and there are a lot of players in the pot. *Big cards play better against fewer players.*

Again, a pair of aces is the strongest starting hand before the flop. With only two cards, there is nothing higher. But aces do not always stand up as the winning hand after the flop. The weakest starting hand is an unsuited seven and deuce. There are five gaps between the two cards, making a straight impossible. Because they are not suited, you cannot make a flush either.

Many players in low-limit games will play any ace regardless of the second card. Many players have found themselves a loser when an ace flops and they are beat out by a player with a bigger kicker. A kicker is an unpaired card in your hand that will determine the winner in the event of a tie. Example: If the winning hand were a pair of aces and you held A-K and your opponent held A-J, your king would beat his jack. In this example the king and jack are the kickers.

Some players will just play any two cards. They are looking for miracle flops to improve their hands. Although it is possible to get a miracle flop, more often than not you *won't* get it.

> **Please Note:** *To be a consistent winner, a player needs to learn the correct starting hands.*

The Hold'em Arrow

When I started playing Texas Hold'em there were only a handful of books written about the game. David Sklansky was the first to publish a table of the starting hands in his book *Hold'em Poker* in 1976. The table ranked the starting hands and gave an explanation as to the proper position from which to play them. This list of starting hands has become more or less the standard for knowledgeable players. There are some hands that can be played differently depending on the number of players, the type of the game, and whether or not the pot was raised before your turn to act. A player will need to tighten up or loosen these guidelines accordingly.

As I studied the table of starting hands, I thought a graphic representation would be easier to understand. I started to draw out some ideas on graph paper. I wanted a design that would help me understand the hands in relation to the dealer button.

I started drawing out different configurations of the starting hands and finally thought of a linear design. I drew a dealer button on the right side of the sheet. I then started drawing the pairs on the line next to the button. Since the player to the left of the dealer acts first, I put the pair of aces to the immediate left with the rest of the pairs in descending order with the deuces being the furthest hand on the dealer's left side. The hands closest to the dealer's left would be the early position hands. Since a table is circular, as you get closer to the right side of the dealer button, you will be in later position. These are the hands toward the left side of the sheet.

I proceeded to fill in the other starting hands. I placed the suited cards on the top of the line of pairs and placed the unsuited hands underneath. When I finished I noticed that the chart looked like an arrow. It also showed how the number of starting hands increased in the later positions. I found

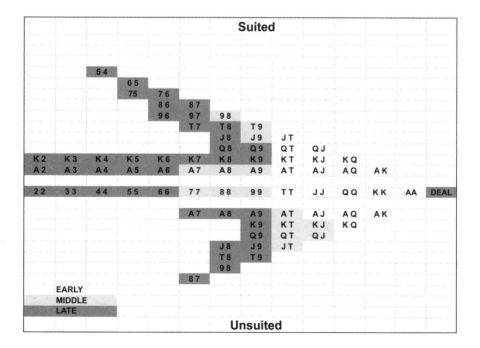

this chart helped me visualize the hands in the order I was looking for. I color-coded the hands for early, middle, and late positions.

These positions are not written in stone and can be adjusted for the type of game I am playing in. For example, in a very loose, passive game I might consider playing the pair of 9s or 8s in early position instead of the middle position. In an aggressive game, the suited queen-10 may move to middle position.

CHAPTER 5

Suited Cards

The biggest mistake novice players make is playing any two suited cards from any position in hopes of making a flush. It doesn't matter to them if the cards have too many gaps to form a straight or has no potential to win if they make a pair. I have seen players call the pot from early position with a hand such as a 4S and 8S.

Making a Flush

In order to play winning poker you have to know about odds and probability. Let's take a look at a few cold facts concerning the realities of a flush draw.

Being dealt two suited cards as a starting hand is a fairly common occurrence. The probability of being dealt this hand is about 23.5 percent. This means there will be a lot of opportunity for those players who will play a hand containing any two suited cards. Making a flush with this hand is a lot more difficult than most players realize.

The Flop

The probability of flopping three of your suit, thereby giving you a complete flush, is 0.842 percent. The odds against you are 118-to-1.

The probability of flopping two of your suit for a four flush is 10.944 percent. The odds are 8-to-1 against you.

The probability of only flopping one of your suit is 41.6 percent. The odds are 1.4-to-1 against you.

The Turn

If you have a four flush after the flop, the probability of making a flush on the turn or river is 34.97 percent. The odds against you are 1.86-to-1.

The River

If you have a four flush after the turn, the probability of making a flush on the river is 19.6 percent. The odds against you are 4.1-to-1.

Turn and River Runner

If you flop only one of your suit, the probability of hitting your suit on the turn and the river is 1.7 percent. The odds against you are 55-to-1.

Finally for all the possibilities if you start suited and stay to see all seven cards (your two and the five board cards), the probability that you will make a flush is 5.77 percent. The odds against you are 16.3-to-1.

Simply put, for every time you play two suited cards, you will only make your flush about once in 16 tries. If you play low suited cards, you still have to worry about a bigger flush beating you. There is also the likelihood that you could be "counterfeited."

In poker, your hand is counterfeited when a card falls on the board that lessens the value of your hand. This happens when you play two suited cards and four suited cards are on the board. Suppose you play the 3 and 8 of spades in the hand mentioned above.

- You make a flush on the flop with the 10, 7, and 2 of spades
- The turn is the jack of hearts
- The river is the four of spades

Your flush has been counterfeited if anyone has a spade higher than your 8 in the hole. With three low cards on the flop, it is likely that someone holding two "overcards" may have stayed in the hand. A player holding the ace of spades and jack may have called a bet on the turn with the top pair and then made the nut flush with four spades on the board.

A Costly Mistake

When you start with two suited cards you will flop two or more of that suit only about 11 percent of the time. That means you are an 8-to-1 underdog before the flop. You will flop a complete flush only 0.84 percent of the time. The odds are 118-to-1 against this happening.

If you start suited and stay through the river card, you will make a flush about 5.77 percent of the time. That means that about 94 percent of the time when you start suited, you will not make your flush if you stay to the river card. This type of hand will cost you a lot of money if you consistently play it without regard to the value of the suited cards.

Assume you are playing in a $3/6 game where the pot is never raised. It will cost you $3 each for the pre-flop and flop and $6 on the turn for a total of $12 to see the river card. You play this hand 100 times. You will win six times and lose 94 times. It will cost you $1,128 to play this hand 94 times. To break even you would have to win an average of $188 dollars each of the six times that you did win, which will not happen in a limit game.

This is an overly simplistic example, because there are plenty of other hands that could be made from two starting cards. I just want to point out that because your two starting cards are suited doesn't necessarily mean that you should play any two suited cards from any position.

Many players lose with this type of hand and then try to justify playing it by pointing out that the cards were suited. In reality, just being suited is the wrong reason to play these types of hands. Sometimes a player will beat you when they do make the occasional flush with this type of hand. If this happens don't get upset, because you can be confident that you will win more money from this type of player in the long run.

The players who play their hands incorrectly are the players you win money from.

CHAPTER 6
Any Ace Won't Do

In the last chapter, I wrote that the biggest mistake that losing Texas Hold'em players make is to play any two suited cards from any position. The second-biggest mistake is playing a single ace from any position. In my logbook I put the acronym SAP for this type of player, and that is what many of them end up being when they play a single ace—saps.

Pocket aces just about play themselves. You can play them from any position. There is not much thought involved, as the only decision you have to make pre-flop is whether or not to raise. However, playing single aces needs a little more thought.

In Texas Hold'em, a single ace is not as powerful as some players would like to think. Many players look down and see a single ace in one of their starting hands and get all excited. They think they have found a winning lottery ticket that they need only to bet to cash in. This is partly due to the fact that you will only have an ace in your starting hand about 15 percent of the time. But a single ace is not as strong as some players think it is.

Please Note: *You can't play a single ace with a low kicker from any position if you want to be a winning player, especially if it is unsuited.*

Everyone loves to see aces in their stating hands. You will be dealt at least one ace about 15 percent of the time before the flop, which means that 85 percent of the time you won't have an ace. Maybe that is the reason that some players get so excited when they see an ace.

The chances of one of your opponents holding an ace at the same time you do is directly related to the number of players in the game with you. This chart shows the *absence* of aces before the flop based on the number of players. The figures in the chart are expressed in percentages.

Number of Players	Probability that no player has an ace (including yourself)	If you have an ace, the probability that no other player has an ace.	If you have NO ace, the probability that no other player has an ace.
2	71.87	88.24	84.49
3	60.28	77.45	70.86
4	50.14	67.57	58.95
5	41.34	58.57	48.60
6	33.76	50.41	39.68
7	27.27	43.04	32.05
8	21.76	36.43	25.58
9	17.13	30.53	20.14
10	13.28	25.31	15.61

If you are playing at a full table with 10 players and hold a single ace, the probability that there is no other player also holding an ace is 25.31 percent. That means that when you have an ace, one of the nine other players will have an ace about 75 percent of the time. This is why you need to consider your kicker to go with that single ace.

Playing an ace with a small kicker is referred to as playing a "weak ace." When you do this, you are setting yourself up to be beaten by a player who holds an ace with a higher kicker. If you hold the ace of diamonds and five of clubs and the flop is the ace of spades, 10 of hearts, and 8 of diamonds, if one of your opponents holds an ace, your chances of winning with your five as a kicker are very slim.

Your opponent would have to hold a four, three, or deuce in order for you to win. There are only 12 cards that he could hold that would make you a winner, and along with three other fives that would make a tie. If your opponent held any other card, you would be beaten if it went to the river with no improvements to either hand.

Also, you have to consider that you are just as likely to pair your kicker instead of the ace. In the above example, if you paired your 5, you would have a small pair with an ace kicker. However, if you played your single ace with a bigger card there would be situations where you would almost rather pair your kicker than your ace. If you hold the ace of clubs and queen of hearts and the flop is the queen of spades, 8 of clubs, and 5 of hearts, you now have the top pair with the best kicker.

Anyone else holding a queen is sure to give you action with this flop. You might also get action from players holding the single ace who are looking for an ace to appear on the turn or river. If this happens you will still have them beat with two pairs.

"Suited" Aces

Suited aces play well against a large field. In late position in an unraised pot you can play a suited ace because of its flush potential. If you do make a flush, you will have the nut flush, but you have to remember that you will only make a flush about 5.77 percent of the time when you start suited. This is why you want to play your suited ace in a hand with many players. Playing a suited ace with a small kicker from early position is not advisable.

If you are in a game and notice that many of the players are playing a single ace, then you have the opportunity to make some money from them if you only play an ace with a strong kicker. Many players will refuse to fold a pair of aces even if they have a weak kicker. These players will call you all the way to the river, only to be beaten by your strong kicker.

When there are five or more players in the hand, a pair of aces will only hold up about 35 percent of the time. A single ace will win even less often, but still many players will stay in the hand with a single ace and call all the way to the river. If you want to be a winning player you will avoid playing an unsuited weak ace from any position.

Please Note: *Don't be a SAP! Learn to throw away those single aces when you are out of position. You will see a big improvement in your game and your wallet.*

CHAPTER 7

Early Position

I can't stress enough that Texas Hold'em is a *positional* game. When you are in early position you need a strong hand to enter the pot. You have no idea what the players who follow you will do. It is extremely costly to enter the pot with marginal cards only to be raised or reraised. This is where the category of big cards definitely comes into play, but not all big cards can be played in early position. When you are in early position, you want to play a hand that can hopefully stand up to a raise. This is especially true if you are under the gun as the first player to act.

When I am under the gun, I will limit my play to big pairs or an ace with a jack or higher. In a very passive game, I may loosen up just a bit, but it is usually better to play tight when you are under the gun. Here are some of the other hands playable from early or any position.

Pair of Aces

Pocket Rockets, Bullets, American Airlines—no matter what you call them, a pair of aces by any other name is still the best starting hand you can have. If this were two-card showdown, you would be a winner every time. But this is Hold'em, and you still have a ways to go before you rake in the chips. With aces, your hand will hold up against one or two players most of the time but will win about 35 percent of the time with five or more players in the pot. Getting your pair of aces beaten is known as getting your aces "cracked." It happens and is a fact of the game. Because of this, you want to thin the field if possible, but you also want to get as much money in the pot for the times that your hand does win.

> **Please Note:** *It's okay to raise from any position with aces.*

When you raise from early position, you will have a good shot at thinning the field. Players with marginal drawing hands will probably fold.

But there are some considerations on how to maximize the money in the pot without giving your opponents the proper odds to draw out on you. Most players will not fold their hand to a raise once they have entered the pot. In middle position you want to raise to drive out any of the players acting after you who might hold marginal hands while getting more money from those already in the pot. If the pot has already been raised when it gets to you, go ahead and reraise. It's okay to cap the betting if you get reraised again. Most of the time you will raise with aces, but sometimes you may want to mix up your style of play.

In late position if most of the players have entered the pot you may want to just call when you are in the blinds with a pair of aces. When you raise from the blind, you are letting everyone know that you have a strong hand. Sometimes you may be better off using a little deception. By not raising you can see the flop and either bet in hopes of being raised or slow-play the hand and go for a check-raise if the flop hits you.

After the flop you must look at the board carefully. If the flop brings all little cards, your aces may still be the best hand. If there has been a lot of action before the flop and the flop brings a king or two or more face cards, you might have a problem. If one of your opponents was raising with a pair of kings, they now have a set. If they were holding two face cards, they could have flopped two pairs. If you bet and are raised you will have to proceed with caution.

Pair of Kings

When I first started playing Hold'em, I heard some players refer to "paint" cards and had no idea what they were talking about. I soon found out that paint cards were the cards that I called "picture" cards, with the picture of the king, queen, or jack. I suppose they do resemble paintings more than they do pictures. Anyway the king is the big paint card, and when you start with a pair of them, you have the second-best starting hand. Only a pair of aces can beat you at this point.

The probability of being dealt any pair is 220-to-1 (0.45 percent) or less than one-half of a percent, so the probability of one of your opponents holding a pair of aces when you are dealt a pair of kings is slim, although obviously it does happen. However the probability of a player holding a single ace before the flop is about 15 percent. If an ace appears in the flop, you could lose out to a player who will play any ace. Because of this you want to play the kings as aggressively as possible.

Please Note: *It is advisable to raise with a pair of kings from any position.*

If the pot has been raised, go ahead and reraise. Cap the betting if you can. If no ace appears on the flop, go ahead and raise again. You want to make it very expensive for anyone holding a single ace to stay in the pot.

Some players try to get fancy and slow-play their kings in hopes of maybe raising on the turn or river, when the betting limits go up. This will backfire on you when an ace shows up on the turn or the river and you lose to a player holding a hand like A-6 off suit.

> **Please Note:** *You should never slow-play a single pair, as they are too vulnerable in a multiway pot.*

If an ace or two high cards—such as J-10 or higher—should flop, you could be in trouble if someone raises. If there is a raise when an ace flops, it's more than likely that someone was playing a single ace. However, because it is correct strategy to play high cards in your starting hands, a flop containing two or three high cards may give your opponent two pairs, a straight, or a straight draw. You shouldn't automatically fold when there is betting, but you do need to reassess the situation if there is a raise going on.

Many players get married to a pair of kings (will not fold) when the flop brings two or more high cards. The reasoning is that it is possible to draw another king on the turn or river. This may hold up against two pairs, but you might find that you are drawing dead against a straight. Because being dealt a pair of kings doesn't happen that often, it's natural to want to play them to the end. However, there are times when you just have to let it go and fold the big guys. A winning player is one who can do this.

Pairs of Queens or Jacks

Queens and jacks are the "baby paint" cards. Obviously queens are a little stronger than jacks, but both of these are vulnerable to the single aces and kings that many low-limit players will play if an overcard shows up on the flop. (An overcard is any card higher than the ones you hold.)

Pocket queens are the third-most-powerful starting hand; however, strong starting hands do not necessarily win the pot.

In most games, from *any* position, you definitely want to raise to thin the field. The only exception is in very low-limit games where the table consists of very loose players and calling stations. In late position with six or more players, you may only want to call with this hand as, you only have about a 20 percent chance of winning. You will have to pay attention to your opponents' play. I have probably saved more money by not raising pre-flop with these hands in most low-limit games.

A pair of jacks is a hand that looks good but can be beaten often, especially in low-limit games, because many players in low-limit games will play any aces or kings, and your jacks are susceptible to overcards on the flop. You should raise with them from early position to try to narrow the field. However, in late position depending on the number of players, you might just want to call. In a no-limit game you can raise enough to drive other people out, but in a limit game you will just be making the pot odds bigger giving everyone the correct odds to make the call.

If you hold pocket jacks, the odds of a higher card coming on the flop is 59 percent.

If you see an overcard on the flop, you shouldn't hesitate to bet the hand, but be wary if there is a raise. The problem with starting with a pair of jacks is that you usually need to flop a set or a straight or straight draw to improve your hand, as you are vulnerable if there are overcards on the flop.

If you see an overcard on the flop you shouldn't hesitate to bet the hand, but be wary if there is a raise. If no card higher than your queen or jack appears on the flop, you should raise with the top pair if a player ahead of you bets. You want to make it expensive for anyone who might be holding a single ace or king. If you should happen to flop a set of queens or jacks, then you might want to just call if there is a bet and then go for a raise on the turn when the betting limits are higher.

Pair of 10s

Tens are actually the start of the medium pairs. Since most players will play any face cards, they can easily be beaten if any overcards appear on the flop. Pocket 10s can be played in early position in loose, passive games, but you might want to pass if the game is very aggressive.

> **Please Note:** *Since all straights require the use of a 10 or a 5, holding 10s does have an advantage if the flop brings cards that may need a 10 to complete a straight draw.*

Since you have two of them, it is unlikely that another player will have the other ones. If the flop brings all low cards, making your 10s the top pair, you should raise if anyone bets before you after the flop. You need to make it expensive for anyone holding overcards to stay in the pot. If the flop contains aces or faces, you will probably be best to fold your 10s if you have no other outs, such as a straight draw.

One Ace–One King

The combination of ace-king is sometimes referred to as "Big Slick." Most experts agree that A-K, either suited or unsuited, is one of the most mis-played hands in Limit Hold'em.

An ace and a king are two of the best cards you can hold when they are paired, but when you have a single of each, you have a drawing hand. You need to improve this hand to give it any value. Many players will play A-K as though they were holding a pair of aces or kings. If you do pair one of your cards on the flop, you will have the top pair and top kicker. You will flop an ace or a king about 30 percent of the time. Many players look at that statistic and think it's a high percentage, but look at the other side and you will realize that you *won't* flop either an ace or king 70 percent of the time. This figure is the same for any two unpaired cards you hold before the flop.

In early position, you should raise with A-K suited and call with an unsuited combination. The suited cards will give you the potential of having the nut flush if you make a flush. If you feel that raising will limit the field, then you can raise with A-K unsuited as well. If the pot is raised ahead of you, reraise with A-K suited and with A-K if you think it will limit the field.

If the flop does not help you out and there is a bet and a raise, your two overcards will not have much value. I have seen players play A-K all the way to the river when there is betting and raising going on. If there are several players in the hand, you are probably going to be drawing dead if you do pair your ace or king.

> **Please Note:** *Players who refuse to abandon A-K and play it to the end in hopes a catching a pair on the river lose more money by doing so.*

Ace with Queen or Ace with Jack

An ace with a queen or of an ace with a jack is a playable hand from early position. You have a strong kicker if there is an ace on the flop, or you will have a big pair with the best kicker if a queen or a jack should flop. When these cards are suited you will have the added potential for making a flush. If, however, the pot is raised ahead of you and you have an unsuited A-J, you may be in for trouble since a player raising from early position may have a big pair. You have to consider who is doing the raising.

Ace with 10

In blackjack, A-10 is the best hand, but in Texas Hold'em it's not as strong as some players would like to believe. From early position an A-10 suited is playable, but the unsuited A-10 is a middle-position hand. Although a 10 is considered a big card, it is not extremely powerful, as many players will be holding face cards.

Big Connectors and Gappers

From early position, a hand of K-Q is the only other unsuited connector to play. You can play suited connectors K-Qs, Q-Js, and J-10s. You can also play suited gappers K-Js, K-10s, and Q-10s. With these hands you can flop the nut straight or a large flush. If the pot has been raised, you would be best to forgo these smaller gapped hands.

> **Please Note:** *In this book a small letter S next to a pair of cards signifies that they are the same suit.*

Remember when you are in early position and the player under the gun or another player raises, it usually means that they have a powerful hand. If the raise comes from a solid player it would be best to err on the side of caution and throw away some of the lower hands. Just because a hand is considered playable from early position, it does not mean you will play it in all types of games. A hand that you would play in a loose, passive game may be unplayable in a tight, aggressive game.

For early position here is a quick reference:
Raise and reraise with a pair of aces and kings and with A-K suited. If you are in a tight game and think it will narrow the field, or you are the first to act in late position, you can raise with A-K and also a pair of queens or jacks.

Hand	Call or Raise	If Raised
A-A	Raise	Reraise
K-K	Raise	Reraise
A-Ks	Raise	Reraise
Q-Q	Raise—Narrow Field/Late	Call
J-J	Raise—Narrow Field/Late	Call
10-10	Call	Call
A-Q	Call	Call
A-Js	Call	Call
A-10s	Call	Call
K-Qs	Call	Call

Hand	Call or Raise	If Raised
K-Js	Call	Call
K-10s	Call	Call
Q-10s	Call	Call
Q-Js	Call	Call
J-10s	Call	Call
A-K	Raise—Narrow Field/Late	Call
A-Q	Call	Call
A-J	Call	Call
K-Q	Call	Call

s denotes that the cards are suited.

Please Note: *Fold everything else.*

CHAPTER 8
Middle Position

In middle position you can obviously play all the early position hands. The additional hands that are playable in middle position are drawing hands. They are not likely to win a pot without some sort of improvement. You also can play a few more hands because you will have more information about your situation.

If a player in early position raises, you know there is a potentially strong hand in front of you, and you will need to tighten up your starting requirements. If there has been a reraise, you may want to bail out altogether.

In middle position you can also start to judge how many players will be active in the hand. If everyone has called when it gets to you, then you know you will have a multiway pot. In a 10-handed game, middle position is the player in the five, six, and seven seat after the dealer button. Players one and two are the blinds, so if you are the number five player, there are only two players acting before you before the flop. If there is a raise in front of you, it will usually mean you are up against a big hand.

Anytime you call from middle position, you are adding to the pot odds making it appropriate for callers with weaker hands to enter the pot. Calling a raise will add additional money to the pot and may entice even more players to enter because of the size of the pot. You will be getting better pot odds, but you will be up against more players, decreasing your chances of winning.

Medium Pairs

Pocket 9s, 8s, and 7s are considered medium pairs. They are not the strongest pairs you can start with, and they require you to play them a little selectively. You have to be extremely careful when the flop brings overcards.

You will usually need to improve these pairs on the flop to have them hold up. When you start with a medium or small pocket pair, your chances for improving is a little more limited. You will need to flop a set in most cases for a winning hand. If the pot has been raised before it is your turn to act, you should probably pass on these medium pairs.

I tend to play conservatively before the flop and will fold this hand if it is raised. If you routinely play this hand, calling two or more bets, then you will lose more in the long run. With these pairs, if you don't flop a set or straight draw, you will have to release them if the flop contains overcards and there is a bet. One or more overcards will flop more than 90 percent of the time.

Suited Ace

Ace with a suited 9, 8, or 7 can be added to your stating hands in this position. You are looking to make the nut flush or are hoping for aces up. If there is an ace on the flop and you get action, you might find yourself up against a higher kicker. You don't want to play this hand heads-up against a player who has raised. You are not getting proper odds for your flush draw, and you will end up losing more in the long run.

Big Cards

Unsuited big cards—10s through kings—join the list of middle-position hands. Although these are big cards if you play them against a few players and flop one pair, you may find yourself up against a higher pair with a weak kicker. These are drawing hands.

If there are a lot of players calling in front of you, some of these hands can turn into trouble hands. If the flop contains all big cards, then you must be careful. You would like to flop a straight or a straight draw that utilizes your two pocket cards. If you make two pairs on the flop, you still should be aware of the possibility that someone else has made a straight, because other players may also be holding big cards. Play these big cards in an unraised multihanded pot.

Suited Connectors and Gappers: K-9s, Q-9s, T-9s, 9-8s, J-9s

These are all drawing hands that you want to play in an unraised pot with many players. They are marginal hands that will require you to hit a big flop to continue. I will play these in late middle position only if there are at least four players in the hand. If there is a wild player to my left who has been raising it up, I will usually pass on these hands. T-9s and 9-8s are connectors that you would almost rather make into a straight than a baby flush. K-9s and Q-9s have the possibility of making a big flush.

When you make a flush, the ace of your suit will appear on the flop about a third of the time. If the ace does not appear, and you are raised, you have to be aware that you may be up against the nut flush.

For middle position here is a quick reference:

Hand	Call—Number of Players	If Raised
9-9	Call	Call—Four or More
8-8	Call	Call—Four or More
7-7	Call	Call—Four or More
A-9s	Call—Four or More	Fold
A-8s	Call—Four or More	Fold
A-7s	Call—Four or More	Fold
K-9s	Call—Four or More	Fold
Q-9s	Call—Four or More	Fold
J-9s	Call—Four or More	Fold
T-9s	Call—Four or More	Fold
9-8s	Call—Four or More	Fold
A-10	Call	Fold
K-J	Call—Four or More	Fold
K-10	Call—Four or More	Fold
Q-J	Call—Four or More	Fold
Q-10	Call—Four or More	Fold
J-10	Call—Four or More	Fold
A-J	Call	Call
K-Q	Call	Call

s denotes that the cards are suited.

CHAPTER 9

Late Position

When you are in late position, or last to act, you have a big advantage. You will have the best position for all four betting rounds. You will have more information about your opponents because they have to act before you do. You can enter the pot with weaker starting hands if there have been no raises before it is your turn to act. If you are first to enter the pot, you can sometimes raise with hands that you normally would call with in early position. Late position is the time to raise with queens and jacks and unsuited A-K or A-Q if no one else has called the pot.

Remember this is done to further limit the field or even win the blinds. If there are callers ahead of you, it will not drive any of them out. In low-limit games, once a player enters the pot, he will usually call a raise to see the flop.

If you find yourself in an unraised pot with many players, you can play the weaker suited connectors very cheaply. In late position there is less of a chance that a player acting after you will raise you. If you hit a flop and make a straight, you will have a good chance of scooping a large pot. If you don't, it has only cost you a single bet. If you must cold-call a raise or two, you can easily bail out when you are in late position and save yourself money.

When you are the designated dealer you are "on the button" and last to act before the blinds. If you have a playable hand and no one else has entered the pot, you may be able to steal the blinds with a raise if you don't think the players will defend their blinds. This should not be tried if you have a trash hand.

Please Note: *Being last to act does not make your hand any stronger. It just means that you can enter the pot cheaper because the blinds will usually not raise unless they have a big hand. You should be extremely cautious if you are raised from a player in the blinds. This is a sure indication that they have a strong hand.*

Small Pairs

Play any pair in an unraised pot with at least five callers. If you hold a pair you will flop a set about 11.76 percent of the time. This means the odds are 7.5-to-1 against you. With five callers you are getting close to proper odds. If you do flop a set, you will have a big hand and have the advantage of acting late in the round. If there are six or more players in the hand, you can call one raise. Don't cold-call two raises with a small pair, and be careful if the raise comes from an early position player. If there are less than six players, fold if raised in front of you.

Ace Any: A-6s, A-2s, and A-9, A-8, A-7

You can play any suited ace in late position with enough callers. If you flop a flush, you will have the nut flush or you may flop a nut-flush draw. You will only make a flush about 6 percent of the time, which means that these hands can be trouble.

As with the middle position suited-ace hands, you can be in trouble if an ace appears on the flop, unless you make two pairs. You will have a very weak kicker. If you pair your kicker you will more than likely get beat with an overpair. You can play unsuited A-9, A-8, or A-7 as long as there are no raises in front of you. Again, these hands usually spell trouble if an ace flops. You need to flop two pairs to be secure. If you don't, you may find yourself in the same trouble as the suited-ace hands.

Suited King: K-8s through K-2s

Suited cards with kings play very similar to the ace-suited hands. Your odds of making a flush are the same, but you will not have the nuts if you do make it.

Please Note: *The "nuts" is the best hand possible.*

In the case of a flush, anyone holding the ace will beat you with the nut flush. Keep in mind, however, that one-third of the time you make a flush, the ace will be on the board and you will have the nuts.

Connectors: 8-7s, 7-6s, 6-5s, 5-4s, and T-9, 9-8, 8-7

Little connectors can become powerful hands if the flop hits you. You are looking for a straight or a straight draw if the cards are unsuited and the additional flush or flush draw with the suited connectors. Since many players will continue playing big overcards when the flop contains all small cards, it is possible to build a big pot. Since the value of these hands is dependent on the flop, it is important that you get in cheaply and release them quickly if the hand does not develop. These hands do not develop often, so you want to make sure that you have many players in the pot to make it worthwhile. Never play these hands against fewer than five players.

Gappers: Q-8s, J-8s, T-8s, 9-7s, and K-9, Q-9, J-9

When your starting two cards have a gap between them, it will make it even more difficult to make a straight. When the hand contains cards with values 10 and below, I will rarely play them with more than one gap unless I am in the small blind. The hands containing one big card with two gaps are playable but with caution, as they are marginal at best.

The suited gappers will give you the added potential for making a flush. Since you are playing these hands in multiway pots with five or more players, the other hands can present trouble if you only pair one of the cards. If the flop contains big cards, you will have a weak kicker with kings, queens, or jacks. If you pair your 9 or 8, it will probably not hold up against a large field.

While playing in late position gives you the opportunity to play more hands, you still must be selective.

For late position here is a quick reference:

Hand	Call—Number of Players	If Raised
6-6	Call—Five or More	Call One Raise—Six or More
5-5	Call—Five or More	Call One Raise—Six or More
4-4	Call—Five or More	Call One Raise—Six or More
3-3	Call—Five or More	Call One Raise—Six or More
2-2	Call—Five or More	Call One Raise—Six or More
A-6s	Call—Five or More	Call One Raise—Six or More
A-5s	Call—Five or More	Call One Raise—Six or More
A-4s	Call—Five or More	Call One Raise—Six or More
A-3s	Call—Five or More	Call One Raise—Six or More
A-2s	Call—Five or More	Call One Raise—Six or More
K-8s	Call—Five or More	Fold
K-7s	Call—Five or More	Fold
K-6s	Call—Five or More	Fold
K-5s	Call—Five or More	Fold
K-4s	Call—Five or More	Fold
K-3s	Call—Five or More	Fold
K-2s	Call—Five or More	Fold

Hand	Call—Number of Players	If Raised
Q-8s	Call—Five or More	Fold
J-8s	Call—Five or More	Fold
T-8s	Call—Five or More	Fold
9-7s	Call—Five or More	Fold
8-7s	Call—Five or More	Fold
7-6s	Call—Five or More	Fold
6-5s	Call—Five or More	Fold
5-4s	Call—Five or More	Fold
A-9	Call—Five or More	Fold
A-8	Call—Five or More	Fold
A-7	Call—Five or More	Fold
K-9	Call—Five or More	Fold
Q-9	Call—Five or More	Fold
J-9	Call—Five or More	Fold
T-9	Call—Five or More	Fold
9-8	Call—Five or More	Fold
8-7	Call—Five or More	Fold

s denotes that the cards are suited.

CHAPTER 10

Blinds

The blinds have the advantage of being in late position before the flop but the disadvantage of being in early position after the flop. Many players feel that because they put money in for the blinds, they must defend the blinds no matter what starting cards they hold. They will routinely call all raises even with hands that they would not play from any other position.

You must realize that once you put the money for the blinds into the pot, it is no longer your money; it belongs to whoever eventually wins the pot. Many players lose a lot of money from misplaying hands when they are in the blinds. In a 10-handed game, the blinds will account for two-tenths of your total hands. Playing every hand without regard to the action in front of you is no better than playing with the "any two cards can win" attitude, which is essentially what you are doing.

There are instances where you will want to defend your big blind against aggressive players who you know are just trying to steal your blinds. If other players discover that you do not always defend your blinds, they may just start making a positional raise every time you are in the blinds. This can be frustrating, but in many cases you can get the player to back down. To do this you must wait for a playable hand. Then when the aggressor tries for a steal by raising the pot, you will reraise him.

In most cases a player will only try for a steal from late position when no one else has entered the pot. This means that you will most likely be heads-up with this player. Since you will be the first to act after the flop you must come out betting. Unless the flop hits the other player, he will usually fold and then think twice about attempting a steal in the future.

Big Blind

In an unraised pot, playing the big blind is easy. You have a free ride. You have already made a bet, so you only need to consider whether you want to raise or merely check your blind bet. In most cases you will probably want to just check. The reason for not raising with a strong hand is for deception.

When a player raises from the big blind he is announcing to everyone that he has a powerful hand. You may find that you will not get too much action after the flop. If there are only one or two players, then you might consider raising to get more money in the pot, but you might be better off just calling and then trying a check raise after the flop.

If the pot has been raised, you need to determine where the raise came from and who made it. If the raise was made from a tight player in early position, you can pretty much determine that you are up against a strong hand. If a reraise occurs before it is your turn to act, you should not call unless you have a powerful hand of your own. If, however, the raise has been made from late position when no one else has entered the pot, you may be up against a player trying to steal and should treat it as such

In a raised pot from the big blind with two or more players, you can call a raise with any pair, connectors, suited ace, or other middle-position hands. Don't call a raise with a hand like J-2 or Q-5 or other hopeless hands. You want to defend your blind only if you have a chance of winning the pot, not because you have already put one bet in.

Small Blind

One consideration that you will have to take into account when playing from the small blind is the limit of the game and the size of the small blind. In most Texas Hold'em games, the small blind is half the size of the minimum bet, but there are some low-limit games where it is less than half.

In a $2/4 game the small blind is $1. In a $4/8 game the small blind is $2. In these games, to call from the small blind you will only be putting in half of a bet. In this situation, with an unraised pot, you can play a little looser. You can play all of the late-position hands. You can also play hands that include any two suited cards, smaller suited or unsuited connectors, or one-gapped hands. In the small blind in an unraised pot, you can also play any ace or king. This does not mean that you would play a completely hopeless hand. A starting hand of 2-7 off suit is still the worst hand in Hold'em, whether you are in the small blind or not.

In the $3/6 game the small blind is only $1 in most card rooms. This means that you would have to put in two-thirds of a bet if you want to call. If this is the game you are playing, you should consider the small blind as being a late-position hand. In a multiway pot you can also play small gapped hands.

For the small blind here is a quick reference:

Hand	Call—Number of Players	If Raised
T-7s	Call—Five or More	Fold
9-6s	Call—Five or More	Fold
8-6s	Call—Five or More	Fold
7-5s	Call—Five or More	Fold
J-8	Call—Five or More	Fold
T-8	Call—Five or More	Fold

When the pot has been raised before you, don't think that you should immediately call just because you have a partial bet in the pot. In the $3/6 game it will cost you $5 to call a raise. Why would you want to invest $5 on a hand that you would not call a $3 bet with just because you already put $1 into the pot? With a raised pot you should play the small blind as you would if you were playing from middle or late position.

Chopping

There will be times when all of the players fold and the players in the blinds are the only ones left to act. In this situation there is an option called "chopping" that is allowed in most card rooms.

> **Please Note:** *Chopping entails the big and small blinds folding their hands and taking back their blind bets.*

The hand is over, the button is moved, and the next hand begins. Chopping is a personal decision that you must make. I have heard arguments on both sides as to whether or not a player should or should not chop. Some players always chop, while other players never chop.

The argument for chopping in a low-limit game is that there is not enough money with just the blinds to make it worthwhile to play out the hand. In a $3/6 game there is only $4 in the pot. There is only $3 in a $2/4 game. Some players feel that this is not worth the time or the risk to play the hand out.

There are some players, however, who never chop. Players who regularly play tournaments don't like to chop because they feel that this heads-up play will give them experience when they make it to the final table in a tournament. This is a valid point on their part. Whether you decide to chop or not, you should stick with your choice for the entire session.

Live Straddle

There is a situation that you will encounter from time to time where the player next to the big blind raises the pot before the cards are dealt. This is known as a "live straddle." Players who put up a live straddle are there to gamble. Most of the time the player making the straddle bet has just won a few pots and feels invincible or is trying to intimidate the other players. Sometime the player may be on tilt or intoxicated. No matter what the reason, it is a bad bet that smart players don't make. When you encounter this situation, you should play tighter than you normally would because it will cost you more money to enter the pot. If you have pocket aces or kings, you can confidently raise and know that the straddler will call your raise.

CHAPTER 11

Game Plan for a Strong Foundation

As a new player, trying to remember all of the starting hands to play from each position is fairly difficult, even if you use the arrow chart to help you remember. There are so many variations of starting hands based on your position and the number of active players in the hand. Many new players tend to guess and lean toward playing weaker starting hands. Consequently, they play too many hands and lose more than they win.

> **Please Note:** *If you are new to Hold'em or have not been successful playing the game, you should limit the starting hands that you play even more than those recommendations in the previous pages.*

What you are about to read is probably the most important concept in this book. It is easy to understand but will be difficult for some to execute. It is the key to winning play, and if you follow this advice, you will build a strong foundation, which will become your base for making you a winning player. From this base you will add all the other principles you learn about the game of Hold'em, and soon you will be playing better than many of your opponents.

Fifty hours may seem like a long time to some. If you play only a few hours once a week, you will be playing this style for a little more than four months, but over the course of your poker lifetime, investing 50 hours of time is a small price to pay for the future dividends you will collect. The following advice is not merely about hand selection. It will help you develop a strong personal commitment to playing a solid winning game.

The starting hands in the suggested positions here may seem a little too tight to players who are used to playing any two cards in loose games. In reality, these hands are too loose for new players or players who have been playing indiscriminately and have not been getting the desired results from their play.

The most important traits a player needs to develop in order to win at poker are patience and discipline. Limiting your hand selection will help you do this. You will be throwing away many more hands than you will be playing. Waiting for the right hands to play will teach you patience. If you can discipline yourself to do this, you will develop a strong basic foundation that will improve your game.

The suggested hands to play are the 20 strongest hands that can be played from early position along with a few additional hands added in late position. Although these are early position hands, they are spread out into the middle and late positions.

In Early position:
- Raise with A-A, K-K, and A-Ks from any position.
- Call with A-K, A-Qs, K-Qs, and Q-Q and fold everything else.

In Middle position:
- Call with J-J, 10-10, 9-9, 8-8, A-Js, A-10s, Q-Js, A-Q, and K-Q.

Late position:
- Call with A-Xs, K-10s, Q-10s, J-10s, A-J, and A-10 (note *X* denotes any card).

Also:
- Play any pair and suited connectors if there are more than five players.
- If you play small pairs, you must fold if you don't flop a set.
- Fold if the pot is raised.

By limiting your play to these hands, it will allow you to concentrate on other fundamentals of the game. Use the time when you are not active in a hand to observe the other players and practice reading the board. This is an excellent opportunity to observe what hands your opponents are playing.

To be honest, using these tight standards will be boring. You will be watching other players entering pots with pure garbage hands and thinking it might be time to loosen up a little. Don't do it! You are on a quest for excellence.

Please Note: *The reality is that playing winning poker is boring because you need to be selective with the hands you choose to play.*

If you find you are getting bored, you should take a break. Get up and stretch your legs, go to the bathroom, grab a soda, or just take a walk around the room. When you sit back down, try to concentrate more on reading the board, the players, and other aspects of the game.

Many players have no concept of pot odds. While you are limiting your play, you can also count the number of players in each hand and practice calculating the money in the pot. If you find you are still losing your commitment to your game plan, you should leave and call it a day. This is about patience and discipline. When you start to lose your patience, you need to have the discipline to leave the game.

There is nothing wrong with playing a tight game. Many low-limit games have enough action that will allow you to win a substantial number of chips using solid, tight play. There may be instances when you are playing with knowledgeable players and your tight play will be detected. If this happens they will not call you as often when you do play a hand, but don't worry too much about it. This is offset by the number of players in low-limit games that have no concept about the style of their opponents' play. Many hands will go to the showdown in Low-Limit Hold'em games. You want to make sure you have the best hand at the showdown. You improve your chance when you start by playing strong, solid hands.

Game Plan

Even after your initial 50 hours of playing this way is over, you may choose to use this tight playing style as your primary game plan. When you sit down to play with unfamiliar players, you can start off in this tight mode until you get a feel for the other players in the game. As the game progresses you can expand your starting hands, but make sure to always play the hands from their proper position.

In a loose game, starting tight and then playing a few more hands can convey the impression that you are actually playing the same loose game as everyone else. In reality you will be still playing solid starting hands, but most players will not catch on to this.

Having disciplined yourself to the tight playing style, you can switch back to the tighter mode at a moment's notice if the game starts getting too wild. It's like a fighter who can switch from righty to southpaw to keep his opponent off balance.

CHAPTER 12

Understanding Pot Odds

The "pot odds" are the relationship between the money in the pot and the price of a bet you must make to call. If the pot contains $36 and the size of the bet you must call is $6, we divide the $36 by $6 and we get 6, which means that the pot odds are 6-to-1.

Many low-limit and even some higher-limit Texas Hold'em players have no concept of pot odds and how it can affect their profitability. They don't understand the reasoning for playing drawing hands against a large field of opponents. Some hands that are profitable against many players will be losing or break-even hands with fewer players in the game.

There is a little experiment that you can try to give you an idea of how the number of players can affect your winning with a hand that has the exact same odds. This experiment simulates how the number of players will affect a hand that has odds of 3-to-1 against you. First of all, get a deck of cards and take out the four aces, 2s, 3s, and 4s. You will have 16 cards. Then get coins or chips to use for the experiment.

There will be four players in the game. Put out a stack of chips for each player. Each player puts one chip in the pot. Shuffle the 16 cards and deal a card. You can be player number one. Each time an ace is dealt you win. If a 2 is dealt, then player number two will collect the money in the pot. Likewise if a 3 or 4 is dealt, the respective player will win the pot. Put another chip in the pot for each player and deal again. Keep repeating this until all 16 cards have been dealt. Notice the results:

- Each time you won a hand you won three chips (one from each of the other players).
- Each time you lost a hand you lost one chip.
- You played 16 hands.
- You won four hands and lost 12.
- You won 12 chips for the four hands you won and lost 12 chips for the 12 hands you did not win.

- You broke even.
- The odds of winning were 3-to-1, and the pot odds were 3-to-1.

Now you will repeat the process, but player number four will not bet. Any time a 4 wins, put the three chips from the pot (yours and the two other players' chips) aside.

At the end of the 16 hands notice the results:

- You won the same four hands. But this time you only won eight chips.
- You lost 12 hands and lost 12 chips.
- You are down four chips.
- Your odds of winning were still 3-to-1, but the pot odds were 2-to-1.

Now put out another stack of chips. This time number four will again play as in the first round, and a fifth chip will be put in the pot to simulate an additional player who will not win.

At the end of 16 hands notice the results:

- You won four hands, but this time you won 16 chips.
- You lost 12 hands and lost 12 chips.
- You won four chips.
- Your odds of winning were 3-to-1, but the pot odds were 4-to-1.

With this example you can see how a hand offering the same odds can be profitable when there is more money in the pot but be unprofitable when there is less money in the pot.

How to Determine Pot Odds

Many players feel that trying to keep track of the money in the pot is a difficult thing to do. I thought so too at first, but I came upon an easy way to do this.

First of all, it is easier to keep track of the number of bets instead of the actual money in the pot. After each betting round the dealer announces how many players are active in the pot. If there have been no raises, you know how many bets have been put in by the number of players active in the hand. During the first betting round before the flop, it is uncommon for players to fold once they enter the pot. If there has been a raise, just double the number of players, and you know the total bets before the flop.

After the flop, count the bets put in by the players in front of you during each round. When it is your turn to act, you will have an accurate determination of your pot odds up to that point. You do not know what the players acting after you will do.

On the last two betting rounds, the limits double and you must adjust your count to reflect this. It is easy to do. Just divide the number of bets that were made in half. Using the $3/6 game, if there were 10 $3 bets in the pot before the turn, it would now be converted to five $6 bets.

Implied Odds

There is a concept called "implied odds" for money you are sure will go into the pot after you act. This means that after you compute the odds before you act, you can add your opponents' future bets if you are sure there will be no raises.

A simple example of implied odds would be if you held a small pair before the flop. If there are five players who have entered the pot before it is your turn to act, you are getting 5-to-1 odds. The odds for making a set are 7.5-to-1, which means you are not getting proper odds for this hand at this time. If you are sure that the players acting after you will call or that there will be a bet made after the flop, you can consider these bets into the pot odds. These are then *implied* odds.

This means you would try to calculate what you would win if your opponent bets and you make your hand and win the pot. If you were heads-up on a flush draw with one card to come, you would have nine outs, and the odds against you would be 4-to-1, which means that there should be $24 in the pot to give you proper odds. If there were only $21 in the pot you would only be getting 3.5-to-1 odds and would not call. If, however, you know that your opponent will call a $6 bet if you make your flush, you can then add this to the $21 already in the pot, thereby giving you an implied pot of $27. You then would be getting 4.5-to-1 odds for your $6 bet.

Calculating Your "Outs"

The reason you need to be able to calculate pot odds is because you will compare them with the odds of drawing a winning hand.

Please Note: *In poker your outs are the unseen cards that will complete or improve your hand to make it the winning hand.*

When you figure your outs, you will use that information to help you determine the odds of having the winning hand. Once you know that information, you compare the pot odds you are getting to the odds of making your hand. This will determine whether or not you continue with the hand or fold.

Each additional card or out will improve the probability of making your hand. You will compare the odds of making your hand to the pot odds to make a determination as to whether or not it is profitable to continue with your hand.

Probability and odds are actually the same thing, although they are expressed differently. Probability is the amount of times an event will occur and is expressed as a percentage. In Texas Hold'em you will be dealt a pocket pair once in 17 hands or 5.88 percent of the time. The odds tell you the number of times an event will not occur. The odds against getting a pocket pair are 16-to-1. You subtract one from the amount of times something will happen to get the odds against it not happening. So in this case you subtract one from 17 to get 16-to-1.

Where did this figure of 16-to-1 come from? First we divide 100 percent by 5.88 percent and get 17.006. So the probability of the event happening is once in 17 attempts. The odds are 16-to-1 against it happening.

When you figure your outs, you will use that information to help determine the odds of having the winning hand. Once you know that information, you compare the pot odds you are getting to the odds of making your hand. This will determine whether or not you continue with the hand or fold.

Luckily you don't have to do the math to figure out your odds for each out. The out chart below has all the information you need. If you are playing online, you can print out the chart and have it sitting next to your computer. All you have to do is determine your odds and compare it with the amount of money in the pot to quickly compute your pot odds. If you are playing live, you will need to memorize the odds for the number of outs.

> **Please Note:** *As a rule of thumb, if you have eight or more outs in a multiway pot you will usually be getting the correct pot odds to continue with your hand. Therefore you only need to learn the odds for seven or fewer outs.*

Some outs you will quickly recognize:
- If you have a four flush you have nine outs.
- If you have an opened straight it is eight outs.
- An inside straight is four outs.
- Improving a pair is two outs.

Outs Chart

Number of Outs	After Flop Two Cards to Come		After Turn One Card to Come	
	Percentage	Odds-to-1	Percentage	Odds-to-1
1	4.3	22.4	2.2	44.5
2	8.4	10.9	4.3	22.3
3	12.5	7	6.5	14.4
4	16.5	4.1	8.7	10.5
5	20.3	3.9	10.9	8.2
6	24.1	3.1	13	6.7
7	27.8	2.6	15.2	5.6
8	31.5	2.2	17.4	4.7
9	35	1.9	19.6	4.1
10	38.4	1.6	21.7	3.6
11	41.7	1.4	24	3.2
12	45	1.2	26.1	2.8
13	48.1	1.1	28.3	2.5
14	51.2	0.95	30.4	2.3
15	54.1	0.85	32.6	2.1
16	57	0.75	34.3	1.9
17	59.8	0.67	37	1.7
18	62.4	0.6	39.1	1.6
19	65	0.54	41.3	1.4
20	67.5	0.48	43.5	1.3

The Rule of Four-Two

The rule of four-two is an easier way to figure the odds for any situation where you know your outs. It is not completely accurate, but it will give you a quick "ballpark" figure of your chances for making a hand. Here is how it works:

With two cards to come after the flop, you multiply your number of outs by four. With one card to come after the turn, you multiply your number of outs by two. This will give you a quick figure to work with. If you have a four-card flush after the flop, you have nine outs. With two cards to come, you multiply the nine by four and you get a 36 percent chance of making the flush. The chart shows the true odds at 35 percent. With one card to come, you multiply nine by two and get 18 percent. The chart shows that the true figure is 19.6. It is not completely accurate, but it is pretty close, and it is an easy calculation to do in your head.

When you are playing Texas Hold'em you will be a winner if you play a mathematical game based on your understanding of the odds of making a winning hand. The odds charts on the next few pages will give you a better understanding of this concept by showing you the odds for many common situations.

CHAPTER 13

Odds Charts

Here are a few charts that will show you the odds for certain hands that you will encounter while playing Texas Hold'em.

Starting Hands

There are 1,326 two-card combinations that can be made from a deck of 52 cards. Here are the odds for some of the stating hands.

The Probability of Holding...	Percent	Odds Against
A Pair before the flop	5.9	16-to-1
Suited cards	23.5	3.25-to-1
Off-suit cards, no pairs	70.6	0.4-to-1
Pocket aces—or any specific pair	.45	220-to-1
All ace-king combinations	1.2	82-to-1
Ace-king suited	.3	331-to-1
A-A, K-K, or A-K	2.1	46-to-1
Single ace	14.9	5.7-to-1
Premium hands—A-A, K-K, Q-Q, A-K, A-Q, K-Q	5	19-to-1

The Flop

With two cards in your hand, there are 19,600 three-card combinations that can appear on the flop. Without considering your two pocket cards, there are 22,100 three-card combinations that can be made from a deck of 52 cards. This chart is based on 52 cards.

The Probability That the Flop Will Contain...	Percent	Odds Against
Trips—three of a kind	0.24	424-to-1
A pair	17	5-to-1
No pair	83	0.2-to-1
Three of the same suit	5	18-to-1
Two of the same suit	55	0.8-to-1
Rainbow—three different suits	40	1.5-to-1
Three in sequence	3.5	28-to-1
Two in sequence	40	1.5-to-1
No sequences	56.4	0.8-to-1

Pocket Pairs

As noted the probability of being dealt a pocket pair is 16-to-1. Being dealt a specific pair is 220-to-1. Your odds of getting pocket deuces are the same as getting pocket rockets. But the two hands couldn't be farther apart. Here are some odds for your pocket pairs if you chose to continue to play them.

Holding a Pocket Pair the Probability the Flop Will Contain...	Percent	Odds against
At least a set or higher	11.8	7.5-to-1
A set—one of your cards on the flop	10.8	8.3-to-1
Full house	0.74	136-to-1
Quads	0.25	407-to-1

After the Flop the Probability of...	Percent	Odds Against
Set improving to full house—two cards to come	33	2-to-1
Set improving to full house—on the turn	15	5.7-to-1
Set improving to full house—on the river	22	3.6-to-1
Pair improving to a set—one card to come	4.4	22-to-1
Pair improving to at least a set—if played to the river	19	4.2-to-1

Unless you hold pocket aces, there is always a chance that a higher card can appear in the flop. The lower your pocket pair, the more likely an over-card will flop.

Probability a Higher Card Will Flop When You Hold:	Percent	Odds against
Kings	23	3.3-to-1
Queens	43	1.3-to-1
Jacks	59	0.7-to-1
10s	71	0.3-to-1
9s	81	0.2-to-1
8s	88	0.1-to-1
7s	93	0.07-to-1
6s	97	0.03-to-1
5s	99	0.01-to-1
4s	99.7	0.003-to-1
3s	99.1	0.0002-to-1

Two Cards of Different Ranks

The majority of your starting hands will consist of two off-suit cards of different ranks. These hands can improve in several ways.

Holding Different Ranks, the Probability of Flopping...	Percent	Odds Against
One pair	29	2.5-to-1
Two pairs	2	49-to-1
Trips	1.4	73-to-1
Full house	0.1	1087-to-1
Quads	0.01	9799-to-1
At least a pair	32	2.1-to-1
No pairs	68	0.5-to-1

With Two Cards to Come, the Probability of...	Percent	Odds Against
No pair improving to at least one pair	24	3.2-to-1
No pair improving to two pairs or trips	1.4	71-to-1
Pair improving to two pairs or better	20	3.9-to-1
Two pairs improving to full house	17	5-to-1
Trips improving to full house	33	2-to-1

Suited Cards

Whenever there are suited cards on board, there is a possibility of a flush. You will be dealt suited cards 23.5 percent of the time. Here are the odds for making a flush.

With Two Suited Cards, the Probability of...	Percent	Odds Against
Flopping two for a four flush	11	8.1-to-1
Then making the flush with two cards to come (nine outs)	35	1.9-to-1
Flopping three for a complete flush	0.84	118-to-1
Flopping one of your suit	41.6	14-to-1
Flopping one and making flush on the river	4.2	23-to-1
Flopping none of your suit	46.6	1.1-to-1
Making a flush of a different suit (five suited cards on board)	0.2	548-to-1

Connectors

There are many combinations of cards that you can use to make a straight. It is easiest when you start with maximum connectors. Max connectors are two cards adjacent to each other with three cards open on each end. There are seven sets of max connectors. They are 4-5, 5-6, 6-7, 7-8, 8-9, 9-10, and T-J. The chart below shows the odds for certain situations.

With Maximum Connectors, the Probability of...	Percent	Odds Against
Starting hand. All - suited and unsuited	8.5	11-to-1
Starting hand. Suited only	2.1	46-to-1
Flopping an open-ended straight draw	9.8	9-to-1
Then making a straight with two cards to come (eight outs)	31.5	2.2-to-1
Flopping an inside-straight draw	21.6	3.6-to-1
Then making a straight with two cards to come (four outs)	16.5	5-to-1
Flopping a straight	1.3	76-to-1

In some cases the numbers have been rounded instead of using two decimal places.

CHAPTER 14

Calling

The main reason that poker players lose money is that they call too much with marginal hands. In Texas Hold'em the big blind constitutes a bet. After looking at your first two cards, you can fold your hand, call the blind bet, or raise it. The expression "limping in" is used when you enter the pot by just calling the blind bet.

> **Please Note:** *Whether or not you enter a hand will depend on two important considerations. These are your position and how many players have entered the pot in front of you.*

If you limp in from an early position, you have to take into account that a player may raise the pot after you. If this happens, you have to call the raise, fold, or reraise. In low-limit games, most players will call the raise rather than fold once they enter the pot.

In deciding whether to play a hand, you should ask yourself if you are willing to call if the pot is raised. If it is a marginal hand, you may want to dump it instead of calling. In later position you will have more information about your opponents and the possible strength of their hands.

Number of Players

In middle and late position, the number of players who have called before you will affect your decision whether or not to play your opening hand. Big pairs can stand up on their own, but when you have a small pair, connectors, or an ace with a small suited card, you will need to improve on the flop. These are drawing hands. You won't make them often, but if the flop hits you, they can turn into powerful hands.

Suppose you are holding an ace and a 6 of spades. If an ace flops, you have a pair of aces with a small suited kicker, but if you flop three of the suit, you now have the nut flush. If you do make a flush draw and proceed to make your flush, you will have the nuts. Similarly, a small pair will probably not win on its own without improvement. In most cases, you will need to flop a set in order to win.

With these types of hands, you want to get into the pot with a minimum bet when possible. More times than not, you won't improve your hand, but if you do make your hand when there are a lot of people in the pot, the amount of money you make will compensate you for the times that you don't make the hand.

If you have a drawing hand, you want at least four people in the pot when you are in middle position and five if you are in late position. Most low-limit players do not give any consideration to the number of players in a hand; this is a concept that is either overlooked or ignored. Remember your big cards and pairs will win more against fewer players. Your drawing hands will play best against a lot of players. You need to know how many players are in the hand before you call.

Calling a Raise

When the pot is raised before the flop, you need to determine how your hand compares to that of the raiser. If the pot is raised before it is your turn to act, you will have to call the original bet and the raise. This is known as "cold-calling." If the pot were reraised before it is your turn to act, you would have to cold-call three bets in order to enter the pot.

> **Please Note:** *Unless you have a very powerful hand, you should not cold-call any raises.*

You need a stronger hand to call a raise than you do to initiate one. If you have to cold-call three bets, you better have an extremely strong hand, such as a pair of aces or kings or A-K suited, because you can pretty much figure that the player who reraised has a very strong hand. These are the only hands you should cold-call a reraise with.

In low-limit games many players cold-call two raises with hands such as unsuited K-J, Q-10, A-10, or weaker. This can be very costly.

The problem with hands like these is that even if you make a pair after the flop, you may only have the second-best hand. If you hold no pair you will pair one of your cards about 32 percent of the time. That means the odds are about 2-to-1 against you pairing one of your pocket cards. If someone has a hand strong enough to reraise, they more than likely have you beat even if you pair one of your cards.

Since you don't have any money invested in a pot that is raised before it is your turn to act, you can merely fold and wait for another hand. Why take the chance of playing a marginal hand against a raise? If you are thinking about calling the raise you must consider the following:

What Position Was the Raise Made From?
If a raise comes from early position, you have to assume the player has a strong hand and he is trying to narrow the field. Most players raising from this position don't fear being reraised. If the raise comes from middle position in an unraised pot, the player could have a semistrong hand and could be trying to narrow the field. If a player is raising from middle position in a pot that has been called by several others, it is another indication of a strong hand. If the raise comes from late position in an unraised pot, a player may be trying to steal the blinds.

Who Raised?
It is very important that you know who made the raise. If the player doing the raising is a very tight player who only plays strong hands, you should have a powerful hand to consider calling. If the player is a maniac who is just looking for action, then he might be raising with any hand.

How Many Players Have Called?
The number of players who call a raise before you will determine whether you call the raise. If there are only a few players you don't want to call with a drawing hand. If there are many players in the pot and it has been raised, then you may be getting the proper pot odds to call. Sometimes the pot will get so big that it becomes what is known as "a protected pot." This means that you can be sure someone will be calling all the way to the end.

What Is Your Position?
Before you call a raise, you need to determine how many players will be acting after you. Will any of them reraise the pot? If you fear a reraise, then your hand is not strong enough to call a raise.

What Do You Have?
Try to determine how strong your hand is compared to the raiser. Do you think you are beat gong in? Here again, it helps to know your other players. If you have a drawing hand and there are many players in the pot, you should be drawing to the nut hand if you are calling a raise. You won't make

your drawing hand very often, but when you do, you don't want it to be second-best.

Be Selective

Just as you are selective about your starting hands, you need to be equally selective about which hands you will call a raise with. Many players feel that once they call a raise, they must call a reraise or two even though they are not getting proper odds to do so.

CHAPTER 15

Raising

Any player can raise the pot with any hand. This does not mean that you should just raise the pot on a whim. There are five reasons to raise the pot when you are playing Texas Hold'em:

1. To get more money in the pot
2. To narrow the field by eliminating other players
3. To bluff
4. To get a free card
5. To gain information

Please Note: *The two best reasons to raise before the flop are when you think you have the best hand and want to get more money in the pot or when you want to narrow the field.*

Bigger Pots

If you have the best hand, you want to get as much money into the pot as possible. Before the flop this includes your big pairs like aces and kings. Don't hesitate to raise or reraise with these hands. A pair of aces is the strongest hand you can hold before the flop, and a pair of kings is the second-best hand. These big pairs will not always hold up, especially against a lot of players. For this reason you want to get as much money in the pot for the times when they do hold up to win.

In a low-limit game you should be careful with pairs of queens and jacks. Because many players will play a single ace, you may find yourself in trouble with these hands if an ace appears on the flop. Unless you think you can narrow the field, you may be better off calling with these hands.

Many times players will raise with hands containing any two big cards such as K-J off-suit, only to see all little cards in the flop. They eventually end up folding when another player bets out or raises when the flop fits their particular hand. They could have saved a bet by simply calling before the flop.

> **Please Note:** *When you raise without a strong hand, you may just be making the pot bigger for someone else to win.*

Narrowing the Field
- You raise the pot when you want to narrow the field.
- Big pairs hold up better against fewer players.
- The more opponents you can drive out, the better your chances of winning with a large pair.
- With many players involved in the pot, the chances of getting drawn out with a straight or flush are greater.
- Your position will greatly influence how many players you can drive out with a raise.
- Before the flop, if you raise under the gun or from early position, you may drive out players who are holding marginal hands.

If there are a lot of players who have already called, your chances of chasing any of them out with a raise in a low-limit game are slim. You will find that once a player has called a single bet, they will not fold until they have seen the flop.

Stealing the Blinds
If you are in late position or on the button (designated dealer), there is a chance that you can steal the blinds by raising if no one else has entered the pot before you. If you notice that the players to your left have previously folded their hands to a raise when they were in the blinds, this may work. You may have to test them.

You should wait until you have a semi-strong hand to do this, in case they will staunchly defend their blinds with any hand. Many players feel that if they have money in the pot, they should play the hand no matter if it was raised or not. Some players will try an outright bluff by raising from early position. If you are in an extremely tight game, this may work, but for the most part bluffing with a raise before the flop should be avoided in a low-limit game.

Getting a Free Card
At first glance, the concept of raising to gain a free card may seem a little confusing, but it can be a good value. Your position is a very important

factor when making this play, and it works best when you are in later position when there are few players acting after you.

When a player raises, it usually means that he is holding a strong hand. In many instances, other players will check to the raiser on the next betting round for fear of being raised if they bet. If you have raised from late position and it is checked to you, you can also check and have the opportunity of seeing the next card for free.

This play is used a lot of the time on the flop when the betting limits are lower. In a $3/6 game, the betting limit on the flop is $3. If you raise, it will cost you $6. The next betting round the limit goes to $6. If everyone checks to you on the turn because you raised during the previous round, you can also check, and you will get to see the river card for the price of your raise on the flop, which is $6. If you merely bet on the flop and then someone bets in front of you on the turn, it will cost you $9 to see the river card. By raising on the flop, you have increased the likelihood that it will be checked to you, and you will see the turn card for free.

If you raise before the flop from late position, there is a chance that you can see all the way to the river card for free. You raise before the flop, and then it is checked to you after the flop. If you check, you will get to see the turn card for free. In a tight game the players may again check to you after the turn card, which means that you can see the river card for free as well. You try to get a free card when you have a drawing hand and want to try to make your hand as cheaply as possible. However, you need to remember that while you are receiving a free card, all of your opponents are getting one as well. There is an equal chance that they will make their hands with the free cards.

Raising is a powerful tool. Whenever you have a legitimate hand you should consider raising instead of just calling. Of course this will be dependent on the other players in you game. If you are in a game with a lot of players who will call any bet or raise, then you may not want to raise unless you think you have the winning hand.

CHAPTER 16

Bluffing and Semibluffing

Bluffing

A bluff is a bet or raise made with a hand that has no chance of winning. The purpose is to win a pot when your hand is not strong enough to do so on its own. You are essentially representing a big hand when, in reality, you have nothing. Bluffing is a very valuable weapon to have in your poker arsenal, but you should make sure you use it correctly and don't overuse it.

The popularity of the television coverage of many of the large no-limit tournaments has led to a lot of misconception about the frequency of bluffing in poker games. Showing bluffs is big drama and makes for very exciting entertainment in these shows. The TV producers make sure they are shown in the final edits of the show.

Bluffing is more prevalent in no-limit poker and tournaments because the players are playing their opponents and their stack size. Bluffing does have a place in some limit poker games as well, though, and can be profitable in situations where it is used correctly. However in Limit Hold'em you will usually have to show down the best hand. Bluffs work best when you are heads-up against another player, especially if the other player plays a tight game.

In most low-limit games, bluffing is futile. For an extra dollar of two there is someone who will want to keep you honest. If there is even one calling station in the game, you should not attempt to bluff. Players in low-limit games also tend to stay if they have caught even a piece of the flop, such as a low pair. Trying to run a bluff by them won't work, as they will call all the way to the river.

In mid- or higher-limit games a bluff has a better chance of being successful if the pot is small. Once the pot gets big the players may be getting the correct odds to stay in. You also may have better success in shorthanded games, as there usually will not be a lot of money in the pot, and a player on a flush draw may not want to continue because they are not getting the right odds to do so.

Your position is important when you contemplate a bluff. If you are on the button and everyone has folded, you might be able to steal the blinds with a bluff. However, you should not try this too often. If you keep raising all the time on the button, the players in the blinds will eventually play back at you. Some players will defend their blinds no matter what they have. If this is the case, this type of bluff will not work.

If you are in the blinds in a shorthanded game and no one has shown any strength before the flop and the flop has been checked around, you may be able to win with a bet by being the first one to bet. You have a better chance of this working if there are no connecting cards on the board or two suited cards.

Some players feel that they should bluff as a way to advertise that they do bluff, in hopes of getting called later when they are not bluffing. They will bluff and then show their hand if they win. Too much advertising can be expensive, and you should avoid bluffing if this is your only reason. While a pure bluff will occasionally work, you should use it very sparingly when you are in a limit game.

Please Note: *The number one rule when attempting a bluff: your bluff must be believable in order for it to have a chance of working.*

Semibluffing

Author David Sklansky coined the term *semibluffing*. It is a profitable technique that is used instead of an outright bluff. Unlike a bluff when you have nothing, semibluffing is done when your hand is not strong enough to win the pot at the time but has the chance of improving to the best hand. If you bet, you are hoping that the other players will fold and you will win the pot without going any further. If you are called, then you still have a chance that your hand will improve to be the best hand.

Many semibluffing situations will come when you have a flush or straight draw. Betting if you are first to act or raising on the flop could win you the pot or get you a free card. If you held the ace and 9 of diamonds and the flop was the king of diamonds, the 9 of clubs, and the 3 of diamonds, then if you bet and no one else had a king, they may figure you for a pair of kings and fold. If you are called you have a pair of 9s, that can be beat by anyone holding a king. However, you have many ways of improving your hand. There are nine diamonds that will make you a flush. There are three aces that will make you two pairs and two 9s that can make you trips or quads, and you even have the possibility of a full house if you were to catch another ace and nine on the turn and river.

If you are in late position and someone bets before you act, you can raise with your flush draw. On the next round the player will usually check to the raiser. If you make your flush, you can bet or you can check and see the river card for free.

Raising with A-K before the flop is technically a semibluff. While it would be possible to win with ace-high, you will probably need to improve this hand. If you raise and everyone folds, you win. You can use a semibluff more than you can use a straight bluff, as you do have a chance of improving your hand. Just remember you can only do this when there are more cards to come.

Beware the Bluffer

Just because you will not be doing much bluffing does not mean there won't be any going on in the game. Some players in low-limit games think that bluffing is an important part of the game and will try it whenever possible.

Be aware that many players will try to bluff on the river. If they have a busted draw, they may try betting or raising to win the pot. If you have a legitimate hand and there is substantial money in the pot, you should call. If the pot contains $90 and it will cost you $6 to call a raise, you are getting 15-to-1 odds. It is better to lose $6 if you call and lose than to forfeit $90 if you toss away the winning hand.

CHAPTER 17

Slow Playing and Check-Raising

In Texas Hold'em you are not trying to win a lot of pots; you're trying to win the most money. In fact the players who win the most pots will usually be losing players, because they are playing too many hands. Two ways you can increase the money you win is with "slow playing" and "check-raising." Both of these tactics have sometimes been referred to as "sandbagging" (especially in home games), but there is nothing underhanded about either tactic. They are acceptable practices used by smart players to maximize their winnings.

Slow Playing

Slow playing is when you play a strong hand weakly by checking or calling instead of betting or raising, to deceive your opponents. When you slow-play you're trying to entice the other players to bet or give them a chance to draw into a hand that will be second best. For example, after the flop, if all the players check to you and you check because you think everybody will fold if you bet, you are essentially giving them a free card. You are hoping that the next card will improve your opponents' hands but not be enough to beat yours.

When you slow-play you are trying to set a trap for the other players, but sometimes this can backfire on you. You must know when to and when not to slow-play a hand. To be successful:

- Your hand must be very strong.
- There must be a good chance that everyone will fold if you bet.
- It should be unlikely the free card will give the player a hand that will beat you.
- There should not be a lot of players in the hand, and the pot must be small.

For example, if you raise before the flop with the ace of hearts and the jack of spades and you get two callers, and the flop is the ace and jack of diamonds and the jack of clubs, you have a full house. Unless someone holds the other two aces (which is unlikely, because you probably would have been reraised), you have the best hand. A player with K-Q, K-10, or Q-10 has a straight draw. In this situation you don't mind checking and giving a free card.

If it is bet, and there are players still to act after you, just call, because a raise may drive out the other players. You are hoping that someone will make a hand that will be second-best to your full house. You will also get action from anyone holding a single ace who has made top pair or a jack who has just made trips.

Mistakes

One of the biggest mistakes that many players make is to slow-play before the flop with pocket aces and kings. Instead of raising, they just call with their big pocket pairs and then complain when they get beat by someone who would have folded if they had raised.

> **Please Note:** *Big pocket pairs play best against a small field, so you raise to narrow the field.*

If you are in early or middle position and decide to slow-play your hand, it could be a costly mistake. If you merely call with A-A, you are allowing everyone into the hand for a single bet. The more players in the hand, the more likely it is that one of them will flop a hand that can beat you.

Slow playing can be a valuable tactic, but many players use it too often when they flop a good, but not great, hand such as top pair, two pairs, three of a kind, or a set. Many players will decide to slow-play a set rather than bet it. If there are two suited cards or a straight draw on the board, chances are somebody will be chasing a flush or a straight. In the long run you will make more money by just betting your set rather than trying to slow-play your set. It is always better to rake in a small pot than to lose it completely by giving your opponent the chance to draw out on you.

Check-Raising

Check-raising is when you check your hand and then raise when another player bets. In home games the idea of check-raising is considered sandbagging and is frowned upon or even not allowed. However, it is allowed in casino poker rooms and is a powerful tool to help you extract more money from your fellow players.

Check-raising is a good way to get more money in the pot when you think you have the best hand. When you have a hand that can't be beaten, you want to slow play, but if your hand is susceptible to a stronger hand, you may want to utilize the check-raise. When you check-raise you are also looking to eliminate some of the players, thus narrowing the field.

If you are in early position and know a player in late position will bet, you can attempt to narrow the field by using a check-raise. If the player in late position has raised before the flop, there is a good chance that many of the players will check to the raiser. When you check-raise, you are getting more money in the pot from the original bettor, but you are also forcing some players acting after you to cold-call two bets. You should do this when you have a good hand but one that could be beaten by a player on a draw.

Suppose you are in the big blind and there are five players in the pot when a player in late position raises. You have the 8 and 7 of hearts. The flop is the king of spades, 8 of diamonds, and 7 of clubs. You have made the middle and bottom two pair. You have flopped a strong hand but not one that you want to play against a lot of players.

You check, and unless a player holds a single king, it is likely they will all check to the original raiser. The original raiser may have raised from late position with a pocket pair or two high cards, in which case he will bet. You raise and now force all the other players to cold-call two bets. A player holding only two big cards, or someone on a straight draw, will not be getting proper odds to call the double bet. You will narrow the field to a heads-up situation where you become a favorite to win. If a player does pair the king and bets, you can still raise to get more money into the pot.

Another situation where you may want to use a check-raise is to tame an aggressive player to your left. If you have been playing a tight game, checking and folding on the flop, you may become the target of a player who has taken notice of this. The player will refuse to allow you a free card by betting every time you check. All you have to do is check the next time you have a strong hand and then raise the player when he bets. If you do this a couple times, he will think twice about betting the next time you check, not knowing if you have a legitimate hand or not.

In order for a check-raise to work, you have to be certain that a player who acts after you will bet. If you check a good hand with the intention of check-raising and everyone after you checks as well, you have defeated the purpose. Worse still, you have given all the other players a free card, which could make hands that beat you. If you have any doubts that a player acting after you will bet, you are better off just coming out and betting the hand. This will assure that anyone on a draw will either have to pay up or get out. You don't want to give free cards to players who could beat you and turn what would have been a small win into a major loss. When in doubt, bet it out!

CHAPTER 18

The Flop

The flop is the first three community cards turned over by the dealer. Choosing to play a starting hand is the biggest decision you will make while playing Texas Hold'em. Deciding whether to continue playing after seeing the flop will be your second-biggest decision. It can also be one of the most costly decisions if you continue after the flop with an inferior hand.

There are 19,600 three-card combinations that can appear on the flop. Combined with the two cards in you hand, there are 2,598,960 five-card combinations. The sad reality is that after waiting patiently for a good starting hand, you probably won't like the flop.

The flop defines your hand, because after the flop your hand will be 71 percent complete. Where does this figure come from? Assuming you play your hand out to the end, it will consist of seven cards. After the flop you have seen five cards or 5/7 of the final hand, which is equal to 71 percent. With this much of your hand complete, you should have enough information to determine whether to continue.

Author Shane Smith coined the phrase "Fit or Fold." You will want to use this criterion when deciding to continue playing the hand. If the flop fits your hand, you will continue playing. If the flop does not fit your hand, you should fold. The flop can fit your hand in three different ways:

1. **It improves your existing hand.** The flop may make you a complete hand that is capable of winning the pot without any further improvement. You could make top pair, two pair, trips, or any other complete hand.

2. **It gives you a good drawing hand.** The flop may give you a good hand to draw to. This could include a four-card flush or straight draw. With three or more players in the hand, you will be getting correct odds to draw to this hand.

3. **Your hand beats the board.** This means that the cards in your hand will beat the cards on the board. If you hold an overpair to the board, you have top pair in the pocket. (An overpair is a pair that is higher

than the highest card in the flop.) Sometimes you can continue playing with just overcards higher than the board cards.

This may sound very simplistic because there are other considerations you need to evaluate even if the flop fits your hand. The makeup of the flop will be a determining factor as to whether you continue playing or not. Many players in low-limit games will play any two suited cards. If the flop shows two cards of the same suit, there is a good chance one of the other players could be on a flush draw.

Before knowing how to proceed, there are several questions you need to consider when the flop comes.

How many players are in the hand?
If you are on a draw you want enough players in the hand to make it worth your while to continue. If you have top pair you want to limit the field if possible, because the more players in the hand, the bigger the chance that someone will complete a drawing hand.

What is your Position?
You should always be aware of your position. The number of players acting after you may have a bearing on whether you check, bet, or raise. Any time you are in late position you have an advantage.

Was there a raise?
If there was a raise during the previous round, you need to know who made it and what position the raiser is in. Is this player a solid player or a habitual bluffer? If there is a raise on the flop, you need to read the board carefully. Many times a player will raise with a flush draw in hopes of gaining a free card on the turn. You will need to determine if this may be the case.

How much money is in the pot?
You need to know approximately how much money is in the pot at all times to determine if you are getting the correct pot odds to continue playing. Usually three or more players will give you the odds you need after the flop.

Learning to read the board is an important skill you need to develop even if you follow the fit-or-fold method for playing your hand. You need to determine how strong your hand is compared to the best hand on the board. This is not to imply that someone will have the nuts for every hand, but you need to determine the strength of your hand compared to all of the possible hands.

Please Note: *The best hand after the flop is a huge favorite to be the winner at the end.*

Take the Lead

If you decide to continue playing once you see it, then it is time for you to become the aggressor and take the lead. If you are first to act, then you should bet. Many losing players will check in hopes of seeing the turn card for free. The problem with this strategy is that all of your opponents will also get to see the turn for free, and they might draw a card that will beat you. You can't determine the strength of anyone else's hand by checking. If you bet and are raised, then you can determine that they have a strong hand and you can fold, call, or raise accordingly. Since the betting limits are still low, the flop is the time to use a bet to determine the strength of your opponents' hands. If you are in later position and have a strong hand or a good draw, you may want to raise to narrow the field or to get a free card on the turn.

Winning players have no problem with folding a hand after seeing the flop. Losing players will stay in to see one more card. The amount of money they waste on calling the flop could ultimately be the determining factor in their quest to become a winner

Here are two common mistakes that are made by players after the flop:

1. **Continuing with a small pair.** Small pairs are lousy hands if they do not improve to a set on the flop. If there are overcards and more than one player, you should throw away your hand if there is a bet in front of you. There are only two cards in the deck that will help you. The odds are 11-to-1 against making a set on the turn and 22-to-1 on the river. These are not good odds, so go by the rule: *No set, no bet!*

2. **Betting out with nothing.** After the flop you have nothing. Everyone has checked to you. Many players will bet in this situation in hopes of stealing the pot. Don't waste your money. The reality is that in a low-limit game with a multiway pot, you will find someone chasing. Save your money and take a free card.

CHAPTER 19

Reading the Board

Many low-limit and newer players come to the poker table wearing blinders. They look at their two starting cards and the community board cards, and if they see something that makes any type of hand, they just start betting or calling. They do this without regard to what the other players may have. This is wrong and is a good way to quickly go broke.

It is extremely important that you can determine how your hand stacks up against the other possible hands that your opponents may hold. This is known as "reading the board." In Texas Hold'em, your ability to accurately read the board is one of the most important skills you can develop.

Because Texas Hold'em players use the same five community cards, you can easily determine what the best possible hand will be. The best possible hand is called "the nuts." This is not to say one of the players will always have the nuts, but by knowing what the best hand is, you can determine the strength of your own hand compared to it. Once you determine the strength of your hand, you will have more information to make your decision about how it should be played.

How to Read the Board

Reading the board is not difficult. You look at the community cards and then determine what possible hands can be made if you add two additional cards. The two additional cards are the hole cards held by the players. You start with the highest possible hand and then work your way down to the lowest hand. Look at the example below. (Note: x denotes any other card.)

The possibilities for this hand in order are:

- **Three of a kind**
- Aces if you have A-A
- Jacks if you have J-J
- Sevens if you have 7-7
- Fives if you have 5-5
- Deuces if you have 2-2
- **Two pairs**
- Aces and jacks if you have A-J
- Aces and sevens if you have A-7
- Aces and fives if you have A-5
- Aces and deuces if you have A-2
- Jacks and sevens if you have J-7
- Jacks and fives if you have J-5
- Jacks and sevens if you have J-2
- Sevens and fives if you have 7-5
- Sevens and deuces if you have 7-2
- **Pairs**
- Aces if you have A-x
- Jacks if you have J-x
- Sevens if you have 7-x
- Fives if you have 5-x
- Deuces if you have 2-x

That is a pretty innocent and straightforward set of board cards with limited possibilities for a big hand. Other boards you read will have many more possibilities. Knowing some of the red flags makes it easier to quickly evaluate how your hand will stack up against your opponents.

Suited Cards

Any time the board contains suited cards there is the possibility of a flush. Many low-limit players will play any two suited cards. When you see a third suited card appear on the board and there is betting and raising, you know that someone has made their flush.

Please Note: *Without three suited cards, no one can make a flush.*

Pair on the Board

Whenever there is a pair on the board, there is a possibility that someone has four of a kind. Although that is not common, there *is* a strong possibility that someone has made a full house. This is especially true if the board contains mostly high cards.

Double-Paired Board

If there are two pairs on the board, it doubles the chance of a four of a kind and greatly increases the chances of a full house.

In the board above, if you hold an ace, your chance of winning will be slim if there are many players in the hand. Any time there are two pairs on the board, the chances of a full house are greatly increased. If there is a lot of raising, you have to consider this fact. Tens and 9s are common cards for a player to have in their hand.

Straights

Straight draws are very deceptive and sometimes difficult to read. Whenever there are three sequenced cards or two cards with a gap of three or fewer, there is a potential for a straight. In fact, all flops that don't contain a pair can make a straight on the fourth card except for K-8-3, K-8-2, K-7-2, and Q-7-2.

Many players will play starting hands that have connectors suited or unsuited or two cards with a single gap. If you see three cards in sequence and there is action, you should be thinking *straight*. If you hold connectors at the low end of the sequence and make a straight, you may be in for a big loss if someone holds the connectors for the higher end.

Determining Your Outs

Be aware of the unseen cards that can improve or make your hand. These are your outs. The only way to determine your outs is by reading the board. Once you determine your outs, you can assess how strong your hand will be if you do improve. Sometimes even if you make a hand it may not be strong enough to win.

Changing Your Evaluation

The best hand after the flop will not necessarily be the best hand at the river. You must reassess the board every time another card is added.

Practice

Learning to read the board correctly only takes a little practice. If you are new to the game, all you have to do is get a deck of cards and deal some practice hands. Start by turning over three cards to represent the flop and determine the best possible hand. Then turn up a fourth one for the turn and see what possibilities you can make with this card. Finally turn over a fifth card for the river and repeat the exercise.

If you are playing in a live game, you can practice reading the board even when you are not involved in a hand. Since you will not be playing many hands as a tight player, this will keep you occupied. It will also give you some valuable information about your opponents and the types of hands they play when you see their cards at the showdown:

- Will they bet out with a middle or bottom pair?
- Will they raise or semibluff with suited cards after the flop?
- Do they only bet or raise with a strong hand like top pair?

All of this information can be determined by reading the board and watching the other players at the showdown.

When I was in school there was a sign hanging on the classroom wall that said: READING IS FUNDAMENTAL. That was good advice for the classroom, and it is excellent advice in the card room as well.

CHAPTER 20

The Turn

In Limit Texas Hold'em, the turn is the turning point in the hand. The betting limits are doubled, and you have seen 86 percent of your final hand. With one card to come, you now have a big decision to make—whether to play or fold. Many times if you call on the turn, you will also end up calling on the river. Marginal hands that could be abandoned on the turn could end up as costly hands on the river if you lose. In an unraised pot a bet on the turn costs you the same as the pre-flop and the flop bet added together.

This is the time to start looking at the pot odds to determine if it will be profitable to continue. Since the betting limits double on the turn, the pot odds are now cut in half. In a $3/6 game, if there were $30 in the pot, you would be getting 10-to-1 odds on a $3 bet. Now that the bets are $6 you are only getting 5-to-1. You might not be getting the correct odds to stay in with a drawing hand. For example, if you get to the turn and you are trying to draw to an inside straight, you only have four outs. The odds are 10.5-to-1 against you. If you are only getting 5-to-1 in pot odds, you should give it up.

The Best Hand

I ran a computer simulation to determine how often the best hand at the turn held on to be the winning hand. In a field of 10 low-limit players, the best hand at the turn held up about 79 percent of the time. With the addition of the turn card, there are more possible hands that can be made by the cards on the board. This is where your board-reading skills will be important. You want to know where your hand ranks compared to the best possible hand that can be made from the board. It's impossible to cover every situation, but there are a few general guidelines for playing your hand on the turn.

Checking

If you have an open-ended straight or flush draw you want to see the river as cheaply as possible. In this instance it is usually best to check. If someone bets and it is raised, you can get out without putting any money in the pot. If there is no raise and there are three or more players, you can call the bet because you should be getting correct odds to do so.

Betting

If you think you have the best hand after seeing the turn card and are first to act, then go ahead and bet. Many players will try to get fancy and attempt to check-raise in this position. If the other players also check, you have lost a bet or two. In low-limit games the straightforward approach is usually the best, as there are plenty of players who will call you. Make them pay. Why give them a free card if you don't have to?

Calling

If you were planning to call a bet if someone makes one before it is your turn to act, this bet doesn't mean that you should automatically call a raise. First you must consider who made the raise and what position he is in. If another player raises on the turn from early position, it usually means they have a strong hand.

If there is a raise on the turn and you hold only one pair, you are more than likely beaten and should fold. If there are three suited cards or cards that can likely make a straight on the board, fold because that pair is beaten.

If you get to the turn and you hold only two unsuited overcards (two cards higher than any cards on the board) with no flush or straight draw, then you should fold if there is a bet in front of you. Too much money is lost by players who hope to catch a miracle card on the river. The best hand you can make with two unsuited overcards is a pair, which will probably lose.

If another player raises on the turn and you hold less than the top pair, you are more than likely beaten and should fold.

Raising

If you have two pairs or better and think you have the best hand, then you should raise. This will get more money in the pot and hopefully narrow the field for you. If you only have top pair and a player bets into you, that means they are not afraid of top pair. You should not raise in this situation. It is better to just call and see what the river card brings.

Make Your Best Decision

More money is lost by losing players who are looking for a miracle on the river. Don't play "wish hands" or hands where you may be drawing dead.

> **Please Note:** *Drawing dead is when you make your hand but are still beaten with a higher hand.*

A winning player knows how to release a marginal hand, and the turn is definitely the time to do it, because betting limits are doubled.

CHAPTER 21

The River

The river is the final community card in Texas Hold'em. If you have been playing properly, you will not see the river card unless you have a strong hand that is a favorite to win or you have a draw to a winning hand. Once the river card is turned over, you know exactly what you have. Playing decisions on the river are easier than during other rounds, but they still require some thought.

If you were drawing to a hand, you know whether you were successful or not. Obviously if you do not make your hand, you will usually fold if there has been a bet and a call. If you do make a hand or had a made hand before the river, then you need to assess its strength to determine how to play.

Mistakes

When you get to the river there are two mistakes that you can make. One is to call a losing bet, which will cost you the price of a bet. The other is to fold your hand, which will cost you all the money in the pot.

Obviously folding your hand will be a far more costly mistake than merely calling a bet. If there is a slight chance you may have the winning hand, you should call. I'm not advocating calling with nothing, but you should call if there is a chance to win. Many times the pot odds will justify making the call.

Pot Odds

In low-limit games the pots can get very large. Many times you will have a lot of players seeing the flop and many staying to see the turn. By the time the river card is dealt, you will probably be getting the correct odds to call with any hand that has a possibility of winning. Look at this example:

You are in a $3/6 game and you get to the river. There is $60 in the pot, and you are last to act. There are two other players still active in the hand. Before any betting takes place you are getting 10-to-1 odds. If the first player bets, there is $66 in the pot. The second player calls and brings the pot up to $72. It will cost you $6 to call as well. You are now getting 12-to-1 odds for your call.

If you made this same call 13 times and lost 12 times but won once, you would be even. You would lose $6 in 12 attempts, or $72 dollars, when you lost, but you would win $72 when you won. If you were to win this bet once in 12 tries, you would be ahead of the game by $6.

Bet It Out

Don't try to get fancy on the river by attempting a check-raise. As with the turn, if you have a strong hand you should bet your hand if you are first to act. If you bet and the other player folds, then they more than likely would have just checked if you had checked in an attempt to check-raise. Many times a player in a low-limit game will call your bet with just an ace-high in hopes that you are bluffing. You want to make this type of player pay, and betting is the only way to do this. On the other hand if you think that you might be beat because of a scare card on the river, it might be prudent to just check and call.

Scare Cards

You should always look closely at the river card and try to determine how it could help someone's hand. If everyone checks on the turn and there is a bet from early position when a third suited card falls, you can be pretty sure you are up against a flush. If the board pairs on the turn, it could give someone a full house. Because of the "any-ace mentality" in low-limit games, you should also be cautious when an ace comes up on the river. A player with a small pair and ace kicker could have made two pairs.

If you hold only top pair and there is a raise with the possibility of a flush on the board, you are beaten. Seldom will a player bluff with a raise on the river when there are three suited cards on the board.

When You Win

When you show your cards you are giving away valuable information. You want to make your opponents pay to see your hand.

Please Note: *Never show your hand if you don't have to.*

If there is a showdown, don't throw your cards into the muck until the pot is pushed to you. If there is a discrepancy about the winning hand and you have mucked your cards, you may end up forfeiting the pot.

PART II: Omaha

CHAPTER 22
Omaha

The recent surge in the popularity of Texas Hold'em has had a rippling effect. As more and more new players are joining the game, many experienced players looking to expand their knowledge are trying their hand at new poker games.

Some Limit Hold'em players are branching out to play No-Limit Hold'em. Quite a few Texas Hold'em players are trying the game of Omaha because it looks very similar to Hold'em. Omaha resembles Texas Hold'em in the fact that it is a game played with five community cards and has four betting rounds. However, Omaha is quite different because the player receives four personal cards, and two of them must be used to form the best five-card hand at the showdown.

There are two variations of the game: Omaha High and Omaha 8 or Better, which is sometimes called Omaha Hi-Lo Split or just Omaha 8. Both versions of the game can be played in three ways: as limit games with structured betting rounds, as no-limit games, or as pot-limit games.

The mechanics of the game are the same for both versions. The only difference is that Hi-Lo is a split-pot game where there can be two winners for a hand.

The most common game found in the card room is Limit Omaha. For this example I will use the $2/4 betting structure. This means the minimum bet is $2 for the first two betting rounds and $4 for the last two betting rounds.

The Opening
As with all games played in the card room, the dealer does not play. There is a "designated dealer" button that rotates around the table to denote who will act last. In Omaha two blind bets are posted to start a new hand. The player immediately to the left of the designated dealer button puts up or "posts" the small blind, which is half the minimum bet. The small blind for the $2/4 game is $1.

The player to the left of the small blind posts the big blind, which is equal to the minimum bet—$2 for this game. The rest of the players do not put up any money to start the hand. Because the button rotates around the table, each player will eventually act as the big blind, small blind, and dealer. It will cost you $3 every time the deal makes a complete rotation around the table.

Pre-Flop

After the blinds are posted each player receives four cards facedown, with the player on the small blind receiving the first card and the player with the dealer button getting the last card.

The first betting round begins with the player to the left of the big blind putting in $2 to call the blind bet, putting in $4 to raise the big blind, or folding his hand. The betting goes around the table in order until it reaches the player who posted the small blind. That player can call the bet by putting in $1 because a $1 bet was already posted. The last person to act is the big blind. If no one has raised, the dealer will ask if they would like the option. This means the big blind has the option to raise or just check.

The Flop

After the first betting round is completed the dealer burns the top card on the deck. This is done to make sure no one could have accidentally seen the top card. The dealer deals three cards and turns them faceup in the middle of the table. This is known as "the flop." These are community cards used by all the players. Another betting round begins with the first active player to the left of the dealer button. The minimum bet for this round is also $3.

The Turn

After the flop betting round, the dealer burns another card and turns a fourth card faceup in the middle of the table. This is called "the turn." The minimum bet after the turn is $4 and begins again with the first active player to the left of the button.

The River

Following the betting round for the turn, the dealer will burn another card and turn a fifth and final card faceup. This is called "the river." Now the final betting round begins with $4 being the minimum bet. There is usually a three- or four-raise maximum during all betting rounds except if the play becomes heads-up with two players.

The Showdown

To determine the winner, the players *must* use two of his hole cards and three cards from the board to form the highest five-card hand.

Omaha 8 Hi-Lo Split

Omaha 8 Hi-Lo is a split-pot game. That means there can be two winners if there is a qualifying low hand. The player with the highest hand will split the pot with the player with the lowest hand.

> **Please Note:** *In order to have a hand qualify as low, there must be no cards higher than 8 in that five-card hand.*

Many players prefer the split-pot version of the game, and it has become so popular that most card rooms no longer offer Omaha High only—in fact, it is slowly becoming extinct. Therefore, this book will only be dealing with the split-pot game.

High Hand

At least half of the pot will go to the player with the highest hand. Since in Omaha you must use two cards from your hand, there must be three cards on the board that are 8 or lower. If there are not three cards on the board that are eight or lower, there can be no low hand. This means there will only be one winner. The player with the highest hand will win the whole pot.

Low Hand

The low hand consists of the five lowest single cards. An ace can be used as either high or low, so it is considered the highest for the high hand and lowest for the low hand. Therefore the lowest hand is A-2-3-4-5. This hand is also called a "wheel."

If two players have the same hand they will split the low half of the pot. This is not uncommon, because many players will play any hand that consists of an ace-deuce.

> **Please Note:** *A flush or straight is ignored when making a low hand; however, it may also be used as the high hand.*

When two players split the low, we refer to it as getting "quartered," as you will only win a quarter of the pot.

High and Low

The ideal situation in Omaha is to have a hand that will win both the high hand *and* the low hand. This is known as "scooping the pot." Since you have four cards in your hand, you can use any combination of two cards for the high hand and low hand. You may use two cards for the high hand and two different cards for the low hand. The other way to win the whole pot is to have the highest hand and have no low hand possible.

CHAPTER 23

Omaha Starting Hands

In Omaha you get four hole cards instead of two. At first glance some players may think that this gives them double the starting-hand combinations, but in reality, with four cards you have six possible two-card combinations.

Here is how it works: You have four cards, A-B-C-D. The combinations are: AB, CD, AC, BD, AD, and BC.

With all these starting combinations, many Omaha players think that this gives them a reason to play more hands. Many players feel that they should see the flop because there are so many possibilities with four starting cards. *If you play every hand, you will go broke.* There are 5,277 four-card combinations that can be dealt with a 52-card deck. When you figure in the suited combinations, there are 270,725 combinations of two-card hands that can be made. Most of these will be losers.

In a 10-handed game you have six combinations of starting hands, but your opponents have a combined 54 (6x9) starting hands against you. Instead of playing looser, you actually need to be more selective in choosing the hands you want to play.

Of course in the low-limit games you will start playing in you will encounter very loose players who will usually see the flop with between 50 to 80 percent of their starting hand dealt to them. In contrast, if you are selective and play the hand with the highest probability of winning, then you will only see the flop between 10 to 20 percent of the time. In a 10-handed game this means one or two hands per round.

Cards Must Work Together

The cards in your starting hand need to be coordinated. This means that the four cards should work together, such as having a straight possibility that may wrap around the flop. Double-suited hands that contain aces are good for the nut flush; however, three or four cards of the same suit are garbage hands, because they diminish your flush possibilities.

Because you want to scoop the pot in Omaha your hand will usually need to hold an ace if you expect to win. Since the ace is the highest and lowest card, there are very few hands that are worth playing if they don't contain an ace, unless you are only going strictly for the high half of the pot.

The best starting hand is A-A-2-3 double-suited. "Double-suited" means that one ace and the 2 are the same suit and the other ace and the 3 are another suit. This gives you a good chance at the nut flush in two different suits. It also has the possibility of making a straight as well. If an ace, 2, or 3 appear on the board, your hand will not be counterfeited and you will have the nut-low hand if three more low cards are on the board.

If you do not hold an ace and are going for the high half of the pot, the four cards in your starting hand should be coordinated. This means they should work together. You want cards that can hopefully form a straight, flush, or full house.

Please Note: *It is a very rare occurrence that a single pair wins the pot in Omaha.*

The Top Ten Starting Hands in Omaha Hi-Low:

1.	A-A-2-3 double-suited
2.	A-A-2-4 double-suited
3.	A-A-2-3 suited
4.	A-A-2-5 double-suited
5.	A-A-2-4 suited
6.	A-A-3-4 double-suited
7.	A-A-2-3 nonsuited
8.	A-A-2-2 double-suited
9.	A-A-3-5 double-suited
10.	A-A-2-6 double-suited

The Other Profitable Starting Omaha Hands

These hands can be double-suited, suited (where only two cards are the same suit and the other two are different suits), or of different suits. Note: The *x* denotes any other card. However, you still want the fourth card to fit with the other three cards. If you had A-A-2-x, you would want the x card to be a low card or suited with an ace.

1.	A-A-2-x
2.	A-A-3-x
3.	A-A-4-5
4.	A-2-3-x
5.	A-2-K-K
6.	A-2-Q-Q
7.	A-2-J-J
8.	A-3-4-5
9.	A-A-x-x
10.	A-2-K-Q
11.	A-2-K-J
12.	A-2-x-x (suited ace)
13.	A-3-K-K
14.	A-3-4-x
15.	2-3-4-5 (fold if there is no ace on the flop)
16.	J-Q-K-A
17.	T-J-Q-K
18.	K-K-Q-J
19.	Q-J-10-9
20.	2-3-4-x (fold if there is no ace on the flop)
21.	Any four cards between 10 and ace

Ace-Deuce Only

Many players look at their starting four cards, and if they see an A-2 they act as if they have just found the Holy Grail. They immediately raise with this hand, which is wrong for a couple of reasons. First is the fact that in order to qualify for low, there must be three or more low cards on the board. This does not always happen, and if three high cards come on the flop you are in big trouble.

Getting Quartered

Another reason raising with an A-2 is wrong is the fact that every other player with A-2 will also be in the hand. If you do make your low, instead of getting half the pot you will get half of the low pot, which is a quarter.

Please Note: *Being quartered will cost you money.*

For this reason you *should not* get into a raising war on the river in a multiway pot with low only, because one of the other players may also have the low. Example: There are three players in the hand. You start raising and you end up putting $20 in the pot, as do the other two players. There is $60 in the pot from the three of you. One player turns over high and collects half the pot, or $30. The other player turns over a low hand that ties you. You get $15 apiece, even though you each contributed $20 to the pot. You lost money by raising. You can save money by not automatically raising with A-2.

Getting Counterfeited

"Getting counterfeited" is a phrase used when your low hand becomes worthless because a card on the board pairs one of the hole cards that you were using to make the low hand.

If you have an A-2 in your hand and there is an ace or deuce on the board, your hand is counterfeited if there are only three low cards on the board. Since you must use two cards from your hand, you will need to have three different low cards on the board or your hand will not count as low.

For example: You have A-2-9-Q. The board is: 3-5-J-K-2. You can't make a low hand because the 2 on the board is paired with the 2 in your hand.

> **Please Note:** *In order to have a valid low hand, you must have five different low cards that do not match.*

Counterfeiting will occur more often if you constantly play the A-2 with no other low cards in your starting hand. In this example the 9 and queen do not fit with each other or with the ace or 2. However, this is the type of hands losers will play. In fact, they will actually raise with this hand.

Odds of Making a Low

The chart below shows the odds of making a low hand based on the number of different unpaired low cards you hold in your starting hand.

Number of Different Low Cards You Hold	Odds of Making Low Before the Flop	Odds of Making Low Two Low Cards on Flop	Odds of Making Low One Low Card on Flop
4	49%	70%	24%
3	40%	72%	26%
2	24%	26%	1%

You may notice an oddity in this chart. There is a slightly larger percentage of making the low hand with three different low cards than four on the flop. This is because with four low cards there is a higher chance of pairing one of your low cards, which will counterfeit it and make it unplayable for the low hand.

Simple Point-Count Strategy

Since choosing a strong starting hand can be difficult for a new player, here is a simple system that assigns a point value to the four hole cards. If your hand totals high enough, you play; if not, you fold. It's easy to learn and will give you a strong foundation as you are learning the game.

Here is the easy counting system you can use to help determine the strength of your starting cards. I found this method was one of the easiest ways to give me a practical estimation of my hand strength and was surprised by how well I did when I used it.

For the High Hand:

Pairs: Aces count as 30 points. Kings = 13, Queens = 12, Jacks = 11, and all other pairs equal their face values. Example: a pair of 5s is worth five points.

Flushes: Two-card flushes count 10 points with an ace. All others without an ace count as four points. Three or four cards of the same suit count as half.

Straights: Two-card straights with no gap or one gap count as two points. Example: 8-9 or 8-10.

High Cards: Unpaired Ace = four points, King = two points.

For the Low Hand:

1.	A-2 = 20 points
2.	A-3 = 15 points,
3.	2-3 = 10 points
4.	A-4 = 10 points
5.	2-4, 3-4 = 5 points
6.	2-3 = 10 points
7.	A-5, 2-5, 3-5, or 4-5 = 5 points

Add up the points for your four cards for the high count and the low count. Add them together. It takes 25 points to call, 40 points to raise, and 50 points to reraise. If you are in the small blind, you can complete your bet with 10 points.

Please Note: *If your hand doesn't add up, you don't play.*

Because you are only playing the strongest hands with this method, you can play these hands that add up from any position.

I found this point-count method to be one of the easiest ways to give me a practical estimation of my hand strength. While it is not the only way to choose a starting hand, it is the best one to use if you are new to the game or even an experienced player who has not been having much success playing Omaha.

It is easy to miss some combinations of hands when you are looking at four starting cards. This point-count method helps put things in perspective. It will also help you avoid some of the pitfalls that Omaha players encounter. The biggest one is overvaluing big pairs or hands containing a single ace with no 2 or 3.

CHAPTER 24

Counterfeited

In Omaha there are some situations that will arise from time to time that will turn a good hand into a loser. This can be very frustrating, but they are part of the game. If you are going to play Omaha you have to be prepared for some evil twists that Lady Luck will throw your way. In many ways, Omaha is not a steady contest or as predictable as Texas Hold'em.

However, you can minimize your Omaha losses by playing correctly.
* Do not automatically raise if you have an A-2.
* Try to avoid getting counterfeited.
* Try not to be drawing dead.

"Drawing dead" is the phrase used when your hand will be a loser even if you draw the cards to complete or improve it. Your ability to read the board will help you determine if you are drawing dead or not. In Omaha, if you are not drawing to the nut hand (best possible hand that can be made), then you are probably drawing dead.

Bad Beats

You have a great hand, and someone beats you! That's a "bad beat." As in, "Too bad you got beat." Omaha is replete with bad beats because of the structure of the game.

Because more players are staying to see the flop, the pots can be very large in Omaha. Players will be getting correct odds to justify staying in a hand. This means there will be more bad beats in Omaha. In Omaha the best hand can change with each new board card, so bad beats occur more frequently. You have to have the emotional fortitude to handle this if you want to play the game.

CHAPTER 25

Reading the Board

To repeat, when you play poker and have the best possible hand that can't be beaten, it's called "the nuts." In Hold'em it is rare that a player will have the absolute nuts after the river, but in Omaha it is a common occurrence.

If you are not drawing to the nuts after the flop, you may find yourself with the second-best hand or worse. Most new players wonder why this happens so much in Omaha. The answer is quite simple. If you are playing in a 10-handed game, each player receives four hole cards for a total of 40 cards. There are five cards on the board, so 45 out of the 52 cards in the deck will be in play.

If you want to win at Omaha, it is critical that you learn to read the board quickly and accurately after each community card is revealed to determine the nut hand. What makes this more challenging is that you must be able to do this for the high hand *and* the low hand. To further complicate this process, your four-card starting hand can make six two-card combinations for both the low hand and the high hand. That means you have to look at 12 different possibilities to determine your best hand. It's no wonder that most novice players lose a few hands simply because they misread the board.

Here is a hand that will confuse some players who are used to playing Texas Hold'em. Look at this hand and board and determine the player's best hand.

Player's hand: Ah, As, Jc, and 10s

The board cards are: Kh, Qh, 7h, 5h, and 5c

What did you determine? The best hand is two pairs—aces and 5s.

Many novices will say that the player had an ace-high heart flush (Ah-Kh-Qh-7h, 5h) or an ace-high straight (A-K-Q-J-10). *Neither of those hands is possible* because it would require using four board cards to make the flush or using three hole cards to make the straight.

Please Note: *The most common mistake that novice players make is not remembering that they must use two cards from their hand and three cards from the board.*

Practice Drill

As simple as it may sound, the best way to learn to read the board is to practice. As with any new endeavor you want to master, it will require some effort on your part. The reward will be profitable once you do master this skill. The best part is you can get all the practice you need for the price of a deck of cards. All you have to do is deal out several hundred practice hands and then determine the best high hand and best low hand. This is called the "Nut Drill," and it will consist of just dealing out the board cards. You don't have to deal out or look at any hole cards during this drill.

Many players get confused when they look at the hole cards and try to determine the nut hand. The purpose of this drill is to determine which two cards will make the best high and low hands. Deal out five cards faceup to simulate the board cards. Now determine which two cards will make you the best high hand and which two cards will make the best low hand.

The board cards are: 4h-2c-5c-9h-Jc

With this board, the nut high would be a flush if a player has A-x of clubs (x denotes any club card). Therefore, the best low would be A-2-3-4-5 if a player holds an A-3.

Keep repeating this drill until you can quickly determine which two hole cards will make the best high and low hands from the five board cards.

After you become proficient using the five board cards, deal them out as if you were playing a live game and determine the nut hand at each stage and what possible hands you can draw to.

Start by dealing three cards for the flop.

These are: Jh-10c-8h

After this flop the best hand is a straight if someone holds a queen and 9. However, with two hearts on the board, there is a draw to the nut flush if someone holds an A-x of hearts.

Now deal a card for the turn.

This will be the 6c.

After the turn the best hand is still a straight if someone holds a queen and 9. However, with two hearts on the board, there is still a draw to the nut flush if someone holds an A-x of hearts. Someone with A-2 has a draw to the nut low.

Now deal a card for the river.

This will be 5h.

The best possible hand for this board would be the A-2 of hearts. A player with those cards would scoop the whole pot with an ace-high flush and would win the low if no other player had an A-2. If another player had A-2, the low half of the pot would be split.

Strange Hands

You will see some strange hands in Omaha. As mentioned earlier, it is quite common for two players to have a tie for the low hand. You will also occasionally see three players tie for low, and I have even seen four players tie for low when they each had an A-2. They received an eighth of the pot.

I once split a pot with another player but not in the usual way. At the showdown we both had a wheel (A-2-3-4-5) for the best low hand, and this straight was also the best high hand. We were tied with the best high *and* low hands. We split the high half of the pot and we split the low half.

Quick Rules

Here are some rules that will speed up the process by helping you eliminate hands.

- If there is not a pair on the board, there cannot be four of a kind or a full house.
- If there are not three suited cards, there cannot be a flush.
- If there are not three low cards, there cannot be a low hand.
- You cannot make a straight without a 5 or a 10.

Cards Speak

When you play in the casino card room there is the rule that *cards speak*, which means that no matter what you say when you flip over your cards, you actually have the best possible hand that you could make with your cards. It's the responsibility of the dealer to point out that a hand is miscalled.

> **Please Note:** *If you are unsure of whether your hand is a winner, you can just turn it faceup and let the dealer determine the hand.*

There have also been situations where other players misread their cards and announce that they have a winning hand when they actually do not. Don't just assume you have a losing hand and toss your cards into the discard pile, because if you do this, your hand will be declared dead. Wait until the dealer pushes the pot to the winner before mucking your hand.

CHAPTER 26
Omaha Post-Flop Strategy

This was mentioned in the previous section on board reading, but it is so vital to playing winning Omaha, I will repeat it again. If you are not drawing to the nuts after the flop, you may find yourself second-best or worse. If you are playing in a 10-handed game, each player receives four hole cards for a total of 40 cards. There are five cards on the board, so 45 out of the 52 cards in the deck will be in play. With so many cards in play, someone is likely to have the nut hand or at least a draw to the nut hand. This is an important paragraph to remember!

The Flop

As with Texas Hold'em you should play the flop using the fit-or-fold criteria. This is even more imperative in Omaha Hi-Lo because there is a greater chance that someone has made a good hand with their four starting cards. If you have high cards and the flop comes with two or three low cards, your hand is not going to be worth much unless you have the nut-flush draw.

Too many people play low cards in Omaha Hi-Lo. Even a made straight will probably be beaten if two or three suited cards fall. There is a very simple strategy you can use for playing the flop that will greatly increase your winning percentage and keep you from suffering big losses.

If you are in a loose game with four or more players seeing the flop, after the flop, continue playing *only* if you have made the nuts or have a draw to the nut hand. Fold everything else. This strategy is simple and effective, but it is difficult to accomplish if you don't have the discipline to stick to the game plan.

The Turn

At the turn the betting limits double. Do you have a chance at the nut hand? Have you made a low hand? How many players are left in the hand? These are all the questions you should be asking on the turn. Again if there are a lot of players still active—and with Omaha, there usually will be—if you have not made a powerful hand or have a draw to the nut hand, you should fold. Remember that in a limit game the betting limits double with the turn, so if you fold a losing hand, you are essentially saving two bets.

The River

The river in Omaha is cruel! More players get drawn out on the river in Omaha than they do in Texas Hold'em. You can have the nut hand after the turn only to find it worthless after the river card is exposed.

For example, the board is: 2d-4s-5s-Jh.

You Hold: Ac-3d-Kc-Kh

You have the nut-low and an A-2-3-4-5 straight, which may be good enough for the high hand as well.

And what happens? The river is As. Your promising hand has just been rendered worthless by the river card! You no longer have a low hand because it has been counterfeited because of the ace pairing your ace. The fact that it is a spade means there are now three spades on the board and someone is likely to have a flush that will beat your straight.

The biggest mistake that Omaha players make on the river is reraising when they have made the low hand. If there are several players left in the hand and you have the low hand, you can almost be certain that another player has tied you for low as well. When this happens, you will be spitting the low half of the pot. In other words you will be quartered. When you get quartered, you lose money because the player with the high takes half the pot, which you have very kindly added money to.

A Cruel Game

In Low-Limit Omaha Hi-Lo there are many bad beats because so many players stay in until the end, and many of them draw out on the river. If you don't have the emotional fortitude to handle this type of bad beat, then you should probably stick to playing Texas Hold'em. However, if you are selective about your starting hands and draw only to the nuts in the subsequent rounds, you will find that Omaha Hi-Lo can be an exciting and profitable game.

CHAPTER 27

You Can't Win Omaha with Texas Hold'em Strategy

When Texas Hold'em players try to play Omaha for the first time, their downfall is that they think they can win at Omaha using Texas Hold'em strategy. Omaha may look like Hold'em because it is played with five community cards, but that is where the similarities end. In Hold'em you can use any five-card combination formed by your two hole cards and the five community cards. I'll repeat, in Omaha you *must* use two cards from your hand and three cards from the board.

Big Pairs Rarely Win

One of the biggest mistakes that Hold'em players new to Omaha make is raising and reraising with a big pair before the flop. While pocket rockets may be a great hand in Hold'em, it will rarely hold up in Omaha in a multiway pot.

In Omaha Hi-Lo, where the pot is split between the high and low hands, every player with an ace and a small card will be playing, which will further diminish the possibility that your pair of aces will be the winner. Omaha is a game in which straights, flushes, and full houses tend to be the winning hands.

Pre-Flop Raises Don't Work

In Hold'em you can sometimes raise from late position and win the pot when everyone folds. In Omaha you will usually have more players staying in to see the flop. This means that a positional raise will not work. With each player holding four cards, many of them will find some reason to see the flop.

The Nuts Win More Often

In Hold'em it is rare that a player will have the absolute nuts (best hand possible) after the river, but in Omaha it is a common occurrence. If you are

93

not drawing to the nuts after the flop, you may find yourself second-best or worse. In Hold'em nine outs will give you a good shot at the winning hand. In Omaha you may need 16 or 20 outs to even stay in after the flop. In most instances you will have to show down the best hand to win.

Because of all the possibilities after the flop, you don't want to slow-play a hand and give your opponent a chance to draw out on you.

Don't Slow-Play or Check-Raise

Slow playing and check-raising are two tactics used in Texas Hold'em to get more money in the pot when you have the best hand. These tactics are unnecessary in Omaha, as most players will call if they have any remote possibility of making a hand. The way to get more money in the pot when you have the best hand is to bet if you are first to act or raise if someone bets before you.

Learn the Game

If you want to be a winner, you must learn to play Omaha correctly. You can't be a winner if you use your Hold'em strategy for this game. Omaha is not Texas Hold'em.

That being said, if you learn to play correctly, Omaha is actually easier to play because it is so straightforward and the pots are usually much larger than in Texas Hold'em. This means it will be more profitable for a winning player.

PART III: Expert Poker Advice from Bill "Ace-10" Burton

CHAPTER 28

Expert Poker Advice: Playing in a Card Room

Playing casino poker is quite different from playing in a home game. There are certain procedures and protocols you will need to understand before you sit down to play. You will find that playing poker in the casino has many advantages over a home game.

One of the biggest advantages to playing in the card room is the availability of games any time you want to play. You won't have to worry if one of your regular players can't make it for the weekly game. You also don't have to worry about time constraints. You can play for as long as you want.

There are some procedures you need to be aware of when you play in a casino. You don't just walk up to a table and sit down. When you enter the poker room, you must sign in at the desk. You tell the host what game you are interested in playing. If there is an opening, you will be seated immediately. If the table is full, they will take your initials and call you when there is an opening. Some casinos have a large board where they will write your name or initials; in some places they will write your name on a list. Either way you will be called when it is your turn.

When your name is called the poker-room host will show you to your table. In some rooms the host will ask you how much you would like to buy in for and get you your chips when you are seated. At other casinos you will purchase the chips from the dealer when you sit down. You are allowed to bring chips from other games. All games have a minimum buy-in, which for most low-limit games is usually $30.

Posting

In many casinos a new player sitting down at the table has to post a bet equal to the big blind if he wishes to be dealt into the next hand. This is not mandatory, and you may elect to wait until it is your turn to be the big blind before you enter the game.

Please Note: *Waiting to play a hand has advantages.*

Waiting will give you time to observe your competition and determine the type of players at your table. Notice the quality of starting hands being played and who is playing them.

Is the table tight or loose? Observing the table while you wait for a seat will give you an insight about your competition. Waiting will also give you a few minutes to settle in and get your mind emotionally prepared for the game. If you can't get immediate seating when you sign in and find yourself on the waiting list for a game, it is advisable to watch the game in progress. Then when you do get a seat at the table, you can post right away, as you will already have a feel for the table.

Table Stakes

In casino poker you play for table stakes. This means that you bet only with the money that you have on the table. You're not allowed to go into your pocket for more money in the middle of a hand. If you run out of chips, you announce that you are "all in" and you will only be eligible for the money in the pot up to that point. Any additional bets made by other players will be put in a side pot. You will not be eligible for this side pot even if you have the best hand. This means that once a player is "all in" it is possible for a player with the second-best hand to win some money from the remaining players in the hand.

You are allowed to buy more chips at any time between hands. You may also have money other than chips on the table that will be counted as part of your table stakes. Say you were to keep a $20 bill under your stack of chips. This would be counted as $20 on the table. In the middle of a hand, if you ran out of chips you would be able to place the money in for a bet and you would be given your change in chips. It counts because it was on the table before the hand was started.

Taking a Break

Sooner or later you will need to take a break. You can get up and leave the table to go to the bathroom, stretch your legs, or take a break for any other reason. What you can't do is take your chips with you if you plan on returning to the game. The chips must stay on the table.

The dealer will deal you out of the hand while you are away from your seat. If you do not miss any blinds, it will not cost you any money while you are away from the table, as you won't be involved in any hands. If you are gone from the table and miss your blinds, a button will be put in front of your chips showing that you have missed a blind. When you return from your break, you will have to make up any blinds you missed while you were gone. You can post it right away or wait until it is your turn to be the big blind again.

If you missed both a big blind and a small blind, the money for the small blind you missed will be put in the pot, and the money for the big blind will act as a live bet. Even if you missed more than one big and small blind, you will only be required to make up one of each in most card rooms.

I used to try and take my breaks after it was my turn to act as the blinds. I noticed one problem with this. I was always leaving the table when I was in late position, giving up the advantage that acting later gave me. I discovered that if I had to leave the table and would miss more than a couple hands I could actually turn this to an advantage. Instead of taking a break after the blind, I now leave the table one hand before I am the big blind when I am going to be under the gun. Since this is the worst position, where you have to act first, I don't mind missing this hand. I then return to the table after the dealer button has passed me. I post my big blind and am then in the late position with the option to check or raise when it is my turn. After the flop, I am second-to-last to act, putting me in extremely good position. Granted I have to forfeit my small blind, but most of the time I fold these if I don't have a playable hand. For the price of the small blind I have bought myself excellent position.

Most of the card rooms are fairly liberal about the amount of time you can be away from the table. Each card room has their policy, but if you are just going to the bathroom or stretching your legs for a while, there will not be any problems. If you are gone for too long, the floor person can pick up your chips and seat someone in your place.

Changing Seats

When you are first seated at a table, you may not have a choice of seats unless it is a new game. This does not mean you can't change your seat once you are in the game. If a player is leaving the table, you can request his seat by telling the dealer as soon as you see him get ready to go.

The main reason to change seats is to get the weaker players to your left and the aggressive players to your right. If you have a player who raises a lot, you want that person sitting on your right. That way, if they raise, you can fold all but your stronger hands. If that person is sitting on your left, you may call with a borderline hand only to find that it will cost you a raise as well. Conversely, you would like to have the weaker player on your left. A weaker player is predictable, and if he is also a calling station, you can profit from raising and knowing that he will call you.

Changing Tables and Must-Move Tables

Game selection is very important. You will find that some games are more profitable than others. You may sit down and find that everyone is so tight that you can't make any money. At other times, you may find yourself at a table with players who you know are more skilled than you.

If you take a seat at a low-limit table and see all the regulars who usually play in the $30/60 game killing time until their game opens up, you may not want to play there. Some card rooms will have more than one game going at the limit you want to play. If, for any reason, you find you don't like the game at the table where you are seated, you can request a table change from the floor person. In some places you may be moved to a different table even if you like the game you are in. This happens when a card room opens up a "must-move" table.

The first table that opens at a particular limit is the main game. If you walk in the card room and want to play $3/6 Hold'em and there is only one game going on, you will be put on the waiting list. If there are enough players on the waiting list, the card room may open up a new $3/6 game. They will designate this table a must-move game. They want to accommodate as many players as they can, but they also want to keep the main game full. Therefore if a seat becomes open at the main table and there is nobody on the waiting list, they will take a player from the must-move table. The player will be determined by the order in which they were seated at the must-move table. The first player seated will be the first one to move to the main game.

Game Selection

In some card rooms, there will be several games being played at the same limit. When you have a choice, you should pick a game that you think will be profitable for you. A game filled with rocks (tight players) who only bet when they have the nuts will not be as profitable as a game with one or two calling stations. You should evaluate the skill level of the players in a game and determine where you fit in. If you feel that you are outmatched by the players at one table, you should look for a different game. Game selection will be a big factor in whether you win or lose.

Bankroll Considerations

One of the most common questions asked about casino poker is how much of a bankroll you should have. Most casinos have a minimum buy-in for each game. This is the minimum needed to sit at the table, but it is usually a lot less than what you may actually need.

In a $3/6 Texas Hold'em game the minimum buy-in might be $30. This is only 10 times the minimum bet of the first two betting rounds. This does not give you much of a cushion if you were to lose a hand or two. If you were to play a hand of Hold'em from start to finish, calling a bet on each round with no raises involved, it would cost you $18 if you lost the hand. Buying in for the minimum would not even cover the cost of two hands.

As a rule of thumb, you should start with about 15 to 20 times the big bet. In a $3/6 Hold'em game you should buy in for $100. This gives you enough money to play with, should you get involved in a big hand. There is nothing worse that running out of money and having to go "all in" when you have the winning hand.

Common Mistakes

Once seated in a game, you want to observe proper table etiquette and be careful not to make any of the common beginner mistakes. Here are a few of the common mistakes made by new players when they sit down to play casino poker for the first time. Actually, some of them are made by experienced players as well.

Betting Out of Turn

You must wait until the player to your right acts. If you bet out of turn, this could give an unfair advantage to a player that did not act yet. If you raise out of turn, a player who might have called could fold. If you fold out of turn, you are giving an advantage to the player on your right who may have folded and now knows you won't raise.

Making a String Raise

If you are going to raise, you should announce "raise" when it is your turn. If you don't announce a raise, you must put the bet and the raise in at the same time. If you put in the bet and then go back to your stack for the raise, you can be called for a "string bet," which is not allowed, and your raise will not be honored.

Not Knowing What the Bet Is

You have to know what the bet is when it is your turn. You must pay attention to the amount of the bet made by the first active player. Then you must be aware if the bet was raised.

Folding Instead of Checking

Sometimes if the player does not like the next card dealt, he will immediately fold when it is his turn. If you are first to act, you can check. If everyone else checks, you get to see the next card for free. The same is true if everyone checks before it is your turn: you should also check instead of folding your cards. The free card may just make your hand. A fold instead of a check essentially gives an advantage to the remaining players. There is now one fewer player in the hand that they need to worry about.

Throwing Chips into the Pot

Place your bet in front of you. This way the dealer sees that your bet is correct. He will scoop them into the pot. You don't throw them into the pot like you would at home.

Not Protecting Your Cards

It is up to the players to protect their cards at all times. Place your hands or a chip on top of your cards. If another player's cards mix with yours when they throw in their cards, your hand will be declared dead. You will see some players bring a special weight or lucky charm to place over their pocket cards. It doesn't matter what you use as long as it is not so large as to interfere with the play of the game.

Make sure to protect your cards until the pot is pushed to you. I once had the winning hand and the dealer pushed the pot to another player and swept my cards into the muck at the same time. I yelled that I had the winning hand. The floor was called and it was ruled that since my cards were in the discard pile I was not entitled to the pot.

Throwing Away a Winning Hand and Discards

The cards speak for themselves. Don't immediately throw in your cards if someone calls out a better hand. The dealer will declare the winner of the hand. Sometimes you may have a better hand than you thought you had. There is also the possibility that the player calling his winning hand has misread his own hand. Let the dealer declare the winner before mucking your hand.

Losing Control of Your Emotions

Keep your emotions in check. The table is not the place for foul language or temper tantrums. It will not be tolerated. Besides, it makes you look foolish. Veteran players as well as newcomers make this mistake. It is one that should not be made by anyone!

Playing Too Many Hands

Many players crave the action. They feel that if they are not involved in the hand they aren't really playing the game. Successful players play fewer hands. It takes patience and discipline to wait until you have a proper starting hand. If you can practice these traits, you will be on your way to becoming a winning player.

Playing Too Long

Playing winning poker takes concentration. You need to pay attention to the game as well as the players at the table. If you play too long, you may get tired or even bored. This can cause you to make mistakes or play marginal hands. If you start to get tired, leave the game. When I started playing, I would set time limits for each session. This helped to keep me focused and also helped me learn discipline by sticking to the limits I had set for myself.

CHAPTER 29

Expert Poker Advice: Reading Your Opponents

We have all watched poker-tournament television and seen some players make reads on their opponents that might have some of us wondering if they were indeed psychic. Two players will bet down to the river card, and one will muck his hand with a comment that his opponent must be holding two specific cards, and sure enough those are the exact two cards that the other player has.

To some viewers it may almost seem supernatural, but in essence it is one of the skills that separates the great players from their competition. Reading your opponent's hand is one of the key skills that must be developed in order for a player to succeed in the higher-limit games and tournaments.

A Vital Skill

Reading your opponents to determine what cards they are holding is part science and part art and psychology. It is not an easy skill to learn. If it were, everyone would be doing it and the games would be a lot harder to beat. It takes hard work and patience to develop your reading skill. It also involves paying attention during the game, even when you are not actively involved in a hand.

Reading the Board

One of the first skills that a Hold'em player must learn is how to read the board to determine the best possible hand. You need the ability to identify all the combinations of hands that can be made from the board cards. It is extremely important that you can determine how your hand stacks up against the other possible hands that your opponent may hold. You can't start trying to figure out what your opponent might be holding without knowing what hands can be made from the board cards.

Narrowing the Hands

The first thing you must do is to analyze your opponents' action during each betting round of the hand—whether they call, raise, or fold based on the cards that have been dealt faceup so far. You need to use logic to help understand why they are making their play based on the information that you have seen.

You then have to work backward from the current point and look at all the preceding action that came in the previous betting rounds to help narrow your conclusions as to what they might have. You will have more information as the play unfolds.

Start a Checklist

One of the best ways to start reading other players and narrowing the hands they may have is to make a checklist that you can use in sizing up the players during a game.

There are certain questions I will ask myself at the table as I watch each player. This has helped me improve my reading skills, and if you start doing this during the game, it should help you out as well. When you watch the other players, note the following:

How many hands are they playing?

It is very easy to tell if a player is loose or tight just by the number of hands they play. Even if they don't stay in until the end, you should note the number of times that a player will enter the pot.

What cards did they show down at the end?

As I noted earlier, each time you show a hand you are giving away information. You want to know the types of hands your opponents are playing and file this information for later. Do they like to play any suited cards, single aces, suited connectors, or big cards?

What position were they in during the hand?

You want to note the position the players were in when they entered the pot. Are they playing weak hands from early position? Loose players will play weak hands out of position, and this is something you want to note. If a player is tight and then comes in with a raise from early position, you can determine that they have a big hand.

Did the player raise or call before the flop?

You need to know the types of hands that a player will raise with or call a raise with. Any time a player raises you should note their position and the hand they raised with. You should also look at the other players acting after the raise and determine what types of hands they will call a raise with.

Was the player the aggressor, or did he check and call?

You should note whether players are aggressive or passive by the number of times they raise or just limp in pre-flop. You also want to know the types of hands they may raise with or the hands they simply call or check with after the flop. Picking up on their betting patterns is crucial in reading players.

Did the player slow-play or bluff?

Some players like to slow-play hands or bluff more often. You should note if players limp in with pocket aces. Did they flop a big hand and try to trap the other players? Some players like to bluff or semibluff at specific times. Make a note any time you catch a player doing this.

When you ask yourself these types of questions after every hand, you can very quickly gauge whether your opponents are good, whether they are tight or loose, and whether they are aggressive or passive players.

Beating the Bad Players

As poker continues to grow in popularity, the casino card rooms have seen the influx of new players who want to give poker a try. Most of these new players have little or no knowledge of the game other than the basic rules. The majority of them have never read a single book about poker strategy. Many of them have gotten all of their education from watching the tournaments on TV.

The Maniacs

Some of these players with their TV educations sit down in a low-limit game and play the way they have seen players play the final table of a televised no-limit tournament. They think that they can win a low-limit game by bluffing and raising. They play like maniacs, and they are really easy to spot.

The Meek

The second type of player is the meeks. They are weak, passive players who will sit down in a game and play a lot of hands but rarely raise or fold.

Both the maniacs and the meek players have something in common: they don't know how to play the game properly. They rarely have any concept of starting-hand requirements, pot odds, or even how to read the board. Some of them will use the "any two will do" strategy while others will wait for two suited cards. Many of the new players think that a single ace is the Holy Grail and constitutes a raise every time they have one. They will cold-call raises with hopeless hands and chase all the way to the river looking for a miracle card.

The number of new players has actually been a double-edged sword for the knowledgeable player.

Please Note: *Bad players are profitable for good players.*

In low-limit games you will make more money from your opponents' mistakes than you will from your own fancy play. This is because most of the new players are only interested in their own cards. Few of them even notice what type of hands the other players are playing.

Strategy Against Bad Players

In the long run a good player will beat the clueless players; however, with all these new players in the game, you will also suffer more bad beats than you would in a game full of skilled players. This has frustrated many veteran players.

In the last few months, I have received numerous emails from players who have been used to winning and now all of a sudden find that they are getting clobbered by the new players in low-limit games. They are angry that the damn new players don't know how to play the game. They want to know what to do about it. Some of these players have even told me they have had heated arguments with the newbie players.

I have witnessed this at the tables where I play. I saw an argument break out that I thought was going to turn into a physical altercation. A player with pocket aces flopped a set and lost to a straight by a player who cold-called a raise with 2-5 off-suit. The "veteran" player started screaming obscenities at the new player, who started yelling back that he had the right to play whatever cards he wanted to.

The dealer finally got the players settled down, but the player who suffered the bad beat continued making snide remarks about the new player. A few minutes later, the new player, who had been donating money to the table, got up and left the game. This is exactly what you don't want to happen.

Don't Educate Them

Bad players are overall losers. You don't want to educate them at the table, and you definitely don't want to chase them away. There is a wealth of books, software, and other information available to a player who wants to learn to play the game properly.

If a new player wants to get his education by playing at the table in a live game, you should make sure that he "pays" for this education by the money he loses chasing almost hopeless hands. Why would you want to give this player any free advice that he can use to beat you in the future? When a player gets lucky and wins a big pot, you should tell him, "Nice hand."

> **Please Note:** *Always encourage bad players to continue to play as they do by complimenting them on a win.*

Sure it hurts when you are on the receiving end of a bad beat, but a good player knows how to control his emotions and not let it affect future hands. Avoid making any derogatory remarks aimed at the new player. If you are really upset, get up and leave the table until you calm down. When you get angry, you are one step closer to going on tilt, which can be devastating for you and your bankroll.

Adjust Your Strategy

When you are playing in a game filled with new players, you will need to make some adjustments to your strategy. You need to adjust your play based on the players in your game at the moment.

If you are in a game with a lot of aggressive players, you will want to tighten up from early position. If you are in a passive game with a lot of loose players, you will want to play a few more hands.

In a game with a lot of callers, you will win fewer pots, but you will win more money in the pots that you do win. It is up to you to learn how to adjust your strategy to play and win against the new players.

Here are a few tips to help you in these types of games:

Play aggressively from early position with the big pairs, but realize that they won't hold up as often. Pocket aces will win the majority of times against a small field but will only hold up about 35 percent of the time against a full table of calling players (also known as a "calling station").

Don't try to slow-play or get fancy. Bet the best hand if you have it. The straightforward approach is usually the best, as there are plenty of players who will call you. Make them pay. Why give them a free card if you don't have to?

Don't try to bluff. If you are in the game with even one calling station, you shouldn't try to bluff. You will be called by some player who wants to keep you honest.

Play more connectors from late position. In a game with many players in the pot, your drawing hands go up in value. You will be getting correct odds to see the flop with these hands, and when you do hit, you will be rewarded with a good-sized pot.

In Short: Be Thankful for Bad Players!

Don't complain about new players. Encourage them and make them feel wanted. The rewards are immense. If you learn how to play against them, they will thank you by leaving some of their money behind for you to take home.

CHAPTER 30

Expert Poker Advice: Losing Streaks

It doesn't matter how good a poker player you are. Sooner or later you are going to run into a losing streak. One thing is certain: a losing streak can affect you psychologically. It can wreak havoc with you emotionally, causing you to second-guess and question your own abilities and your play. How you handle a losing streak will be a true test of your poker abilities.

All players at one time or another will experience a losing streak. When this happens players need to determine if the losing was brought about by bad play on their part or just by a negative fluctuation in the luck of the draw. When you start losing, the first thing to do is to look at your game thoroughly.

If the losing streak is being caused by bad play, you need to take action to correct the situation. There are several things you should ask yourself:

- Did you loosen your standards for starting hands?
- Are you misreading the board?
- Are you playing too loose or too aggressively?
- Did you move up in limits?
- Are you playing too long?
- Are you multitasking while playing online?

Common Problems

Many players going through a losing streak may find that they have loosened their standards for starting hands. They have had great success and many winning sessions, and soon they think they are invincible. They start entering the pot by playing hands out of position. They tend to take more chances and end up playing too many hands.

It's common for players to move up in limits as they become more proficient. Many times when you move up, you will encounter players that are more skilled—some far more skilled.

If you find that your losing streak started when you moved up, you may want to drop back down to a lower limit. It's much better to be a winning player in a low-limit game than a losing player at the higher limit.

I play a lot of Sit & Go tournaments online. After coming into the money 16 out of 20 tournaments, I went into a losing streak and went 0-for-15. I finally moved down in the limits just to preserve my bankroll until the losing streak ended and I started winning again.

Players on a losing streak may find that they have been playing more aggressively. They may be raising more or bluffing more to try and bully their opponents. In reality, they are just throwing away money and compounding their own losses.

One of the biggest problems with playing online is that there are so many other things you can do while you play. Talking on the phone, watching TV, answering emails, or reading a magazine while you play can be the cause of your losing streak. Making mental errors such as misreading the board or not noticing that the guy who just raised you has only played three hands in that last hour will contribute to your losing. You have to give the game your full attention.

Playing too long may also be a factor in your losing sessions. When you play too long, you lose concentration or can even get bored and find yourself not giving the game your full attention. If you have been losing after playing marathon sessions, then cut back the amount of time you play.

Bad Luck

If you can honestly say that you have not been making any of the mistakes above, then it may be that you were just suffering a string of bad luck. If your losses are being caused by a bad run of the cards, then it's time to weather the storm.

There is nothing worse than finding you have the second-best hand time after time. We've all been there when small sets are beaten by larger sets, straights are beaten by flushes, and flushes are beaten by full houses. It's ugly, but it does happen to everyone from time to time.

> **Please Note:** *Bad luck is a part of any game, even if you have an edge at that game.*

One thing you don't want to do is make any radical changes in your play. When players get into a losing streak, they sometimes start playing differently. They tend to second-guess some of their play. A player who has had success playing aggressively may become timid and start calling instead of raising or hesitating while making a play for fear of losing.

> **Please Note:** *You can't forsake your winning strategy to compensate for a run of bad cards.*

Going on Tilt

Some players will go on tilt—that is, go somewhat crazy—during a long losing streak. This will only add to your problems. If you find yourself playing differently or starting to play recklessly, then it might be best to just take a few days *or weeks* off and get away from the game for a while.

When players become upset and lose control of their emotions, they start making poor decisions and playing badly. Players on tilt will start to play any starting hands and call bets when they should not. If they have just suffered a bad beat, this could trigger them to go on tilt. They have lost money and are trying to make it back in one or two hands by playing overly aggressively with weak hands. *Their play becomes irrational.* Like a child having a temper tantrum, they act out in anger, throwing chips in the pot trying to intimidate the other players. This will usually just lead to more losses.

Sometimes players will get to the point where they just don't care how much money they have lost. Poker expert Mike Caro calls this "crossing the threshold of pain." A player may be down a few hundred dollars and then think, *What the heck does another hundred matter?* It will matter a lot the next day to most players.

Players can go on tilt when they direct anger at another player. This particular opponent may have beaten them out of a hand, and they are now on a vendetta to get that person. They will raise and reraise in hope of beating this player and getting their money back. This usually will backfire.

> **Please Note:** *Poker is not a game of revenge. It is a game of making money.*

Often you can make money from players who are on tilt. They will be throwing money around, and it is up to you to catch it. Some may argue that it's wrong to kick someone when they're down, but a player on tilt is fair game in a casino poker game. Just make sure it is not you who is on tilt.

Poker players are predators, and a player on tilt is perfect prey.

CHAPTER 31

Expert Poker Advice: Money Management

The true essence of money management in poker really comes down to bankroll management. It is how you handle your money to ensure that you will not go broke. You can't play poker if you don't have any money to get in a game. Anything you do that causes you to lose money and is a detriment to your bankroll is commonly referred to as a "leak" in your game.

A "leak" in poker is defined as:

1. A gambling situation in which you engage on a regular basis with a negative expectation.
2. Lack of discipline and/or knowledge that causes consistent losses in your poker game.

The first leak that many poker players have is that they like to play other casino games. I know a few players who will hit it big at the poker table and then blow their money at the craps or blackjack tables.

If you insist on playing other games, then the best way to manage this is to have a separate poker bankroll and set aside other money for "entertainment" that you will lose in the casinos.

The second type of leak that causes lost money comes from your own playing abilities. Playing in games that are above your bankroll limits and/ or your skill level can definitely cause you to lose money. Some players make the same mistakes repeatedly and then wonder why they are losing at the tables. The first and most basic step that you need to take in order to fix any problems in your game is to identify and isolate your problem.

Some common leaks are:

- Playing too many hands
- Playing any ace
- Calling too much
- Not knowing how to figure pot odds

Getting input from more experienced players will help you to identify how you can fix your play. Keeping good records of each game that you play is vital in tracking your wins and losses and may help you identify some of your problems, especially if you play in different-limit games. If you can't beat a $10/20 game, move down to a $5/10

Plugging leaks in your game is a vital step in money management.

Stop Losses

One of the most debated topics when discussing money management in poker is that of "stop losses." Because most casino games have a negative expectation, players are advised to set a win goal and stop loss. This ensures that they will not go broke during any given session and will hopefully not give back all the profits if they do win.

Some argue that the concept of money management is nothing more than smoke and mirrors because if you play a game with a negative expectation, you will lose in the long run. Setting a stop loss is just a way for a casino player to hold on to their money a little longer.

Poker has a positive expectation, and most of the pros and experts will tell you setting win goals or stop-loss limits are useless because poker is one big game with a few interruptions to eat, sleep, and work between hands. It doesn't matter if you quit when you are ahead or losing, as you will be coming back to the game eventually. They say that if the game is good, it doesn't matter if you are down, because you will win money back in the long run if you are a good player.

I agree with this up to a point. I still think that you should have some sort of stop loss for each session.

The main reason I advocate a stop loss is for psychological reasons. If you are losing and suffering bad beats or just being dealt rag hand after rag hand, there will come a point where this will start affecting your mental game. When this happens you are no longer able to play your best game. You may find yourself making poor decisions or playing hands that are below your standards. When this happens, it's time to quit.

I suggest that you buy in for a reasonable amount of money. In a limit game I will buy in for a minimum of 20 big bets. If I lose this, I will usually call it a night. If the majority of the loss came from losing only one big hand, then I will evaluate the game and my own state of mind. I might take a break if I am going to continue playing.

Another factor I consider when deciding to quit or not is the length of time that I have been playing. When I first started playing, I found that I could not keep total concentration on the game for more that a couple hours. I then would limit my sessions to a certain time period and then quit, whether I won, lost, or broke even.

Each of us has our own endurance level. Some people can play at peak performance for hours on end. Others might lose concentration after an hour. You have to decide what is best for you. One way to determine your performance level is to look at your logbook. Compare your win/loss record with your playing time and see if the amount of time you spend at the table is having an effect on the outcome of your play.

Whether you call it money management or bankroll management, it all comes down to having the money you need to play poker added to the skills you need to be a winning player.

PART IV: Advantage Pai Gow Poker

CHAPTER 32

The Basics of Pai Gow Poker

[The voice in this section is John "Skinny's."]

Pai Gow Poker is certainly *not* one of the most popular casino table games. It comes in way behind blackjack, craps, roulette, and those carnival games such as Caribbean Stud, Let It Ride, Three-Card Poker, and Four-Card Poker. Indeed, some casinos will only have a few tables for the game, some just one, and some will have none. That is sad because Pai Gow Poker is a fun game, it is a social game, and, most important, it can be beaten.

> **Please Note:** *Pai Gow Poker is a game where the player can get an edge over the house. Played properly the smart player can win in the long run.*

There are three ways the player can get an edge at the game of Pai Gow Poker.
1. The player can get a *mathematical advantage* based on his betting choices.
2. The player can get a *monetary advantage* based on the value of his comps.
3. The player can get an edge mathematically and monetarily with comps, which is a double-barreled advantage over the casino.

In this section, I will show you what you need to know to win money at the game of Pai Gow Poker. Those of you reading about Pai Gow for the first time should carefully go over how the game is played so you are familiar with it. Pai Gow Poker is a simple game, as are all casino games or many people would not be able to play them.

There is nothing as much fun as playing a game where you have the edge. Come on, we all know playing can be fun, but winning is the most fun!

If you are familiar with the rules of the game, you can skip over the next section where I describe how the game is played for those who have never played before or for those who need a refresher. For those familiar with the game, skip down to the section that begins, "Start here if you already know how to play Pai Gow Poker."

The game is played with a standard deck of 52 playing cards plus a joker for a total of 53 cards. The joker is not a true wild card. It can only be used to make a straight, flush, or straight flush. If you are not using it for that purpose, it is automatically an ace.

Each player and the dealer are dealt exactly seven cards. On each deal there are a total of seven hands dealt out with four cards left over. The basic layout has room for six players plus the dealer. Some layouts allow for a dragon hand, which is an extra hand that can be played by the players. On those layouts there is only room for five players because the dragon hand uses one of the spots.

The cards are dealt out to all the positions on each deal, whether someone is playing that spot or not. The dealer puts the four cards left over and any hands that don't have a player playing them into the muck pile. At that point each player is allowed to pick up his hand and set his cards.

Each player is required to arrange his seven cards into a five-card poker hand and a two-card hand. The object is to make the two best poker hands.

Please Note: *The only rule for setting the hands is the five-card hand must beat the two-card hand.*

After setting his cards into two hands, each player places them facedown in the area designated for the hands on the layout. After all the players have set their hands, the dealer sets his hand faceup in front of him. The dealer then compares his hands against those of the players, one by one. As a player, your five-card hand plays against the banker's five-card hand, and your two-card hand plays against the banker's two-card hand.

Please Note: *I will explain the difference between the dealer and the banker shortly.*

The player wins if both the five-card hand and the two-card hand beat the banker's five-card and two-card hands, respectively. A player's winning hands pay even money less a 5 percent commission. The banker wins if both his five-card *and* two-card hands beat the player's corresponding hands. If the player loses both hands, his total wager is lost. However, if one hand wins and the other hand loses, it is a push, and no money is exchanged.

If a player and the banker have the same two-card hand and/or the same five-card hand, it is called a "copy hand," meaning each hand is "copying" the other hand. The banker wins all copy hands. Copy hands occur approximately 2.65 percent of the time.

Please Note: *The copy hand gives the banker a natural edge over the players.*

Hand ranks:*
1. Five aces (four aces, one joker)
2. Royal flush (A-K-Q-J-10 suited)
3. Straight flush* (five consecutive suited cards)
4. Four of a kind
5. Full house (three cards of one rank and two of another)
6. Flush (five suited cards)
7. Straight* (five consecutive unsuited cards)
8. Three of a kind
9. Two pair
10. One pair
11. Highest card

***Please Note:** The highest straight is 10 through ace; however, in Pai Gow Poker, the second-highest straight is ace through 5.*

Start here if you already know how to play Pai Gow Poker.
Let us start with a bit of history about the game. Pai Gow Poker is based on the ancient Chinese domino game of Pai Gow. Pai Gow is played with domino-shaped tiles and was brought over to the United States in the 1800s.

Pai Gow Poker was developed in the early 1980s and combined the popular tile game with elements of poker. It was first introduced at the Bell Club in Bell, California, using standard playing cards. When discussing the card game, one should say "Pai Gow Poker," because strictly speaking, Pai Gow is the name of the tile game, not the card game.

Pai Gow literally means "make nine" and refers to the tile game where tiles that can "make nine" are premium. Pai Gow is the original version of baccarat or chemin de fer, again where nine is the premium hand.

In Pai Gow Poker you will often hear people describe a poor hand as a Pai Gow, or they will root for the banker to have a Pai Gow. Since the worst possible hand in Pai Gow Poker is a nine-high hand (9,8,7,5,4,3,2) that does not contain a flush. I suppose rooting for a Pai Gow for the banker would be hoping the banker makes a nine-high hand.

However, in Chinese the word *lop* means "nothing." So it is better to wish for a "lop-lop" or to describe a bad hand as a "lop-lop."

Please Note: *A Pai Gow Poker hand with nothing in the two-card hand and nothing in the five-card hand is a "lop-lop" or virtually a nothing-nothing hand.*

The first thing you want to know about Pai Gow Poker is the best way to arrange your cards so that it is easy to set them into two hands. You should get in the habit of sorting your seven cards in your hand from low to high or high to low and doing it the same way every time.

After sorting the cards, look to see if you can make a straight or flush with them. After that it should be relatively easy to determine which two cards you want to put in the two-card hand and which cards go into the five-card hand. For example, suppose you are dealt the following after you spread them out in your hand.

Determine how you would set these cards into a two-card hand and a five-card hand before reading any further.

9♦, 7♣, K♦, 2♥, 7♠, 6♦, 5♥

It is certainly possible to look at them and figure out how you want to set them. But if you are distracted or a bit tired after playing for a while, it is a lot easier to make a mistake if you do not sort your cards. If you sort them as I have described, you are much less likely to make an error that could potentially cost you money.

I learned this technique through discussions with dealers in different venues. Several have told me it is best to sort your cards as I described above. Since then I have been more observant of the procedures followed by dealers in different casinos and noticed that most sort the cards first.

Please Note: *If casinos require dealers to sort their cards to avoid mistakes, don't you think it makes sense for you, as a casual or even frequent player, to do it that way?*

By now you should have figured out how to set the above cards. Next I will show you the same cards sorted. Look at the sorted cards and decide whether it is easier to determine how to set the cards with them sorted or unsorted.

$$2\heartsuit, \ 5\heartsuit, \ 6\diamondsuit, \ 7\clubsuit, \ 7\spadesuit, \ 9\diamondsuit, \ K\diamondsuit$$

Once the cards are sorted and you determine there is no straight or flush in the cards, it is easy to see that these cards have a single pair of 7s.

Therefore you would put your next two highest cards (9$\diamondsuit$, K$\diamondsuit$) in the two-card hand; the pair and remaining three low cards (2$\heartsuit$, 5$\heartsuit$, 6$\diamondsuit$, 7$\clubsuit$, 7$\spadesuit$) go in the five-card hand.

The next thing you should know about Pai Gow Poker is the probability of a win, loss, or push as a player.

Please Note: *When you are playing against the banker, you can expect to win approximately 28.61 percent of the deals, lose 29.91 percent of the deals, and push 41.48 percent of the deals.*

Some of the figures depend on the strategy you use and what "house way" the casino is using for setting the dealer's hands. But it will roughly equate to winning 30 percent, losing 30 percent, and pushing 40 percent of the deals, with the banker having an approximate 1.3 percent edge over the player due to the copy hands that the banker wins. You should be able to see from this that Pai Gow Poker is a slow game, because approximately 40 percent of the hands result in a push. Even without having an edge, the low number of hands played is a bankroll saver for the players.

This brings us to the two components that make up the total house advantage (I'll use HA to stand for *house advantage* from now on). One component is the copy hands, which give the banker a 1.3 percent HA over the player. The other component is the 5 percent commission one pays on one's net win.

Please Note: *Since you only pay a commission on a winning hand and you win slightly less than 30 percent as a player, the HA for the commission comes to approximately 1.4 percent.*

You are therefore working against an overall 2.7 percent HA as a player. With the small number of hands, such an HA is not a killer as it would be in a fast-paced game such as blackjack or mini-baccarat.

As an aside, some casinos allow you to prepay the commission, and then they do not collect the full commission on a winning hand. For example, if you were to bet $105 you would be paid $100 on a winning hand rather than

$99.75. It is a good idea to do this if allowed, because it reduces the effective rate of the commission from 5 percent down to 4.76 percent—yes, every little bit helps!

By now you are probably saying to yourself that I told you I was going to tell you how you could play this game with an advantage. Up to now all I have done is tell you how much of an HA the casino has against you as a player.

So here goes:

The key to reducing the overall HA and to getting an edge is the fact that all players are allowed to be the banker when it is their turn to do so. Some casinos do not allow banking, and I would not recommend playing at those casinos. California also has different rules regarding banking, but I will not discuss those here. The vast majority of the casinos that allow banking use one of two methods:

- The around-the-table method
- The zigzag method

With the around-the-table method, the casino rotates the option to bank to each of the players around the table counterclockwise. If a player passes his option, the next player in order may choose to bank. With the zigzag method, the casino must bank every other hand in between the player opportunities to bank.

As banker, you are allowed to wager against the dealer up to the amount of the last bet you made when the dealer was the banker. In addition, if there are other players in the deal, they will be playing against you as the banker, and you need enough money on the table to cover their bets plus your wager against the dealer. As banker you are only required to cover the basic wager of the other players. Any side bets, such as the Fortune Bonus or Envy Bonus—which I describe later—are between the other players and the casino and paid by the casino.

> **Please Note:** *Banking gives you the advantage because the banker wins all copy hands.*

Therefore you want to play for as much as your bankroll can afford as banker. You also want to be the banker as often as the rules allow you to bank.

CHAPTER 33

How to Reduce the House Advantage

One: If you are able to find an empty table where you can play head-to-head against the dealer, you can bank every other hand. This will essentially eliminate the HA for copy hands because you will alternate being banker. The only HA will be for the commission component.

The overall HA reduces to 1.46 percent on average when you play head-to-head against the dealer, alternating being banker. If you get comps for your play, that will reduce the HA even further and might even bring in more money in comps than your expected loss at the game. This type of advantage is called the "monetary edge," as more money is coming back to you than is actually going to the casino.

It is also fun to turn your cards over faceup, one at a time, to add to the suspense of seeing the hand, and it allows the dealer to be involved in rooting for you. Since you are playing by yourself, most dealers will not object to turning your cards this way, and it makes the game more interesting for them to deal as well.

Two: The second way to reduce the HA is a lot of fun, and we call it a "table takeover." If you have five other friends who like to play Pai Gow Poker, the six of you can sit at an empty table and take up all the playing spots. You will all play against the dealer, who banks on the first deal. After that, each player will take the bank when it is his turn to be the banker, and the other friends will sit out because they do not want to bet against their friend when he is the banker.

It is a lot of fun because you can root for each other as you play. Plus when you are the banker playing one-*on*-one against the dealer, you can usually turn your cards over one *by* one so that all your friends, as well as the dealer, can root for you. It makes for a very social game when played this way. It also reduces the hit of the house edge! Relax and have fun playing this way. The suspense of slowly turning over card after card increases the thrill of the game. It's a great method!

With a table takeover, you are effectively playing head-to-head against the dealer because you are sitting out when your friends are banking. Thus the table takeover reduces the HA to 1.46 percent, the same as that for playing head-to-head.

You may even be able to do a table takeover with as few as three to five players. Most casinos will allow you to play two hands as long as they are adjacent to each other on the layout. When it is your turn to bank, the casino will only allow you to bank one hand, but you can normally bank up to the total combined amount you played on the two hands against the dealer.

Please Note: *If you played two hands against the dealer, each $100, you can bank for $200 even if you are not allowed to bank twice. The casinos do not want you to bank twice in a row.*

With three players, each of you should play two hands against the dealer as the banker, taking up all six spots. Then bank one hand for the amount you played on the two hands combined. With four or five players, take up all the spots with some players playing two hands and some playing only one hand.

It is a good idea to play two hands whenever you can, even when playing head-to-head, because you will reduce the variance by spreading the risk for one-half the amount on each of two hands when the house has the advantage as the banker. Then when you have the advantage as the banker, you play for the combined amount. Some casinos do not allow you to combine amounts as banker when you play two hands. In that case you should not play two hands; only play one.

Please Note: *Remember if you are playing two hands, each hand is half your total bet. So if your normal bet were one hand of $50, you would bet two hands of $25 each.*

Three: So how can you get a *real mathematical edge* at the game? The third and most effective way to reduce the HA is when you get to play with strangers at a table who are willing to play against you when you bank. Of course you need the bankroll to cover the bets of all the players. But if you can afford it, you may actually be able to eliminate the HA entirely and/or play with a positive HA for yourself. That advantage can get pretty high for you, depending on how much money is bet by the other players against you.

Not only do you get the edge on the copy hands against the dealer when you are banking but also against all the other players as well. Furthermore, the commission you pay is only on your own net win.

For example, you are banking against the dealer and against four other players all playing for the same amount. If you win three hands and lose two hands, you will have a net win of one hand and only have to pay the commission on the one hand.

CHAPTER 34

The 13-to-1 Advantage

Since you have the edge in your favor when you bank against the dealer and other players, it is to your advantage to play for the minimum against the dealer when the dealer is banking and had the edge in his favor.

> **Please Note:** *If you are playing on a full table with six opponents (five players and the dealer) and can get to bank for 13 times the amount you wagered against the dealer, you can completely eliminate the HA.*

Let me repeat. You will have the HA as the banker on the copy hands, and with 13 times the amount you wagered as a player, you will offset the HA on the commission. To eliminate the mathematical edge of the house, you need to have the six players at the table betting 13 times more than your single bet against the dealer when the dealer banked.

This is not that difficult. To demonstrate this, say you are playing for $10 as the player when the dealer is the banker. When you take the bank on the next hand, you are allowed to play against the dealer for $10. If there are five other players at the table playing against you for $25 each, you will be playing for a total of $135 as the banker. That would be enough to give you a 0.11 percent positive advantage.

Here's the truly great part: if you are able to get players who will play for more than 13 times the amount you played against the dealer, you can get the edge. That's right. If the other players are betting $140 against your $10 wager, you have the mathematical edge over the house!

Just remember, your bet against the dealer when he is the banker must be $10 in this scenario. If you are betting $100, then the other players must bet $1,300+ for you to get the edge!

Each additional unit wagered as banker against six players will gain you 0.21 percent. For example, at 18 times, you would have a 1.05 percent positive mathematical advantage. It just keeps going up from there.

The more money the players bet against you, the higher your edge. Just keep this in mind: you must have enough to be able to pay the other players' winning bets. Don't bank if you can't afford it. Even with an edge, you can still lose.

An interesting fact to notice: Pai Gow Poker players often bet higher than average table-game players, so getting that 13-to-1, 14-to-1, and higher bets is not really that difficult.

The Superstitions of Banking

There are a lot of superstitions that surround gambling in general and Pai Gow Poker in particular. When it comes to banking, you will hear that it is a bad idea to take the bank after the dealer has a bad hand. The superstition is that you will be taking the bad cards from the dealer.

Of course this is complete nonsense. Each game is using a separate deck of cards, and there is no higher order controlling what comes out of the deck except randomness.

Still, I remember one time I had a baccarat player watching me play. He kept track of the hands the banker won and the hands the player won the way they often do in baccarat. He also noted when the banker and player had good or bad hands. Then he advised me whether I should take the bank or not based on his charts and graphs.

He wanted to be involved in my game and would not leave me alone. He was trying to be helpful, so I did not see any need to complain to the casino about him. Instead, I played my game and took the bank every other hand. But I was polite and took his advice if it suited my alternating plan. If it did not, I would point to some supposed flaw and tell him he missed something or other and that, according to his charts, I should do the opposite. He would then go back and study his charts some more.

By the time he figured out what I was saying, the hand was over. If I won I would point out why he could not follow his theory completely and give him some gibberish about the exceptions. Eventually he figured out what I was doing and realized I was not paying any attention to him. He got upset that I was not taking his advice and stormed off in a huff. I was not trying to get him to go away angry; I was just trying to get him to go away! The cards have no memory, and each deal is completely random.

Since the banker has an advantage over the other players, you want to be the banker every time it is your turn to bank. There are no other reasons for doing this! You are playing to win money, not to discover some mystical element to the universe.

I remember a hand that made the advantage of banking very clear to me. I was banking at a full table with strangers playing against me and was dealt an ace-high straight for my five-card hand and a 3-2 for my two-card hand. Of course 3-2 is the lowest possible two-card hand, and I was expecting to see six pushes with this hand. As it turned out, the dealer also had a straight, but it was a lower straight, so I beat the dealer with my five-card hand, *and* the dealer also had 3-2 for his two-card hand. I had a copy hand and won as the banker with the lowest possible two-card hand. Since I won both hands, I beat the dealer with a 3-2 for my two-card hand.

It did not end there.

One of the other players also had an ace-high straight for the five-card hand. Naturally his two-card hand beat my 3-2. But it was a push because I won the copy hand on the five-card hand. This was the first time I saw two copy hands on the same deal—one on the five-card hand and one on the two-card hand. I *won both* because I was the banker.

There is one little wrinkle in the banking at Pai Gow Poker. Some superstitious players think it is bad luck to play against another player who is the bank. These players will sit out, thinking they have a better chance of losing when another player is banking. This is nonsense, but at such tables, you might not be able to get the 13-to-1, 14-to-1, or better wagers against you.

If you can't get to another table where such a betting amount is possible, you still have reduced the house edge remarkably when you bank, and it is quite possible your comps will get you over the top when it comes to the monetary edge. No matter what, always bank when you can!

CHAPTER 35

Other Pai Gow Poker Options

U p to now we have been discussing the basic wager in Pai Gow Poker: the even-money wager between the banker and the player. It is the best bet in the game, and if you play it as I have described above, you can minimize the HA to a very low edge or even turn the HA positive in your favor.

In addition to the basic wager, most layouts have an additional side bet or two that one can wager. Every single one that I have seen or read about comes with a higher house edge than the basic wager. In general they are poor wagers. But the payouts are attractive in relation to your wager. So gamblers are attracted to them for that reason, despite the low probability of winning a large payout.

I already discussed the dragon hand. It is an additional hand that players may wager on after looking at their cards and before the dealer displays his cards. It is an even-money wager, and the hand must be played the house way against the dealer's hand.

There is another superstition with the dragon hand. Some players feel if they have a bad hand, the good cards are in the dragon hand. They take the bet in the hope of winning that wager to offset the expected losing wager on their other hand.

You will recognize the fallacy of this logic. It is no more likely that the good cards will be in the dragon hand than in the dealer's hand. All you would be doing is making an additional wager with a 2.7 percent HA. You cannot combine the dragon-hand wager with your other wager when you bank, so it is a poor wager.

Please Note: *The dragon bet allows the casino to get twice as much money wagered on the table if all the players take that bet. The bet is great for the casino!*

Another popular side bet is Fortune Pai Gow Poker with the envy bonus. I am describing this side bet because I have an unusual story to tell you about it after I describe how it works.

There are two parts to this side bet. It is a single bet with up to two possible payouts. The first one pays you a "fortune" based on the best five-card hand in your seven cards, *regardless of how you set them*. The second part pays you an "envy bonus" based on the strength of the best five-card hand in the seven cards dealt out to the other players in the game. The dealer's hand does not count toward the envy.

There are different pay tables available for the wager, and casinos choose one to use. The HA varies on this side bet depending on the number of players in the game. For the most common pay table, with each additional player available upon which to collect the envy bonus, the HA drops by 0.93 percent based on a $5 bet from –7.77 percent when playing solo down to –3.13 percent when playing at a full table.

Once again you can see this side bet has a high HA and is not a good wager. However, most players make this side bet partly because of the attraction of the 8,000-to-1 payout on the fortune bonus and $5,000 payout on the envy bonus for a natural seven-card straight flush. A $5 side bet can pay a $40,000 "fortune" to the player with the natural seven-card straight flush and $5,000 to anyone else at the table with a $5 side bet for their "envy bonus."

You will have to decide for yourself if it is worth an expected loss of 16¢ at a full table to 39¢ when you are playing alone to go for a one-in–4.8 million chance at the big one. Of course you can collect an even-money fortune bonus with a hand starting at a straight or higher and a $5 envy bonus if one of the other players has a four of a kind or better. But the bigger payouts are for the better and far less frequent hands.

CHAPTER 36

A Horrendously True Tale

An unusual story about the fortune side bet originated in Atlantic City. I had heard this story from several dealers and a few players at different casinos. At first I thought it was another gambling myth that made an interesting story—a very interesting story—but had no basis in fact. Atlantic City, and all casino towns, have their supermythological stories.

I changed my mind when I was telling the story to a Pai Gow Poker dealer in a premium Las Vegas casino.

As I started my tale, he interrupted me and told me he had actually met the person in this story when that player played at his table! The dealer said the gentleman (let's call the player Bill) told him he had become a bit of a legend in Atlantic City because of what happened at a Pai Gow Poker game one day.

Bill said he had been playing for $1,000 a hand and betting the bonus on every hand. Then on his last hand he got distracted by a phone call. Bill put down $1,000 to play the hand but forgot to put up the fortune/envy bonus.

Of course you can guess what comes next.

Bill was dealt a natural seven-card straight flush on the hand and just lost $40,000 he would have won on the bonus. But there were three other players in the hand, and they were each playing the bonus for $5, which entitled them to $5,000 for the envy bonus. Bill showed them his cards and asked if they would be willing to share some of their bonus money with him because of his bad luck in getting distracted and not playing the bonus.

They had been playing together for some time, and the players knew that Bill had been playing the bonus every hand except for this one. Bill thought it was a reasonable request. But according to Bill the players were quite nasty to him and replied, "Hell no! No way!" to his request. This got him even more upset than he already was. He threw his cards facedown in front of him without setting them and told the dealer to "muck" his cards.

Of course all hell broke out at this point. But the rules are simple in this case: if any player mucks his hand, the house is only allowed to count the cards to be sure there are seven cards in the hand. They are not allowed to look at the hand, and all potential bonuses are forfeited. Even though everyone knew Bill had a natural seven-card straight flush, the other players did not collect their $5,000 envy bonus.

The dealer relating the story to me said Bill seemed like a nice guy. In fact, Bill told him he would have understood if the other players had said they needed the money or had been losing so much that this would just bring them back to even. In that case he would have still played out the hand. When they were nasty and rude, he just lost it.

Bill forfeited his $1,000 wager by mucking his cards. But it did not matter to him because he was so angry at the other players. I guess this was an expensive lesson in being polite and following the golden rule, which in Pai Gow Poker is this: some money is better than no money!

CHAPTER 37

How to Play Your Hands

The final thing you need to know about Pai Gow Poker is how to set your cards. There is one optimal strategy for setting your hands, but it is fairly complicated and varies slightly depending on whether you are the banker or player. It is far too complex to discuss in a single chapter, and the difference between several ways of setting certain hands is quite small and, really, as my friends say, "no big deal."

However the good news is that each casino has a standard house way that the dealer is required to follow in setting the cards with no exceptions. Furthermore, you are allowed to ask the dealer what the house way is for setting your cards after everyone has set their cards and placed them face-down in front of them.

The dealer will then tell you the house way, and it is up to you whether you want to set your cards that way or not. As Frank Scoblete likes to say, "Take a look at the money the casino has and the money you have. Would you rather play the house way or your way?"

For the most part Frank is correct. Isn't he always? [*Yes, I am. —Frank.*] In general the house way is an excellent way to set your cards. When it comes to the house way you are liable to hear a lot of stories from players. You probably do not want to pay attention to any of them.

Players like to say that the house is playing against six other players so they set the cards in a way that optimizes play against six players. Since you as a player are only playing against the dealer, you should follow a different strategy. Well the house does not change the way they play when there is only one player at the table, so where is the logic in that? If the house way is not good for heads-up play, why do they follow the same house way when playing heads-up?

I read someplace that casinos choose their house way based on the way players commonly set their hands in their specific casino. Since they have to have a house way for the dealers to set their hands when they first introduce the game in their casino, how would they know how players commonly set

130

their hands, since the game was not played there before? Then after they introduce the game, most players are going to follow the house way for that casino.

Studying the way players play in that casino after that will most likely yield the result that players follow the house way the casino introduced in the first place.

I once had a pit boss tell me that when they brought the game into her casino, they had a choice of different house ways from which to pick. She said the one they chose for their casino was fairly aggressive, while others were more conservative. I suppose it is possible to rank the house ways from conservative to aggressive based on some parameter. But I doubt anyone has done an exhaustive study amongst the various house ways.

I did say there is an optimal strategy when playing as the banker that differs slightly from that of the player. This is because the banker wins the copy hands, so it alters the strategy in certain situations, not because the banker is playing against six players. But even with this, the house does not alter its house way depending on whether it is the banker or not.

The casino needs a standard way for the dealers to set their hands that they can remember and is not too complicated. They do not want the dealer referring to a sheet of paper to determine the house way too often. If it is too complicated to remember, they will lose money due to errors as well.

Players also need a reasonable hand-setting strategy to follow. Whatever criteria a casino uses for determining its house way, I think simplicity is an overriding factor in their choice.

The most common seven-card hands are those that have exactly one or two pair as the best hand that can be made out of the seven cards. Hands with one pair occur approximately 42 percent of the time, and hands with two pair occur approximately 23 percent of the time. Those are the most common hands you will see when playing Pai Gow Poker.

The optimal way to play a hand with one pair is to put the pair in your five-card hand with the three lowest cards. Your two highest cards then go in the two-card hand. A hand with two pairs seems to be the hand where casinos vary the most when it comes to their house way. (At the end of this section, I will give you some simple rules for good ways to set a hand with two pairs.)

For the most part, casinos do not seem to significantly vary the way they play all the other hands. The easiest thing to do is to follow the house way at the casino you are playing in if you have one of those other hands. That would just make the hand-play simple and not hard to remember. After all, how hard is it to say to the dealer, "How should I play this hand?"

> **Please Note:** *House ways for different casinos are not so different that you have to agonize over them. Casinos certainly don't worry about it!*

Following is the house way used by some casinos in Atlantic City:

High card: The second and third highest cards go in the two-card hand. The highest card goes in the five-card hand.

One pair: The two highest cards go in the two-card hand. The pair and the three lowest cards go in the five-card hand.

Two pair: Rank the pairs according to the following groupings:

A. 2 through 6: Low pair = L

B. 7 through 10: Medium pair = M

C. Jack through king: High pair = H

- L-L or L-M: Split pairs, highest in five-card hand, lowest in two-card hand, *unless* you can put a king or ace in the two-card hand and then play two pairs in the five-card hand
- L-H or M-M: Split with high pair in the five-card hand, low pair in the two-card hand, *unless* you can put an ace in the two-card hand and then play two pairs in the five-card hand
- M-H or H-H: Always split with high pair in the five-card hand and low pair in the two-card hand
- Pair of aces and any other pair: Always split

Three pair: Highest pair in the two-card hand; the other two pairs in the five-card hand

Three of a kind: Three of a kind in the five-card hand (*Exception:* With three aces, one ace should be put in the two-card hand, and the pair of aces remain in the five-card hand.)

Straights, flushes, straight flushes, and royal flushes:

- With no pair: When choosing whether to play a straight, flush, or straight flush, play the category that will allow the highest two cards in two-card hand
- With sixth or seventh card: Play lower straight or flush in the five-card hand in order to place the highest cards in the two-card hand
- With one pair: Play pair in the two-card hand only if a straight, flush, or straight flush can be played in the five-card hand
- With two pair: Use two-pair rule
- With three pair: Use three-pair rule
- With three of a kind: Play pair in two-card hand
- With full house: Use full-house rule

Full house: Always split *unless* the pair is 2s and you have an ace and a king to play in the two-card hand

Full house with three of a kind and two pairs: Play the highest pair in two-card hand

Full house with three of a kind twice: Always play the highest pair in two-card hand

Four of a kind: Play according to the rank of the four of a kind:
- 2 through 6: Always keep together
- 7 through 10: Split unless a king or better can be played in two-card hand
- Jack through king: Split unless an ace can be played in two-card hand
- Aces: Always split

Four of a kind and a pair: Play pair in two-card hand

Four of a kind and three of a kind: Play pair in two-card hand from the three of a kind

Five aces: Split aces and play three aces in five-card hand and two aces in two-card hand *unless* you have a pair of kings, then play five aces in five-card hand and kings in two-card hand

You do not have to memorize the list above. I am only showing it as an example of the house way that is used by some casinos.

Improving on the Two-Pair Rules

The two-pair rules above are a reasonable set of rules for playing two pairs in your hands. If you want to improve upon those two-pair rules you could consider trying one of the following:

The rule of 9-15:

Consider the point value of each pair's rank as it corresponds to the face value of the cards. Pairs from 2 through 10 have a value equal to their face value of 2 through 10. Picture pairs from jacks through aces have the value of 11 through 14. Jack = 11; queen = 12; king = 13; ace = 14.

A pair of 2s has a value of 2. A pair of 9s has a value of 9. A pair of queens has a value of 12.

Always split two pair *except*:

(1) If you add the value of each pair, get a sum of nine or less, and have a king and/or an ace to play in the two-card hand. For example, if you have a pair of 6s and a pair of 3s in your two pairs, that'll be a 6+3, which equal 9, and you have a king and/or an ace to play in your two-card hand. You therefore play the two pairs in the five-card hand.

(2) If you add the value of each pair, get a sum of 10 through 15, and you have an ace to play in the two-card hand. So a pair of 6s and a pair of 5s will

equal 11. With an ace, you keep the pairs together in the five-card hand and use the ace in the two-card hand.

By using the rule of 9-15 you take away 0.04 percent from the house edge of some casinos' house way, which gives you additional elbow room in the game—*tiny* elbow room…teeny-tiny elbow room.

The rule of 7-11-16:
Always split two pair *except:*

(1) If you add the value of each pair, get a sum of five, six, or seven, and you have a queen, king, or ace to play in the two-card hand.

(2) If you add the value of each pair, get a sum of eight through 11, and you have a king or ace to play in the two-card hand.

(3) If you add the value of each pair, get a sum of 12 through 16, and you have an ace to play in the two-card hand.

The rule of 7-11-16 is as close to the optimal strategy for playing two pair that can be easily remembered. It is slightly better than the rule of 9-15.

Finally let me give you a little trick I use to evaluate my hand. It sometimes helps me to decide how to play a hand on a close call. The Wizard of Odds has two tables on his website that give the probability that any given player hand will beat the dealer. They can be found at: http://wizardofodds.com/games/pai-gow-poker/appendix/1/

According to those charts a pair of queens in a player's five-card hand will beat the banker 54.2 percent of the time, while a pair of jacks in a player's five-card hand will beat the banker 49.1 percent of the time. One needs a pair of queens or better in the five-card hand to have a better-than-even chance of winning the five-card hand.

The chart for a two-card hand shows that K-Q in a player's two-card hand beats the banker 45.3 percent of the time and A-2 in a player's two-card hand beats the banker 51.9 percent of the time. Thus one needs better than K-Q in the two-card hand to have a better-than-even chance of winning the two-card hand.

Knowing such bits of information is helpful in evaluating the strength of one's cards. It can also be useful in deciding how to play one's hand in certain circumstances. Unfortunately one is not allowed to have a copy of the chart at the tables.

But you can make note of certain hands that you thought could be played differently and then look at the charts later to see which was the best way to play the cards. I have found this helpful over time, because it has given me more insight into playing certain hands.

PART V: Advantage Video Poker

CHAPTER 38

Payback, Return, Variance, and Volatility

[The voice in this section is Jerry "Stickman."]

Two factors determine the winning characteristics of a video-poker game—payback (sometimes called "return") and variance (also called "volatility").

Payback (or return) is the amount of money that is "paid back" or "returned" out of the money that is played through a video-poker game. It is expressed as a percentage such as 99.54 percent. Playing a game that has a 99.54 percent return means that in the long run you will get back $99.54 for every $100 you run through the game. On a $1 game where you play $5 per hand, after 20 hands are played you will have an average of $99.54 returned in the long run. (That means it will take a while for the math to work out to near its probability.)

Another way to talk about this is house edge. The house edge is what the casino keeps from your video-poker play—or any casino game, for that matter. The house edge is the difference between what the player runs through the game and what the game returns. For this example, the house-edge calculation is $100 minus $99.54, which equals 46¢, which is 0.46 percent. Notice how low that house edge is. This is the actual return and house edge for the full-pay version of Jacks or Better video poker. I would venture to say there is not a standard slot machine in any major gaming location that has as low a house edge. This is why video poker is so popular.

Of course not all video-poker returns are this high. Some go as low as 95 percent and—in some very bad situations—even lower. However, some returns are higher—even more than 100 percent! This book will show you which specific games and pay tables give you which specific returns.

Notice that earlier I wrote "in the long run." After 20 hands on a $1 game playing $5 per hand, I guarantee you will *not* have $99.54. You will have $100 or $105 or $85 or any multiple of $5, because that is what the hands pay. You will have ups and downs. Your credit balance will swing up and it will swing down. But after thousands and thousands of hands, the average return will be very close to $99.54 for every $100 you ran through this game.

The swings in bankroll are called "volatility" or "variance." *Volatility* is a generic term that refers to how high or low the bankroll swings. Variance is a mathematical term that puts a number on the volatility. The variance of video-poker games runs from a low of about 12–15 to a high approaching 200.

What difference does volatility make to the video-poker player? Plenty. The higher the volatility, the higher—and lower—the bankroll swings. If you are lucky and hit a large-paying hand early, you will have plenty of money to continue playing. What if you don't hit any large-paying hand early? In a high-volatility game, the player loses much faster than they would on a low-volatility game. So you must have enough cash to ride through the losing streaks. The bankroll requirements for a high-volatility game are much higher than for a low-volatility game because the downs and ups are far more intense.

The next section will discuss bankroll requirements in more detail. For now, just be aware that multiple high-paying hands on a game come with a price. That price is steeper losing streaks and correspondingly higher bankroll requirements.

I suggest the following guidelines for deciding whether to play a video-poker game based on its variance.

From a *bankroll safety* point of view, if the variance is less than 40, it is a fairly safe—albeit possibly boring—game to play.

A variance of 40–80 means it may be an exciting ride, but think carefully about whether you have the bankroll and emotional will to play this game, as there will be significant losing streaks.

If the variance is higher than 80, seriously consider a different game. Unless you are sure you have a large enough bankroll and you can emotionally tolerate potentially *huge* losing streaks, these games may not be for you.

I will alert you when you have machines that give you an advantage by writing **Advantage Alert** and for those machines that are just a shade under break-even with **Almost Advantage Alert**.

CHAPTER 39

Bankroll Requirements

Gamblers play video poker to have fun. While winning is the most fun, a majority of sessions will not be winners. In fact, in video poker losing sessions will probably outnumber winning sessions two-to-one. A video-poker player can be very careful and select the game with the highest return in the casino. It may even be higher than 100 percent, meaning he has an edge over the casino. The video-poker player can put in hours of time learning and practicing the correct strategy to maximize his return on the game. But unless the video-poker player has enough money with him, his lofty ambitions may not be realized.

Having too small a bankroll is the reason players have to quit early—sometimes days early. Let's be clear about what I mean when I say "bankroll." I mean money that is set aside specifically to be used for casino play. I don't mean dipping into a common bank account that is accessed from an ATM with a bank debit card or (even worse) a credit card. We call a bank account that is strictly for gambling a 401(g) (the *G* stands for *gambling*).

The money cannot come from a bank account that is used for paying bills such as groceries, gas, mortgage, heart surgery, and so forth. It must be money that is totally separate and *is kept* totally separate. It is money to be used strictly for casino gambling.

Ideally players will bring this money with them rather than accessing a separate gambling bank account with a debit card. It is far too easy to lose track of your withdrawals or to start chasing losses if you use a piece of plastic to obtain—or worse, replenish—your gambling stake.

Okay, enough about how you should set up a bankroll. How much should the bankroll contain? That is the real question.

Let's assume you have a 401(g) for your casino video-poker play. How much is enough? As is almost always the case, the answer is—it depends.

First, make sure you choose an appropriate denomination of machine to play. If you only have a couple hundred dollars, a $1 machine is not for you. A quarter machine might work if it has a high return and low variance and you will not be playing for too long. If you don't size the game to your bankroll, you are asking for trouble. Losing streaks—even on low-variance games—are common. I once had a streak of 38 losing hands in a row—and this was on a low-variance machine. Playing a quarter machine 38 hands at $1.25 a hand amounts to nearly a $50 lost in less than five minutes. Not fun.

As a standard rule of thumb you need three to four times the amount a royal pays. So if you are playing a 25¢ game where a five-credit royal flush pays 4,000 credits or $1,000, your bankroll should be around $3,000–4,000. This is a good rule of thumb.

Do you need to bring this entire amount with you? Very likely the answer is, no you don't. The three to four times a royal flush is a long-term bankroll requirement. It is normally enough to tide you through until you hit your next royal flush.

Playing three to four hours a day for three or four days is not really long-term—although if you are losing, it can certainly seem as though it is. If you are only at the casino for a few hours and will only be playing two hours, your bankroll requirements are much less than if you are staying three days and playing four hours each day.

Let's take the example of playing for a couple hours. Once a strategy is learned, the rate of play can be anywhere from 200 to 1,200 hands per hour, depending on the player's skill, the type of video-poker game, the complexity of the strategy, and the speed of the machine.

For the sake of this discussion, I will use 500 hands per hour as the rate of play. Two hours of play means 1,000 hands played. If the game played is the same 25¢ game with a 99.54 percent return and a 19.5 variance, $300 is an adequate bankroll to make sure the player doesn't go broke in two hours.

But how much is required for a trip where you play four hours each day for three days? This trip has 500 hands per hour, four hours per day, for three days. The calculation for total hands is 500 hands times four hours per day times three days = 6,000 hands. This is six times the number of hands as the previous two-hour session. Will a bankroll of $1,800 (six times the $300 for two hours) be required? Thankfully, the answer is no. It works out that $900 is sufficient to last for the four hours per day on your three-day trip (usually) without going broke.

Please keep in mind that the return and variance used in the above example is for one of the best all-around video-poker games—9/6 full-pay Jacks or Better. This game is fully examined later in this book. For this chapter only the return and variance are of any concern.

What would happen to bankroll requirements if a higher-variance game were played? Let's look at 9/6 Double Double Bonus Poker—the most popular version of a very popular video-poker game. Again, this game will be fully examined later in the book. What matters are the return of 98.98 percent and the variance of 42.0. Let's use the same playing parameters as above.

First let's see what the bankroll requirement will be for a two-hour session of 1,000 hands. The same bankroll of $300 will be totally wiped out one time in 20 sessions or 5 percent of the time. In order to make sure your entire bankroll is not lost, it needs to be at least $450—fully 50 percent more than for full-pay Jacks or Better.

If the same bankroll of $900 used for the four-hour-per-day, three-day trip playing 9/6 Jacks or Better was used for playing the Double Double Bonus game instead, the player would get wiped out one time in 11 visits or 9 percent of the time. The bankroll required to usually make sure it wasn't entirely lost would be $1,650.

The bankroll requirements for 12 hours of Jacks or Better play is triple the original amount required for two hours of play ($900 versus $300), but the bankroll requirement for 12 hours of Double Double Bonus is three and two-thirds what is required for two hours ($1,650 versus $450).

Variance does make a difference, but in the case of Double Double Bonus Poker, the return is also lower than Jacks or Better, and this also affects bankroll size.

Let's try one more example using a very high-variance game: the 9/7 Triple Double Bonus with a return of 99.58 percent (just about the same as the 99.54 percent return of 9/6 Jacks or Better). The variance is 98.3 (roughly five times the 19.5 variance of Jacks or Better).

To play two hours of Triple Double Bonus requires a bankroll of $600 to usually make sure the entire amount is not lost. Even though this game has nearly the same very good return, the variance doubles the bankroll requirements for two hours of play versus Jacks or Better. The Triple Double Bonus player will need one-third more bankroll for two hours of play than what is needed for Double Double Bonus, even though Triple Double Bonus has a better return.

For a three-day, four-hour-per-day trip, $2,100 is probably required to make sure the player doesn't go bust. This is one-third more than for Double Double Bonus and two and one-half times what is required for Jacks or Better to play the same length of time.

If you are planning a three-day trip to the casino to play video poker, would you rather play 12 hours for $900 or less, or would you rather play 12 hours for $2,100 or less?

I know my answer.

It is clear that variance matters. Don't take it lightly. Return is only one factor in the money-management equation. Variance is perhaps an even more important factor in protecting your bankroll.

CHAPTER 40

How Playing Strategy Is Determined

There are many possible playing styles for the game of video poker. Due to the number of video-poker variations included in this book, it is not possible to give the absolute perfect-play strategy, as such strategies can go on endlessly. Instead the strategies presented are simplified though quite strong ones that ignore some of the picayune nuances while still giving you an extremely high payback. The returns are no more than a small fraction of a percentage point under perfect strategy. You are not giving up much in order to get an understandable method of play.

The playing strategies included in this book are computer-generated and evaluate every possible result for a particular dealt hand. These results are compared, and only the one that gives the highest average return is include for the play strategy.

This detailed strategy is then reviewed, and some of the very minor changes in return are combined into one step to simplify play. In general the combination of strategy lines reduces the return no more than 0.02 percent—2¢ for every $100 played.

As a disclaimer, the strategy charts presented here have been meticulously developed and checked and are believed to be correct. The author, publisher, or anyone else associated with this book cannot be held responsible for any possible errors or typos…if you find an error, it was probably done by some other writer.

CHAPTER 41

Some Common Video-Poker Terms

In order to properly interpret video-poker strategy charts and therefore properly play the game, you must understand the meaning of several terms. There is a complete listing of video-poker terms in the glossary at the end of this section, but certain terms must be understood in order to properly utilize the strategy charts.

Flush: Cards of the same suit—all spades or diamonds, etc.

Four of a Kind: Four cards of the same rank, such as four kings or four 3s.

Gap: This word is used with straights and straight flushes. A gap is a "hole" in the sequence. The sequence 3, 4, 6, 7 has one gap—the 5. The sequence 3, 5, 7 has two gaps—the 4 and 6.

High Card: Similar to the high pair, a high card is a card of any rank that, when combined with another card of the same rank, would make a high pair. In Jacks or Better it would be a jack through ace. In Kings or Better it would be a king or ace. In Nines or Better it would be a 9 through ace.

High Pair: Any pair that is high enough to win some money—usually these pay even money, which means getting back what you bet. In a Jacks or Better game, it is a pair with the rank of jacks or higher. A pair of jacks, queens, kings, or aces would all be considered high pairs in a Jacks or Better game. In a Kings or Better game only a pair of kings or aces would be considered high pairs. In a Nines or Better game, a pair of 9s, 10s, jacks, queens, kings, or aces would be high pairs.

Inside: This is used with straights and straight flushes; it means there are one or more gaps in the sequence.

Low Pair: Any pair that does not win some money. In Jacks or Better 2s through 10s are low pairs.

Open: Used with straights and straight flushes, it means there are no gaps in the sequence and a sequence of five cards can be completed by adding cards on either or both ends of the sequence. Examples of open straights are: 2, 3, 4, 5 and 8, 9, 10, J and 3, 4, 5.

There are certain sequences that might be thought of as open straights, when in reality they are inside straights. Consider the sequence A, K, Q, J. There are four cards in sequence, but the five-card sequence can only be completed with a 10. If the sequence were K, Q, J, 10, it would be an open straight because the five-card sequence can be completed with an ace or a 9.

What about the sequence K, Q, J? Is this an open or an inside straight? In order to be considered a fully open straight, the five-card sequence *must* be able to be completed with cards on either or both ends of the initial sequence. Since there is room for only one card on the high side of this three-card sequence (the ace), this is an inside straight with one gap.

This is an important concept to master when using strategy charts, as the odds of completing an inside straight or inside straight flush are much less than the odds of completing an open straight or open straight flush. Interpreting your dealt hand improperly will cause errors in play and ultimately cost you money.

Pair: Two cards of the same rank. For example, the king of spades and the king of diamonds, or the three of hearts and the three of clubs are pairs.

Penalty: A penalty makes a hand less valuable. There can be straight or flush penalties. A straight penalty is when one of the cards you are discarding would help make a straight. A flush penalty is when one of the cards you are throwing away would help make a flush. It is sometimes advantageous to throw away a card that would help make a straight or a flush in the hopes of making a more profitable hand. If the term "penalty" is used without specifying whether it is a straight or flush penalty, then either type of penalty counts.

Royal Flush: An ace-high straight flush such as the ace, king, queen, jack, and 10 of hearts.

Straight: Cards in sequence; for example, 4, 5, 6, 7, and 8. The cards can be of mixed suits and can be in any sequence as long as they can be arranged from low to high without any gaps. In most cases the ace can be counted as the lowest card in a sequence (A, 2, 3, 4, 5) or the highest card in a sequence (10, J, Q, K, A).

Straight Flush: This is a hand of the same suit with the cards in sequence. An example would be the 5C, 6C, 7C, 8C, and 9C (*C* = clubs).

Suited: All of the cards mentioned are of the same suit—hearts, diamonds, clubs, or spades.

Three of a Kind: Three cards of the same rank, such as three kings or three 4s.

CHAPTER 42

How to Use Strategy Charts

The strategy charts are arranged so the most favorable holds are at the top. Start at the top of the chart. Look at the first line and compare it to your dealt hand. If it matches, hold those cards. For example, if the strategy line says "Two Pair" and your hand is 4H, 3D, 9C, 3H, 4D, you have two pair—a pair of 4s and a pair of 3s. Hold the two 4s and the two 3s and hit the *draw* button.

If the line does not match your hand, continue down the chart until you find the hand you are dealt. The last line in the chart says, "Draw five new cards." If you reach this line, don't save any cards; just hit the *draw* button.

If more than one hand is listed in a line, the hand(s) at the left have priority over hands following them.

Make sure you play the maximum of five coins for each hand, as the strategy charts are based on the bonus for a royal flush when playing five coins. Failing to do so will cause about a 2 percent loss in return. If you can't afford to play five coins each hand, move to a lower-denomination machine.

CHAPTER 43
Specific Game Information Included in This Book

Much research was done in the development of this book. There are dozens of different video-poker games.

For each game included, there is a brief description of the game as well as any unique features. The game's return percentage and variance are also shown. Advantage and almost-advantage games will be especially noted.

Tables showing payoffs for all paying hands, how often each paying hand occurs on average, and how much of the total payback the hand contributes to the total return are included for each game.

After the detailed pay table information, a simplified strategy is listed. Following the strategy is a brief statement concerning the strategy or the game itself.

Multiple (full-pay and short-pay) versions of most games are included. The short-pay versions that are not included have a return that is too low. In almost all cases one or more of the games and pay tables included this book will be available in a casino near you. Remember, always try to find the highest-return and lowest-variance version of the game to play.

You are much better off playing a game where you keep your money longer, thereby giving you a better chance of hitting the "big one." You work hard for your money. Pick a game that will give it the best chance of winning for you.

CHAPTER 44

Jacks or Better–Class Video-Poker Games

The term Jacks or Better refers to the fact that the games require a pair of jacks or higher before any money is returned to the player. Jacks or Better games were among the first video-poker games created. Since the introduction of the original Draw Poker game, variations of all types have flooded the market.

Video-poker machine manufacturers and casino management worked together to improve the fairly humdrum Draw Poker game. The first change was to make a pair of jacks or better the lowest paying hand. Paying even money for two pair was not endearing this game to the gambling public because there were too many very long waiting periods before a hit.

People seemed to want more action, more excitement. To foster just such excitement, the game of Bonus Poker was introduced. This game paid a "bonus" for certain four of a kind hands. By adding a few higher-paying hands, the game became a bit more exciting.

Of course, nothing stops with just one tweak to a game. Before long, several other "more exciting" games were introduced. They carried names such as Double Bonus Poker, Double Double Bonus Poker, Bonus Poker Deluxe, Double Jackpot Poker, Double Double Jackpot Poker, and on and on—ever more options for the hungry video-poker player.

However, even though there were dozens of different games, they were all based on the concept first introduced as Draw Poker. All of these games required a pair of jacks or higher to get any money returned to the player. Jacks or Better–based games are by far the largest group of any type of video-poker game, validating the concept.

The next section reviews many Jacks or Better–based games that are available in casinos today, giving the reader all the information required to play the game at a high level.

Good luck and, more important, good skill.

CHAPTER 45

Jacks or Better
(Full-Pay, Short-Pay)

The original video-poker game was called Draw Poker and required a hand with two pairs in order to get anything back. The lowest-paying hand was soon changed to a pair of jacks or better in order to help make the game more popular. The game became wildly popular and began to be called simply Jacks or Better. Even though hundreds of other variations have been introduced, Jacks or Better continues to be among the most popular video-poker variations.

There are many reasons for this. It has among the highest paybacks of all the games. It has low variance, and the optimum playing strategy is fairly straightforward to remember.

The pay table has only nine lines. The initial offering of most of the pioneer video-poker games were decent paying games, often very near or *higher than* 100 percent payback. As the games became more popular, casinos wanted to get more money from the games, so the pay tables were degraded. The initial high-paying versions of the game became known as "full-pay."

Full-Pay Jacks or Better
The full-pay version of Jacks or Better has the following pay table:

Jacks or Better Full-Pay—Payback: 99.54 Percent, Variance: 19.5					
Hand	*1 Coin*	*2 Coins*	*3 Coins*	*4 Coins*	*5 Coins*
Royal Flush	250	500	750	1,000	4,000
Straight Flush	50	100	150	200	250
Four of a Kind	25	50	75	100	125
Full House	9	18	27	36	45
Flush	6	12	18	24	30
Straight	4	8	12	16	20

Jacks or Better Full-Pay—Payback: 99.54 Percent, Variance: 19.5					
Hand	*1 Coin*	*2 Coins*	*3 Coins*	*4 Coins*	*5 Coins*
Three of a Kind	3	6	9	12	15
Two Pair	2	4	6	8	10
Jacks or Better	1	2	3	4	5

Hand	*Pay 5 Coins*	*Occurs Every*	*% Return*
Royal Flush	4,000	40,390.6	1.98
Straight Flush	250	9,148.4	0.55
Four of a Kind	125	423.3	5.91
Full House	45	86.9	10.36
Flush	30	90.8	6.61
Straight	20	89.1	4.49
Three of a Kind	15	13.4	22.33
Two Pair	10	7.7	25.86
Jacks or Better	5	4.7	21.46
No Win	0	1.8	0

This game is commonly called 9/6 Jacks or Better—so named because a full house pays 9-for-1 and a flush pays 6-for-1. When downgrading a Jacks or Better pay table, the only payoffs that are usually reduced are the full house and flush—usually but not always. If you find a 9/6 Jacks or Better pay table, it is always a good idea to check the entire pay table before assuming it is a full-pay game.

Notice that the payback for all hands is simply the one-coin amount multiplied by the number of coins played. This is true for all hands except the royal flush. The five-coin payback would be 1,250 if this were true. Instead it is 4,000—quite a bonus. For this reason you should always play the maximum of five coins when playing this game (as well as almost all other variations of video poker). The payback, variance, and strategy charts are all based on playing five coins.

Jacks or Better has only one "jackpot"-sized payout—the royal flush. It also has only nine different possible types of winning hands. Because of this the variance is low and the strategy is not very complex, making Jacks or Better a great game for a novice player or for someone with a somewhat limited bankroll. It is also a great game for players not interested in enduring huge bankroll swings.

Strategy for 9/6 (Full-Pay) Jacks or Better
Four of a Kind or Better
Four Cards of a Royal Flush
Three of a Kind or Better
Four Cards of an **Open** Straight Flush—2345-9TJQ Suited
Two Pair
Four Cards of an **Inside** Straight Flush
High Pair (JJ-AA)
Three Cards of a Royal Flush
Four Cards of a Flush
KQJT (Straight)
Low Pair (22-TT)
QJT9, JT98 (Straights)
Suited QJ9, JT9
Four Cards of an **Open** Straight (0 High Cards)—2345-789T
Suited QJ8
Three-Card **Open** Straight Flush—Suited 345-89T
Suited KQ9, KJ9, QT9, JT8, J98
Suited QJ
AKQJ (Straight)
Suited KQ, KJ, AK, AQ, AJ
Four-Card Straight, **Inside**—3 High Cards
Any Three-Card Straight Flush Exc. 0 High Cards & Two gaps
KQJ, QJ
Suited JT
KQ, KJ
Suited QT
AK, AQ, AJ
Suited KT
One High Card (J-A)
Any Three-Card Straight Flush
Draw Five New Cards

To use this strategy chart, compare the dealt hand to the chart starting with the top row and continuing down one row at a time until you find the cards in your hand listed. Hold the cards listed in that row and hit the *draw* button. If you make it to the bottom on the chart without finding your hand, simply hit the *draw* button without holding any cards.

Short-Pay Jacks or Better

Any pay schedule that reduces the payout for any of the hands is considered a short pay schedule. The most common short-pay Jacks or Better reduces the payouts for a full house and flush to 8-for-1 and 5-for-1 from 9-for-1 and 6-for-1 respectively while keeping all the other payouts the same. Other common short pay schedules are 9/5 and 8/6. Still others will reduce the payout for a five-coin straight flush or the five-coin royal flush.

Here is the most common short-pay version of Jacks or Better.

Jacks or Better 8/5 Short-Pay—Payback: 97.29 Percent, Variance: 19.4					
Hand	1 Coin	2 Coins	3 Coins	4 Coins	5 Coins
Royal Flush	250	500	750	1,000	4,000
Straight Flush	50	100	150	200	250
Four of a Kind	25	50	75	100	125
Full House	8	16	24	32	40
Flush	5	10	15	20	25
Straight	4	8	12	16	20
Three of a Kind	3	6	9	12	15
Two Pair	2	4	6	8	10
Jacks or Better	1	2	3	4	5

Hand	Pay 5 Coins	Occurs Every	% Return
Royal Flush	4,000	40,169.8	1.99
Straight Flush	250	9,288.1	0.54
Four of a Kind	125	423.2	5.91
Full House	40	86.9	9.21
Flush	25	91.7	5.45
Straight	20	89.0	4.49
Three of a Kind	15	13.4	22.34
Two Pair	10	7.7	25.86
Jacks or Better	5	4.7	21.51
No Win	0	1.8	0

This version is very common on the Las Vegas strip and other high-end properties. Although I don't recommend playing this version if it can be helped, this may be the best you are going to find. It has a low variance and is relatively simple to play.

Strategy For 8/5 (Short Pay) Jacks or Better
Four of a Kind or Better
Four Cards of a Royal Flush
Three of a Kind or Better
Any Four-Card Straight Flush, Including **Inside**
Two Pair
High Pair (JJ-AA)
Three Cards of a Royal Flush
Four Cards of a Flush
KQJT (Straight)
Low Pair (22-TT)
Four Cards of an **Open** Straight—2345-9TJQ
Suited QJ9, JT9
AKQJ (Straight)
Suited QJ8
Three-Card **Open** Straight Flush—Suited 345-89T
Suited KQ9, KJ9, QJ, QT9, JT8, J98, KQ, KJ
Four-Card **Inside** Straight—Three High Cards
Suited AK, AQ, AJ
KQJ
Four-Card **Inside** Straight—Two High Cards
QJ (Straight)
Any Three-Card Straight Flush Except Two Gaps, 0 High Card
Suited JT
KQ, KJ, AK, AQ, AJ
J
Suited QT
Q, K, A
Any Three-Card Straight Flush
Any Four-Card **Inside** Straight
Draw Five New Cards

While this strategy may look like the full-pay version, there are some minor changes in some hands' priority. Again, to use the chart, start at the top. When you find your hand, hold the card(s) indicated. If you reach the bottom, discard everything and redraw five cards.

CHAPTER 46

Bonus Poker

Bonus Poker differs from Jacks or Better by paying a bonus for some four of a kind hands. Four 5s through kings are paid 25-for-1 just as in Jacks or Better, but four 2s, 3s, or 4s are paid 40-for-1 and four aces are paid 80-for-1.

This game was developed to satisfy the gambling public's desire for larger jackpots. Jacks or Better has only the royal flush as a true jackpot. The four of a kind pays enough for 25 additional plays, so it is not really a jackpot, although it certainly helps out.

Bonus Poker on the other hand pays 80-for-1 for four aces. On quarter machines this amounts to $100 with five credits played. Although this is not a huge jackpot, it is enough to make the player feel as if they have won something substantial. Also, where the royal flush happens only about once every 40,000 hands, four aces will occur roughly once every 5,100 hands—eight times as often. At 500 hands per hour, the Bonus Poker player will get four aces once every 10 hours, on average.

In order to pay for the increased payouts for quads, other payoffs have to be lowered. In Bonus Poker, payoffs for the full house and flush are reduced to eight and five, going down from nine and six respectively, thereby making the "full-pay" version of this game return 99.17 percent. This is not as good as a full-pay Jacks or Better, but it is still not bad.

Bonus Poker 8/5 Full-Pay—Payback: 99.16 Percent, Variance: 20.9					
Hand	1 Coin	2 Coins	3 Coins	4 Coins	5 Coins
Royal Flush	250	500	750	1,000	4,000
Straight Flush	50	100	150	200	250
Four Aces	80	160	240	320	400
Four 2s, 3s, or 4s	40	80	120	160	200
Four 5s through Ks	25	50	75	100	125
Full House	8	16	24	32	40

Bonus Poker 8/5 Full-Pay—Payback: 99.16 Percent, Variance: 20.9					
Hand	1 Coin	2 Coins	3 Coins	4 Coins	5 Coins
Flush	5	10	15	20	25
Straight	4	8	12	16	20
Three of a Kind	3	6	9	12	15
Two Pair	2	4	6	8	10
Jacks or Better	1	2	3	4	5

Hand	Pay 5 Coins	Occurs Every	% Return
Royal Flush	4,000	40,233.1	1.99
Straight Flush	250	9,360.1	0.53
Four Aces	400	5,106.1	1.57
Four 2s, 3s, or 4s	200	1,896.6	2.11
Four 5s through Ks	125	609.8	4.10
Full House	40	86.9	9.21
Flush	25	91.9	5.44
Straight	20	89.1	4.49
Three of a Kind	15	13.4	22.34
Two Pair	10	7.7	25.86
Jacks or Better	5	4.7	21.53
No Win	0	1.8	0

The variance is a little higher because more of the return is tied up in fewer, larger wins, but it is still reasonable. Also the strategy is relatively simple.

Strategy For 8/5 (Full-Pay) Bonus Poker
Four of a Kind or Better
Four Cards of a Royal Flush
Full House
Three Aces
Flush
Three of a Kind or Better
Four Cards of an **Open** Straight Flush—2345-9TJQ Suited
Two Pair
Four Cards of an **Inside** Straight Flush
High Pair (JJ-AA)

Strategy For 8/5 (Full-Pay) Bonus Poker
Three Cards of a Royal Flush
Four Cards of a Flush
KQJT (Straight)
Low Pair (22-TT)
QJT9, JT98 (Straights)
Suited QJ9, JT9
Four Cards of an **Open** Straight (0 High Cards)—2345-789T
QJ8 Suited
AKQJ (Straight)
Suited QJ
Three-Card **Open** Straight Flush—Suited 345-89T
Suited KQ9, KJ9, QT9, JT8, J98
Suited KQ, KJ, AK, AQ, AJ
Four-Card **Inside** Straight—Three High Cards
KQJ, QJ
Three-Card **Inside** Straight Flush—Two Gaps, One High Card
Suited JT
KQ, KJ
Any Three-Card Straight Flush Exc. 0 High Cards and Two Gaps
AK, AQ, AJ
Suited QT
J, A, Q
Suited KT
K
Any Three-Card Straight Flush
Draw Five New Cards

It is getting harder to find full-pay Jacks or Better games. However, full-pay Bonus Poker games tend to be readily available. The full-pay (8/5) Bonus Poker game is a good play when only 8/5 Jacks or Better games are available. The return is relatively high at better than 99 percent, the variance is low, and the strategy is fairly straightforward and matches Jacks or Better fairly closely. Consider playing it when no good Jacks or Better games are available.

CHAPTER 47

Bonus Poker Deluxe

onus Poker Deluxe is another variation of Jacks or Better designed to add some excitement to play with the possibility of getting higher-paying four-of-a-kind hands.

Bonus Poker Deluxe is different than Bonus Poker because all four of a kinds pay the same 80-for-1. This is a relatively popular game because *any* four of a kind pays 80-for-1 to the player. This means many more large payouts, as four-of-a-kind hands show up roughly 10 times as often as a royal flush (once every 423 hands versus once every 42,000 hands).

The pay table has the exact same hands as Jacks or Better, although the pay values are different. The full-house and two-pair payoffs are each reduced by one credit to fund the additional pays on quads. The payback percentage is a full percentage point lower than full-pay Jacks or Better, so the Bonus Poker Deluxe player is definitely paying for the larger pays on four of a kind. Here is the pay table for standard (full-pay) Bonus Poker Deluxe:

Bonus Poker Deluxe 8/6—Payback: 98.49 Percent, Variance: 32.0					
Hand	1 Coin	2 Coins	3 Coins	4 Coins	5 Coins
Royal Flush	250	500	750	1,000	4,000
Straight Flush	50	100	150	200	250
Four of a Kind	80	160	240	320	400
Full House	8	16	24	32	40
Flush	6	12	18	24	30
Straight	4	8	12	16	20
Three of a Kind	3	6	9	12	15
Two Pair	1	2	3	4	5
Jacks or Better	1	2	3	4	5

Hand	Pay 5 Coins	Occurs Every	% Return
Royal Flush	4,000	42,076.8	1.90
Straight Flush	250	9,173.0	0.55
Four of a Kind	400	423.9	18.87
Full House	40	87.1	9.19
Flush	30	90.0	6.67
Straight	20	78.0	5.13
Three of a Kind	15	13.5	22.22
Two Pair	5	7.8	12.83
Jacks or Better	5	4.7	21.13
No Win	0	1.8	0

One advantage of Bonus Poker Deluxe is that the strategy is just as simple as Jacks or Better. There's no distinguishing four aces from four 2s, 3s, or 4s or from 5s through kings. All four of a kinds are equal—just as in Jacks or Better.

Strategy For 8/6 Bonus Poker Deluxe
Four of a Kind or Better
Four Cards of a Royal Flush
Three of a Kind or Better
Any Four-Card Straight Flush, Including **Inside**
Two Pair
High Pair (JJ-AA)
Three Cards of a Royal Flush Except A-High-10
Four-Card Flush
Suited AKT, AQT, AJT
KQJT (Straight)
Low Pair (22-TT)
QJT9, JT98 (Straights)
Suited QJ9, JT9
Four-Card **Open** Straight (0 High Cards)—2345-789T
Suited QJ8
Three-Card **Open** Straight Flush—Suited 345-89T
Suited KQ9, KJ9, QT9, JT8, J98
AKQJ (Straight)
Suited QJ KQ, KJ, AK, AQ, AJ

Strategy For 8/6 Bonus Poker Deluxe
Four-Card **Inside** Straight—Three High Cards
Any Three-Card Straight Flush Exc. 0 High Cards and Two Gaps
KQJ
Four-Card Straight, **Inside**—Two High Cards
QJ
Suited JT
KQ, KJ
Suited QT
AK, AQ, AJ
J
Suited KT
Q, K, A
Any Three-Card Straight Flush
Four-Card Straight, **Inside**—0 High Cards
Draw Five New Cards

The Bonus Poker Deluxe strategy is only slightly more complex than Jacks or Better, making Bonus Poker Deluxe a good game for novices and recreational players who like getting the larger pays on four-of-a-kind hands and are willing to sacrifice some house edge to get it.

CHAPTER 48

Double Bonus Poker
(Full-Pay, Short-Pay)

Double Bonus Poker takes Bonus Poker one step further and doubles the bonuses for four-of-a-kind hands. Four aces pay 160-for-1 rather than 80-for-1. Four 2s, 3s, or 4s pay 80-for-1 rather than 40-for-1. And four 5s through kings pay 50-for-1 instead of 25-for-1.

> **Advantage Alert:** *Double Bonus Poker's full-pay version pays back more than 100 percent.*

For all of these factors, Double Bonus Poker is one of the more popular video-poker games. However, because of all the different payouts for four-of-a-kind hands, the strategy is more complex. Also, because much more money is paid out in fewer, higher-paying hands, the variance is higher. To pay for the higher pays for quads, full houses, and flushes, two pairs only pay 1-for-1 rather than 2-for-1 as in Jacks or Better or Bonus Poker.

The full-pay version is commonly referred to as 10/7, referencing the 10-for-1 payoff for a full house and 7-for-1 payoff for a flush.

> **Advantage Alert:** *The payback on a 10/7 Double Bonus Poker game with perfect play is 100.17 percent.*

Full-pay versions of Double Bonus Poker can't be found everywhere. A short-pay 9/7 (9-for-1 for a full house and 7-for-1 for a flush) version is more common, paying 99.10 percent with perfect play—still a relatively good bet. Pay tables for both versions of this game follow.

Double Bonus Poker 10/7 Full-Pay—Payback: 100.17 Percent, Variance: 28.3					
Hand	*1 Coin*	*2 Coins*	*3 Coins*	*4 Coins*	*5 Coins*
Royal Flush	250	500	750	1,000	4,000
Straight Flush	50	100	150	200	250
Four Aces	160	320	480	640	800
Four 2s, 3s, or 4s	80	160	240	320	400
Four 5s through Ks	50	100	150	200	250
Full House	10	20	30	40	50
Flush	7	14	21	28	35
Straight	5	10	15	20	25
Three of a Kind	3	6	9	12	15
Two Pair	1	2	3	4	5
Jacks or Better	1	2	3	4	5

Hand	*Pay 5 Coins*	*Occurs Every*	*% Return*
Royal Flush	4,000	48,048.0	1.67
Straight Flush	250	8,841.4	0.57
Four Aces	800	5,030.4	3.18
Four 2s, 3s, or 4s	400	1,908.2	4.19
Four 5s through Ks	250	622.0	8.04
Full House	50	89.4	11.19
Flush	35	66.9	10.47
Straight	25	66.6	7.51
Three of a Kind	15	13.9	21.66
Two Pair	5	8.0	12.47
Jacks or Better	5	5.2	19.24
No Win	0	1.8	0

Double Bonus Poker 9/7 Short-Pay—Payback: 99.10 Percent, Variance: 28.5					
Hand	*1 Coin*	*2 Coins*	*3 Coins*	*4 Coins*	*5 Coins*
Royal Flush	250	500	750	1,000	4,000
Straight Flush	50	100	150	200	250
Four Aces	160	320	480	640	800
Four 2s, 3s, or 4s	80	160	240	320	400
Four 5s through Ks	50	100	150	200	250
Full House	9	18	27	36	45

Double Bonus Poker 9/7 Short-Pay—Payback: 99.10 Percent, Variance: 28.5					
Hand	*1 Coin*	*2 Coins*	*3 Coins*	*4 Coins*	*5 Coins*
Flush	7	14	21	28	35
Straight	5	10	15	20	25
Three of a Kind	3	6	9	12	15
Two Pair	1	2	3	4	5
Jacks or Better	1	2	3	4	5

Hand	*Pay 5 Coins*	*Occurs Every*	*% Return*
Royal Flush	4,000	48,035.0	1.67
Straight Flush	250	8,837.5	0.57
Four Aces	800	4,567.0	3.50
Four 2s, 3s, or 4s	400	1,908.2	4.19
Four 5s through Ks	250	623.5	8.02
Full House	45	94.1	9.57
Flush	35	65.7	10.66
Straight	25	66.6	7.51
Three of a Kind	15	13.7	21.86
Two Pair	5	8.4	11.89
Jacks or Better	5	5.1	19.67
No Win	0	1.8	0

The strategies for these two versions of the game vary slightly. In fact there is only one play that is different between them. Because of that, the strategy table that follows has been designed to incorporate both strategies. This should help you, as you only need to learn and possibly carry one strategy to play both games.

Strategy For 10/7 and 9/7 Double Bonus Poker
Straight Flush or Better
Four Cards of a Royal Flush
Three of a Kind or Better
Any Four-Card Straight Flush, Both **Open** and **Inside**
10/7=>Two Pair -Then- AA; 9/7=>AA -Then- Two Pair
Suited QJT, KQJ, 0–1 Penalties
Four-Card Flush—Three High Cards
Suited KQJ, QJT, Two Penalties

Strategy For 10/7 and 9/7 Double Bonus Poker
Suited KQT, KJT, 0 Penalties
Four-Card Flush—Two High Cards
High Pair (JJ-KK)
Three-Card Royal Flush
Any Four-Card Flush
Four-Card **Open** Straight—2345-10JQK
Low Pair 22, 33, 44 Only
Suited JT9, QJ9
Low Pair (55-TT)
Three-Card Open Straight Flush, 0 High Cards—345-89T
AKQJ (Straight)
Suited QJ8, QT9, JT8, J98, KQ9, KJ9
Four-Card **Inside** Straight—Three High Cards
Suited QJ, KQ, KJ
Three-Card Straight Flush—One Gap, 0 High Cards
Three-Card Flush—Two High Cards
Three-Card Straight Flush—Two Gaps, One High Card
Suited AK, AQ, AJ
Four-Card **Inside** Straight—Two High Cards
KQJ, QJT
Four-Card **Inside** Straight—One High Card
Suited JT
QJ
Three-Card Straight Flush—Two Gaps, 0 High Cards, 0 Penalties
Three-Card Flush—One High Card
Suited QT
KQ, KJ
Three-Card Straight Flush—Two Gaps, 0 High Cards, One Penalty
A, J
Suited KT
Q, K
Four-Card **Inside** Straight—0 High Cards
Three-Card Flush—0 High Cards
Draw Five New Cards

Because more payback money is concentrated in the much-higher-paying four-of-a-kind hands, the variance for Double Bonus Poker is higher than any previously discussed game. Higher variance is not a problem per se, as long as the player has a sufficient bankroll to ride out the dry spells that will occur.

With the proper bankroll and proper practice with the strategy, Double Bonus Poker can be a great game to play. Plenty of large payoffs from four of a kinds and a positive payback expectation on the full-pay version make for fun and excitement and often long-term profits on those advantage varieties.

CHAPTER 49

Double Double Bonus Poker

Double Double Bonus Poker is still another variation of Jacks or Better. Like Bonus Poker and Double Bonus Poker, this game pays a premium for four-of-a-kind hands. However, in order to generate even higher payouts for certain hands, the concept of a "kicker" is introduced in this game.

A kicker is a card from a certain set of cards. For Double Double Bonus, four aces pays 160-for-1. However, four aces with a kicker of a 2, 3, or 4 pays a whopping 400-for-1—two and a half times what is paid for four aces. Getting four aces with a kicker pays half as much as a royal—and it occurs two and a half times as often. Four 2s, 3s, or 4s pays 80-for-1. Four 2s, 3s, or 4s with a kicker of a 2, 3, 4, or ace pays double that, or 160-for-1.

Clearly this game is geared toward people who love hitting big wins. Apparently many people do, as this game is popular.

Unfortunately, the full-pay (9/6) version of this game returns only 98.98 percent to the player, making it one of the lower-paying full-pay games. The variance is high at 42.0, caused by so much money being tied up in a few very large hands. Also, the strategy is more complex than any shown thus far due to the very high value of aces and low cards and the presence of kickers.

The pay table for 9/6 Double Double Bonus Poker looks like this:

Double Double Bonus Poker 9/6 Full-Pay—Payback: 98.98 Percent, Variance: 42.0					
Hand	1 Coin	2 Coins	3 Coins	4 Coins	5 Coins
Royal Flush	250	500	750	1,000	4,000
Straight Flush.	50	100	150	200	250
Four Aces w/ 2, 3, or 4	400	800	1,200	1,600	2,000
Four Aces	160	320	480	640	800
Four 2s, 3s, 4s w/ A,2,3,4	160	320	480	640	800
Four 2s, 3s, or 4s	80	160	240	320	400
Four 5s through Ks	50	100	150	200	250
Full House	9	18	27	36	45

Double Double Bonus Poker 9/6 Full-Pay—Payback: 98.98 Percent, Variance: 42.0					
Hand	1 Coin	2 Coins	3 Coins	4 Coins	5 Coins
Flush	6	12	18	24	30
Straight	4	8	12	16	20
Three of a Kind	3	6	9	12	15
Two Pair	1	2	3	4	5
Jacks or Better	1	2	3	4	5

Hand	Pay 5 Coins	Occurs Every	% Return
Royal Flush	4,000	40,799.3	1.96
Straight Flush	250	9,123.1	0.55
Four Aces w/ 2, 3, or 4	2,000	16,236.4	2.46
Four Aces	800	6,983.4	2.29
Four 2s, 3s, 4s w/ A,2,3,4	800	5,761.0	2.78
Four 2s, 3s, or 4s	400	2,601.4	3.08
Four 5s through Ks	250	613.4	8.15
Full House	45	92.1	9.77
Flush	30	88.0	6.82
Straight	20	78.3	5.11
Three of a Kind	15	13.3	22.58
Two Pair	5	8.1	12.31
Jacks or Better	5	4.7	21.23
No Win	0	1.8	0

Full-pay Double Double Bonus games tend to be widely available. The casino is getting more than 1 percent without degrading the pay schedule. Short pay schedules are present in some casinos, however, so make sure to check the entire pay table before sitting down to play.

Strategy For 9/6 Full-Pay Double Double Bonus Poker
Four of a Kind or Better
Four Cards of a Royal Flush
Three Aces
Full House
Three 2s, 3s, or 4s
Flush
Three of a Kind (5s through Ks)

Strategy For 9/6 Full-Pay Double Double Bonus Poker
Straight
Any Four-Card Straight Flush, Both **Open** and **Inside**
Pair of As
Two Pair
Suited QJT, KQJ
High Pair (JJ, QQ, KK)
Suited KQT, KJT, AKQ, AKJ, AQJ
Four-Card Flush
Three-Card Royal Flush A-High-10
KQJT (Straight)
Pair of 2s, 3s, or 4s
QJT9, JT98 (Straights)
Low Pair (55 through TT)
Suited QJ9, JT9
Four-Card **Open** Straight—2345-789T
Suited QJ8
Three-Card **Open** Straight Flush—Suited 345-89T
Suited KQ9, KJ9, QT9, JT8, J98
AKQJ (Straight)
Suited QJ, AK, AQ, AJ, KQ, KJ
Four-Card **Inside** Straight, 3 High Cards
Any Three-Card Straight Flush **Except** Two Gaps, 0 High Cards
KQJ
Four-Card **Inside** Straight, Two High Cards
QJ, A
Suited JT
KQ, KJ
Suited QT, KT
J, Q, K
Any Three-Card Straight Flush
Four-Card **Inside** Straight
Draw Five New Cards

Getting more high-paying hands is always fun. However, the strategy for Double Double Bonus is fairly complex and the variance is high. Also, the payback is lower than a lot of other full-pay games.

If you choose to play this game, make sure you are aware of these downside issues. Bring enough money with you to make sure you are able to play long enough. Long periods without hitting a large payoff hand will very quickly consume your bankroll. This game is exciting. Make sure you can last long enough to cash in on some of that excitement.

CHAPTER 50

Double Jackpot Poker

Double Jackpot Poker is similar to Double Double Bonus Poker because there is a kicker included in the pay table. Four aces with a king, queen, or jack pays 160-for-1. Four kings, queens, or jacks with an ace, king, queen, or jack pays 80-for-1. Two pairs pays 2-for-1. The full-pay (8/5 meaning a full house pays 8-for-1 and a flush pays 5-for-1) version is the only one to be covered in this book. It returns 99.63 percent with perfect play and has a variance of 22.4.

The complete pay table information is immediately below.

Double Jackpot Poker 8/5 Full-Pay—Payback: 99.63 Percent, Variance: 22.4					
Hand	1 Coin	2 Coins	3 Coins	4 Coins	5 Coins
Royal Flush	250	500	750	1,000	4,000
Straight Flush	50	100	150	200	250
Four Aces w/ K, Q, or J	160	320	480	640	800
Four Aces	80	160	240	320	400
Four Ks, Qs, Js w/A, K, Q, J	80	160	240	320	400
Four Ks, Qs, Js	40	80	120	160	200
Four 2s through Ts	20	40	60	80	100
Full House	8	16	24	32	40
Flush	5	10	15	20	25
Straight	4	8	12	16	20
Three of a Kind	3	6	9	12	15
Two Pair	2	4	6	8	10
Jacks or Better	1	2	3	4	5

Hand	Pay 5 Coins	Occurs Every	% Return
Royal Flush	4,000	40,619.4	1.97
Straight Flush	250	9,620.2	0.52
Four Aces w/ K, Q, or J	800	17,233.4	0.93
Four Aces	400	7,249.5	1.10
Four Ks, Qs, Js w/A, K, Q, J	400	5,721.8	1.40
Four Ks, Qs, Js	200	2,421.2	1.65
Four 2s through Ts	100	633.2	3.16
Full House	40	86.8	9.21
Flush	25	92.8	5.39
Straight	20	89.3	4.48
Three of a Kind	15	13.4	22.34
Two Pair	10	7.7	25.87
Jacks or Better	5	4.6	21.61
No Win	0	1.8	0

Double Jackpot Poker pays a bonus for four of a kinds except for low ones (222-TTT), which have a reduced pay. Four aces or four-of-a-kind high cards with a kicker of a high card garner an extra bonus. Even with the extra pays, the variance for this game still stays in the manageable range at 22.4.

The strategy for Double Jackpot Poker is not that complex, considering there are kickers involved.

Strategy For 8/5 Full-Pay Double Jackpot Poker
Four of a Kind or Better
Four-Card Royal Flush
Three of a Kind or Better
Four-Card **Open** Straight Flush—2345-9TJQ
Two Pair
Any Four-Card Straight Flush
High Pair (JJ-AA)
Any Three-Card Royal Flush
Four-Card Flush
TJQK (Straight)
Low Pair (22-TT)
9TJQ, 89TJ (Straights)
Suited QJ9, JT9

Strategy For 8/5 Full-Pay Double Jackpot Poker
Four-Card **Open** Straight—2345-789T
Suited QJ
Suited QJ8
AKQJ (Straight)
Three-Card **Open** Straight Flush—Suited 345-89T
Suited KQ9, KJ9, QT9, JT8, J98
Suited AK, AQ, AJ, KQ, KJ
Four-Card **Inside** Straight, Three High Cards
KQJ, QJ, KQ, KJ (Straights)
Three-Card Straight Flush, Two Gaps, One High
Suited JT
AK, AQ, AJ (Straights)
Any Three-Card Straight Flush Except Two Gaps, 0 High Cards
One High Card—J, A, Q, K
Any Three-Card Straight Flush
Draw Five New Cards

Double Jackpot Poker is a decent game to play if you can find it with the pay table above. The strategy is relatively simple, variance is fairly low, and return is better than even full-pay Jacks or Better.

CHAPTER 51

Double Double Jackpot Poker

This book will only cover one version of Double Double Jackpot Poker. Double Double Jackpot Poker bumps the larger pays by doubling the Double Jackpot Poker pays for all four of a kinds except 2s through 10s, which are 2.5 times the Double Jackpot version. The pays for full house, flush, and straight are all increased by one. The pay for two pairs is reduced to even money to make up for the increases.

Advantage Alert: *The return for this game is 100.35 percent, but the variance increases dramatically from 22.4 to 38.2.*

The complete pay table information is printed below.

Double Double Jackpot Poker 9/6 Full-Pay—Payback: 100.35 Percent, Variance: 38.2					
Hand	*1 Coin*	*2 Coins*	*3 Coins*	*4 Coins*	*5 Coins*
Royal Flush	250	500	750	1,000	4,000
Straight Flush	50	100	150	200	250
Four Aces w/ K, Q, or J	320	640	960	1,280	1,600
Four Aces	160	320	480	640	800
Four Ks, Qs, Js w/A, K, Q, J	160	320	480	640	800
Four Ks, Qs, Js	80	160	240	320	400
Four 2s through Ts	50	100	150	200	250
Full House	9	18	27	36	45
Flush	6	12	18	24	30
Straight	5	10	15	20	25
Three of a Kind	3	6	9	12	15
Two Pair	1	2	3	4	5
Jacks or Better	1	2	3	4	5

Hand	Pay 5 Coins	Occurs Every	% Return
Royal Flush	4,000	42,885.3	1.87
Straight Flush	250	9,341.1	0.54
Four Aces w/ K, Q, or J	1,600	15,812.1	2.02
Four Aces	800	6,387.8	2.50
Four Ks, Qs, Js w/A, K, Q, J	800	5,851.0	2.73
Four Ks, Qs, Js	400	2,433.5	3.29
Four 2s through Ts	250	638.4	7.83
Full House	45	92.9	9.69
Flush	30	91.2	6.58
Straight	25	64.7	7.72
Three of a Kind	15	13.5	22.22
Two Pair	5	8.3	12.11
Jacks or Better	5	4.7	21.24
No Win	0	1.8	0

The strategy for Double Double Jackpot Poker is more complex than Double Jackpot Poker because certain cards are now worth considerably more.

Strategy for 9/6 Full-Pay Double Double Jackpot Poker
Four of a Kind or Better
Four-Card Royal Flush
Three of a Kind or Better
Any Four-Card Straight Flush
Pair of AA
Two Pair
High Pair—JJ-KK
Any Three-Card Royal Flush Except AhT
Any Four-Card Flush
Any Three-Card Royal Flush, Including AhT
Four-Card **Open** Straight—2345-TJQK
Suited JT9, QJ9
Low Pair—22-TT
AKQJ (Straight)
Three-Card **Open** Straight Flush—Suited 345-89T
Suited QT9, JT8, J98

Strategy for 9/6 Full-Pay Double Double Jackpot Poker
Four-Card **Inside** Straight, Three High Cards
Suited KQ9, KJ9, QJ8
Any Two-Card Royal Flush Except T Low
Four-Card **Inside** Straight, Two High Cards
Any Three-Card Straight Flush, Except Two Gaps, 0 High
KQJ, QJT (Straights)
Four-Card **Inside** Straight , One High Card
QJ (Straight)
Suited JT
KQ, KJ, AK, AQ, AJ (Straights)
A
Suited QT
J, Q
Suited KT
K
Any Three-Card Straight Flush
Any Four-Card **Inside** Straight
Draw Five New Cards

Double Double Jackpot Poker has a great return of higher than 100 percent. The variance is relatively high and the strategy somewhat complex. If this game is available where you play, consider learning the strategy and make sure your bankroll is sufficient to handle the downswings.

Anytime there is a positive-expectation (greater than 100 percent return) game available, serious consideration should be given to taking advantage of it.

CHAPTER 52

Royal Aces Bonus Poker (Full Pay, Short Pay)

Royal Aces Bonus Poker is what the name suggests—aces provide the greatest bonus. In fact, in Royal Aces Bonus Poker, four aces pay the same as a royal flush! Four 2s, 3s, or 4s pays 80-for-1, and four 5s through kings pays 50-for-1. The full-pay version is 9/6 with 9-for-1 for a full house and 6-for-1 for a flush. This is the same as full-pay Jacks or Better.

How can this game afford to pay such large payouts and still pay 9/6? Well, it only pays 1-for-1 for two pairs, but that isn't near enough to cover the additional bonus payments. The answer: a high pair no longer includes jacks, queens, or kings! The only high pair is a pair of aces.

This game concentrates a huge amount of money into very few hands, so even though the payback is 99.58 percent, which is very good, the variance is an astronomical 181.7. In comparison, Jacks or Better has a variance of 19.5, just about one-tenth that of Royal Aces Bonus Poker.

Full-Pay Royal Aces Bonus Poker

The pay table for this version on Royal Aces Bonus Poker looks like this:

Royal Aces Bonus Poker 9/6 Full-Pay—Payback: 99.58 Percent, Variance: 181.7					
Hand	*1 Coin*	*2 Coins*	*3 Coins*	*4 Coins*	*5 Coins*
Royal Flush	250	500	750	1,000	4,000
Straight Flush	100	200	300	400	500
Four Aces	250	500	750	1,000	4,000
Four 2s, 3s, or 4s	80	160	240	320	400
Four 5s through Ks	50	100	150	200	250
Full House	9	18	27	36	45
Flush	6	12	18	24	30
Straight	4	8	12	16	20

Royal Aces Bonus Poker 9/6 Full-Pay—Payback: 99.58 Percent, Variance: 181.7					
Hand	1 Coin	2 Coins	3 Coins	4 Coins	5 Coins
Three of a Kind	3	6	9	12	15
Two Pair	1	2	3	4	5
Aces or Better	1	2	3	4	5

Hand	Pay 5 Coins	Occurs Every	% Return
Royal Flush	4,000	45,968.9	1.74
Straight Flush	500	7,901.4	1.27
Four Aces	4,000	4,058.5	19.71
Four 2s, 3s, or 4s	400	1,883.4	4.25
Four 5s through Ks	250	630.2	7.93
Full House	45	93.5	9.63
Flush	30	66.3	9.05
Straight	20	73.8	5.42
Three of a Kind	15	13.6	22.10
Two Pair	5	8.3	12.01
Pair of Aces	5	15.4	6.48
No Win	0	1.4	0

The strategy for this game is relatively straightforward because there are no kickers.

Strategy for 9/6 Full-Pay Royal Aces Bonus Poker
Straight Flush or Better
Three Aces
Four-Card Royal Flush
Flush or Better
Three of a Kind—222-KKK
Four-Card **Open** Straight Flush—Suited 2345-9TJQ
Straight
High Pair (AA)
Four-Card **Inside** Straight Flush—A234, A345, 2346-9JQK
Two Pair
Suited KQJ, KJT, QJT
Four-Card Flush

Strategy for 9/6 Full-Pay Royal Aces Bonus Poker
Suited AKQ, AJT
Low Pair—22-KK
Three-Card **Open** Straight Flush, 0 High Cards—345-9TJ
Four-Card **Open** Straight, 0 High Cards—2345-10JQK
Three-Card **Inside** Straight Flush, One Gap—234, 235-9JQ
Three-Card **Inside** Straight Flush, w/Ace—A23-A45
A
Any Three-Card Straight Flush
Four-Card **Inside** Straight—2346-9JQK
Three-Card Flush
Suited KQ, KJ, KT, QJ, QT, JT
Two-Card **Open** Straight Flush—45-9T
Two-Card **Inside** Straight Flush, One Gap—34, 35-9J
Three-Card **Open** Straight—345-10JQ
Draw Five New Cards

The high payback and fairly simple strategy make Royal Aces Bonus Poker an easy game to play. The possibility of a royal flush–sized payout roughly every 4,000 hands maximizes the excitement factor of this game.

The very high variance means anyone considering playing this game should make sure their bankroll is sufficient to ride through some very brutal down cycles. With the only high pair being Aces, there is no return every 1.4 hands on average, so be prepared to experience long losing periods.

Royal Aces Bonus Poker—Short Pay

There is another popular version of Royal Aces Bonus Poker that is a short-pay version. Rather than 9/6, it is 9/5 and the return is 98.13 percent. Variance is even higher at 184.1. The pay table for this version is:

Royal Aces Bonus Poker 9/5 Short-Pay—Payback: 98.13 Percent, Variance: 184.1					
Hand	*1 Coin*	*2 Coins*	*3 Coins*	*4 Coins*	*5 Coins*
Royal Flush	250	500	750	1,000	4,000
Straight Flush	100	200	300	400	500
Four Aces	250	500	750	1,000	4,000
Four 2s, 3s, or 4s	80	160	240	320	400
Four 5s through Ks	50	100	150	200	250

Royal Aces Bonus Poker 9/5 Short-Pay—Payback: 98.13 Percent, Variance: 184.1					
Hand	1 Coin	2 Coins	3 Coins	4 Coins	5 Coins
Full House	9	18	27	36	45
Flush	5	10	15	20	25
Straight	4	8	12	16	20
Three of a Kind	3	6	9	12	15
Two Pair	1	2	3	4	5
Aces or Better	1	2	3	4	5

Hand	Pay 5 Coins	Occurs Every	% Return
Royal Flush	4,000	40,693.2	1.97
Straight Flush	500	8,250.0	1.21
Four Aces	4,000	4,037.5	19.81
Four 2s, 3s, or 4s	400	1,884.3	4.25
Four 5s through Ks	250	629.6	7.94
Full House	45	93.4	9.64
Flush	25	71.0	7.04
Straight	20	72.1	5.55
Three of a Kind	15	13.6	22.13
Two Pair	5	8.3	12.03
Pair of Aces	5	15.2	6.56
No Win	0	1.4	0

The slight change in payback for the flush causes a couple of minor changes in the strategy.

Strategy for 9/5 Short-Pay Royal Aces Bonus Poker
Straight Flush or Better
Three Aces
Four-Card Royal Flush
Full House
Three of a Kind—2-K
Four-Card **Open** Straight Flush—Suited 2345-9TJQ
Straight or Better
High Pair (AA)
Four-Card **Inside** Straight Flush—A234, A345, 2346-9JQK

Strategy for 9/5 Short-Pay Royal Aces Bonus Poker
Two Pair
Three-Card Royal Flush
Four-Card Flush
Low Pair—22-KK
Four-Card **Open** Straight, 0 High Cards—2345-TJQK
Three-Card **Open** Straight Flush, 0 High Cards—345-9TJ
Three-Card **Inside** Straight Flush, One Gap—234, 235-9JQ
A
Any Three-Card Straight Flush
Four-Card **Inside** Straight—2346-9JQK
Suited QJ, QT, JT
Three-Card Flush
Suited KQ, KJ, KT
Two-Card **Open** Straight Flush—45-9T
Two-Card **Inside** Straight Flush, One Gap—34, 35-9J
Three-Card **Open** Straight—345-10JQ
Draw Five New Cards

The very high variance of this game combined with the 98 percent payback makes it a game of limited value.

CHAPTER 53

Super Aces Bonus Poker (Full-Pay, Short-Pay)

Super Aces Bonus Poker is another bonus game that favors aces. Four aces pay 400-for-1, four 2s, 3s, or 4s pays 80-for-1, and four 5s through kings pays 50-for-1. The full-pay version is an 8/5 game returning 99.94—almost an even game! This particular game is unique because it pays 60-for-1 for a straight flush instead of the usual 50-for-1.

Full-Pay Super Aces Bonus Poker

The pay table for the full-pay version is shown below.

Almost Advantage Alert: *The full-pay version is an 8/5 game returning 99.94 percent—almost an even game!*

Super Aces Bonus Poker 8/5 Full-Pay—Payback: 99.94 Percent, Variance: 63.4					
Hand	*1 Coin*	*2 Coins*	*3 Coins*	*4 Coins*	*5 Coins*
Royal Flush	250	500	750	1,000	4,000
Straight Flush	60	120	180	240	300
Four Aces	400	800	1,200	1,600	2,000
Four 2s, 3s, or 4s	80	160	240	320	400
Four 5s through Ks	50	100	150	200	250
Full House	8	16	24	32	40
Flush	5	10	15	20	25
Straight	4	8	12	16	20
Three of a Kind	3	6	9	12	15
Two Pair	1	2	3	4	5
Jacks or Better	1	2	3	4	5

Hand	Pay 5 Coins	Occurs Every	% Return
Royal Flush	4,000	39,150.1	2.04
Straight Flush	300	9,694.7	0.62
Four Aces	2,000	4,210.2	9.50
Four 2s, 3s, or 4s	400	1,895.0	4.22
Four 5s through Ks	250	613.2	8.15
Full House	40	92.0	8.70
Flush	25	92.0	5.43
Straight	20	79.0	5.07
Three of a Kind	15	13.3	22.63
Two Pair	5	8.1	12.33
Jacks or Better	5	4.7	21.24
No Win	0	1.8	0

Short-Pay Super Aces Bonus Poker

The short-pay version reduces the payoff for a full house to 7-for-1. This reduces the payback to 98.85 percent, which is still not too bad. The variance stays virtually the same at 63.2. Here is the pay table for the short-pay version of Super Aces Bonus Poker.

Super Aces Bonus Poker 7/5 Short-Pay—Payback: 98.85 Percent, Variance: 63.2					
Hand	1 Coin	2 Coins	3 Coins	4 Coins	5 Coins
Royal Flush	250	500	750	1,000	4,000
Straight Flush	60	120	180	240	300
Four Aces	400	800	1,200	1,600	2,000
Four 2s, 3s, or 4s	80	160	240	320	400
Four 5s through Ks	50	100	150	200	250
Full House	7	14	21	28	35
Flush	5	10	15	20	25
Straight	4	8	12	16	20
Three of a Kind	3	6	9	12	15
Two Pair	1	2	3	4	5
Jacks or Better	1	2	3	4	5

Hand	Pay 5 Coins	Occurs Every	% Return
Royal Flush	4,000	39,112.3	2.05
Straight Flush	300	9,675.4	0.62
Four Aces	2,000	4,211.0	9.50
Four 2s, 3s, or 4s	400	1,895.0	4.22
Four 5s through Ks	250	613.2	8.15
Full House	35	92.0	7.61
Flush	25	92.0	5.44
Straight	20	79.0	5.07
Three of a Kind	15	13.3	22.62
Two Pair	5	8.1	12.33
Jacks or Better	5	4.7	21.24
No Win	0	1.8	0

As the tables show, there is very little difference in the "Occurs Every" and "% Return" columns. There is coincidentally very little difference in the strategies for the two versions. A combined strategy chart is included below.

Strategy for 8/5 Full-Pay and 7/5 Short-Pay Super Aces Bonus Poker (Unless indicated, strategy lines applies to both)
Straight Flush or Better
Three Aces
Four-Card Royal Flush
Three of a Kind or Better
Any Four-Card Straight Flush
High Pair (AA)
Two Pair
** 7/5 Only ** Suited KQJ, QJT
High Pair (JJ-KK)
** 8/5 Only ** Three-Card Royal Flush
** 7/5 Only ** Suited Ahh, AhT, KQT, KJT
Four-Card Flush
Four-Card **Open** Straight, One to Three High Cards
Low Pair—22-TT
Suited JT9, QJ9
Four-Card **Open** Straight, 0 High Cards—2345-789T
AKQJ (Straight)

Strategy for 8/5 Full-Pay and 7/5 Short-Pay Super Aces Bonus Poker (Unless indicated, strategy lines applies to both)
Three-Card **Open** Straight Flush, 0 High Cards—345-89T
Suited QT9, J98, KQ9, KJ9, QJ8
Suited AK, AQ, AJ, KQ, KJ, QJ
Four-Card **Inside** Straight, Three High Cards—AhhT-KQJ9
A, KQJ
Any Three-Card **Inside** Straight Flush Except Two Gaps 0 High
KQT9, QJ98 (Straights)
KQ, KJ, QJ
Suited KT, QT, JT
K, Q, J
Any Three-Card Straight Flush
Any Four-Card Straight
Draw Five New Cards

Super Aces Bonus Poker has a high payoff for four aces and lesser payoffs for other four-of-a-kind hands. If you are able to locate a full-pay version, it pays almost as well as full-pay Jacks or Better, and you get the thrill of more frequent jackpot and mini-jackpot hits. You pay for it in high variance, so make sure you have adequate funding for your sessions.

CHAPTER 54

Super Double Bonus Poker (Full-Pay, Short-Pay)

Super Double Bonus Poker is different than any variation of video poker we have reviewed thus far. Not only does it pay more for a straight flush (80-for-1 rather than 50-for-1), it also breaks up four-of-a-kind hands into four groups. Four aces pays 160-for-1. The next-highest paid are four jacks, queens, or kings, paying 120-for-1. Next comes four 2s, 3s, or 4s, which pays 80-for-1. Last in the list are four 5s through 10s, paying 50-for-1.

Due to the extra category of quads, the strategy will be a tad more complex. The variance is better than Super Aces Bonus Poker—in fact it is just a bit more than half at about 38.

The full-pay version returns 99.70 percent—an excellent return—and the short-pay version returns 98.69 percent.

Full-Pay Super Double Bonus Poker
Here is the pay table for the full-pay (9/5) version of Super Double Bonus Poker:

Super Double Bonus Poker 9/5 Full-Pay—Payback: 99.70 Percent, Variance: 38.0					
Hand	*1 Coin*	*2 Coins*	*3 Coins*	*4 Coins*	*5 Coins*
Royal Flush	250	500	750	1,000	4,000
Straight Flush	80	160	240	320	400
Four Aces	160	320	480	640	800
Four Js, Qs, or Ks	120	240	360	480	600
Four 2s, 3s, or 4s	80	160	240	320	400
Four 5s through Ts	50	100	150	200	250
Full House	9	18	27	36	45
Flush	5	10	15	20	25
Straight	4	8	12	16	20

Super Double Bonus Poker 9/5 Full-Pay—Payback: 99.70 Percent, Variance: 38.0					
Hand	*1 Coin*	*2 Coins*	*3 Coins*	*4 Coins*	*5 Coins*
Three of a Kind	3	6	9	12	15
Two Pair	1	2	3	4	5
Jacks or Better	1	2	3	4	5

Hand	*Pay 5 Coins*	*Occurs Every*	*% Return*
Royal Flush	4,000	40,619.4	1.97
Straight Flush	400	8,917.1	0.90
Four Aces	800	4,515.1	3.54
Four Js, Qs, or Ks	600	1,707.0	7.03
Four 2s, 3s, or 4s	400	1,897.9	4.22
Four 5s through Ts	250	952.6	5.25
Full House	45	92.3	9.75
Flush	25	91.6	5.46
Straight	20	78.0	5.13
Three of a Kind	15	13.3	22.50
Two Pair	5	8.1	12.28
Jacks or Better	5	4.6	21.67
No Win	0	1.8	0

As mentioned above, the strategy for this game will be a little more complex thanks to four different groups of four-of-a-kind payoffs. Also the differences between the full-pay and short-pay strategies are significant enough to require two separate strategies. Here is the full-pay strategy.

Strategy for 9/5 Full-Pay Super Double Bonus Poker
Straight Flush or Better
Four-Card Royal Flush
Three Aces
Full House
Three of a Kind
Flush
Four-Card **Open** Straight Flush—2345-9TJQ
Straight
Any Four-Card Straight Flush
High Pair (AA)

Strategy for 9/5 Full-Pay Super Double Bonus Poker
Two Pair
High Pair (JJ-KK)
Three-Card Royal Flush
Four-Card Flush
Four-Card **Open** Straight, One to Three High Cards
Low Pair—22-44, 77
Suited JT9
Low Pair—55-66, 88-TT
Suited QJ9
Four-Card **Open** Straight, 0 High Cards—2345-789T
Three-Card **Open** Straight Flush, 0 High Cards—345-89T
Suited QT9, J98, QJ8
AKQJ (Straight)
Suited KQ9, KJ9
Suited KQ, KJ, QJ
Four-Card **Inside** Straight, Three High Cards—AhhT-KQJ9
Suited AK, AQ, AJ
Any Three-Card **Inside** Straight Flush Except Two Gaps 0 High
KQJ
KQT9, QJ98 (Straights)
KQ, KJ, QJ
Suited JT
AK, AQ, AJ
Suited QT
A, K, Q, J
Any Three-Card Straight Flush
Any Four-Card Straight
Draw Five New Cards

The higher pays for four-of-a-kind hands and the relatively high return is somewhat offset by the complexity of the strategy. However, it does return more than full-pay Jacks or Better, and you are awarded several jackpots and mini-jackpots. If you have the time and patience to master the strategy and the bankroll to weather the losing spells, Super Double Bonus Poker may be the game for you.

Short-Pay (8/5) Super Double Bonus Poker

The short-pay version reduces the pay for a full house to 8-for-1, which reduces the payback to 98.68 percent. The variance increases just slightly to 38.6. Here is the pay table for the short-pay version of Super Double Bonus Poker.

Super Double Bonus Poker 8/5 Short-Pay—Payback: 98.68 Percent, Variance: 38.6					
Hand	*1 Coin*	*2 Coins*	*3 Coins*	*4 Coins*	*5 Coins*
Royal Flush	250	500	750	1,000	4,000
Straight Flush	80	160	240	320	400
Four Aces	160	320	480	640	800
Four Js, Qs, or Ks	120	240	360	480	600
Four 2s, 3s, or 4s	80	160	240	320	400
Four 5s through Ts	50	100	150	200	250
Full House	8	16	24	32	40
Flush	5	10	15	20	25
Straight	4	8	12	16	20
Three of a Kind	3	6	9	12	15
Two Pair	1	2	3	4	5
Jacks or Better	1	2	3	4	5

Hand	*Pay 5 Coins*	*Occurs Every*	*% Return*
Royal Flush	4,000	40,594.8	1.97
Straight Flush	400	8,888.2	0.90
Four Aces	800	4,512.7	3.55
Four Js, Qs, or Ks	600	1,537.9	7.80
Four 2s, 3s, or 4s	400	1,898.0	4.22
Four 5s through Ts	250	953.0	5.25
Full House	40	109.2	7.32
Flush	25	91.5	5.46
Straight	20	78.0	5.13
Three of a Kind	15	13.0	23.21
Two Pair	5	9.2	10.90
Jacks or Better	5	4.4	22.98
No Win	0	1.8	0

As with the full-pay version of this game, the strategy is relatively complex. Here it is for your review.

Strategy for 8/5 Short-Pay Super Double Bonus Poker
Straight Flush or Better
Four-Card Royal Flush
Three of a Kind, Jacks through Aces
Full House
Three of a Kind, 2s through Ts
Flush
Four-Card **Open** Straight Flush—2345-9TJQ
Straight
Any Four-Card Straight Flush
High Pair (JJ-AA)
Two Pair
Three-Card Royal Flush
Four-Card Flush
Four-Card **Open** Straight, One to Three High Cards
Low Pair—22-44
Suited JT9
Low Pair—88-99
Suited QJ9
Low Pair 55-77, TT
Four-Card **Open** Straight, 0 High Cards—2345-789T
Three-Card **Open** Straight Flush, 0 High Cards—345-89T
Suited QT9, J98, QJ8
AKQJ (Straight)
Suited KQ9, KJ9
Suited AK, AQ, AJ, KQ, KJ, QJ
Four-Card **Inside** Straight, Three High Cards—AKJT, AQJT, KQJ9
Any Three-Card **Inside** Straight Flush Except Two Gaps 0 High
KQJ
KQT9, QJ98 (Straights)
KQ, KJ, QJ
Suited JT
AK, AQ, AJ

Strategy for 8/5 Short-Pay Super Double Bonus Poker
Suited QT
A, K, Q, J
Any Three-Card Straight Flush
Any Four-Card Straight
Draw Five New Cards

Considering the reduced payback of the short-pay Super Double Bonus Poker game as well as the complexity of the strategy, you may want to seriously consider another game; that is, unless where you play offers only short-pay games and the 98.68 percent return is at least 0.5 percent higher than any other game available. Admittedly, the increased pays for straight flushes and quads are fun to hit.

CHAPTER 55

Super Double Double Bonus Poker (Full-Pay, Short-Pay)

Super Double Double Bonus Poker is for the player who wants lots of different options to win big. If you like kickers, this is the game for you. There are four different categories of four of a kinds with kickers in this game.

First you have four aces with a 2, 3, or 4.

Next comes four aces with a jack, queen, or king.

Following that is four 2s, 3s, or 4s with an ace, 2, 3, or 4.

Finally comes four jacks, queens, or kings with a jack, queen, king, or ace. On top of that there are your standard four-of-a-kind categories: aces, 2s through 4s, and 5s through kings.

Full-Pay Super Double Double Bonus Poker

The full-pay version of the game returns 99.68 percent and has a variance of 51. Here is the pay table.

Super Double Double Bonus Poker 8/5 Full-Pay—Payback: 99.69 Percent, Variance: 51.0					
Hand	1 Coin	2 Coins	3 Coins	4 Coins	5 Coins
Royal Flush	250	500	750	1,000	4,000
Straight Flush	50	100	150	200	250
Four Aces w/ Any 2,3,4	400	800	1,200	1,600	2,000
Four Aces w/ Any J,Q,K	320	640	960	1,280	1,600
Four 2s,3s,4s w/ A,2,3,4	160	320	480	640	800
Four Js, Qs, Ks w/ J,Q,K,A	160	320	480	640	800
Four Aces	160	320	480	640	800
Four 2s, 3s, or 4s	80	160	240	320	400
Four 5s through Ks	50	100	150	200	250
Full House	8	16	24	32	40

Super Double Double Bonus Poker 8/5 Full-Pay—Payback: 99.69 Percent, Variance: 51.0					
Hand	*1 Coin*	*2 Coins*	*3 Coins*	*4 Coins*	*5 Coins*
Flush	5	10	15	20	25
Straight	4	8	12	16	20
Three of a Kind	3	6	9	12	15
Two Pair	1	2	3	4	5
Jacks or Better	1	2	3	4	5

Hand	*Pay 5 Coins*	*Occurs Every*	*% Return*
Royal Flush	4,000	40,167.7	1.99
Straight Flush	250	9,637.3	0.52
Four Aces w/ Any 2, 3, 4	2,000	16,586.2	2.41
Four Aces w/ Any J, Q, K	1,600	15,761.2	2.03
Four 2s, 3s, 4s w/A,2,3,4	800	6,984.5	2.29
4 Js,Qs,Ks w/ J, Q, K, A	800	5,140.8	3.11
Four Aces	800	8,998.7	1.78
Four 2s, 3s, or 4s	400	2,601.1	3.08
Four 5s through Ks	250	718.5	6.96
Full House	40	91.9	8.71
Flush	25	91.8	5.44
Straight	20	79.7	5.02
Three of a Kind	15	13.3	22.64
Two Pair	5	8.1	12.34
Jacks or Better	5	4.7	21.37
No Win	0	1.8	0

As you might expect, the strategy for this game is complex. All the four-of-a-kind and kicker combinations wreak havoc with simplicity. The myriad jackpot-winning combinations come at a price. Here is the strategy for the full-pay version of Super Double Double Bonus Poker.

Strategy for 8/5 Full-Pay Super Double Double Bonus Poker
Four of a Kind or Better
Four-Card Royal Flush
Three Aces
Full House

Strategy for 8/5 Full-Pay Super Double Double Bonus Poker
Any Three of a Kind or Better
Any Four-Card Straight Flush
Pair of Aces
Two Pair
High Pair—JJ-KK
Three-Card Royal Flush
Four-Card Flush
KQJT (Straight)
Low Pair—22-44
QJT9, JT98 (Straights)
Low Pair—55-TT
Four-Card **Open** Straight, 0 High Cards—2345-789T
Suited QJ9, JT9
AKQJ (Straight)
Suited KQ9, KJ9, QJ8, QT9, J98
Suited KQ, KJ, QJ
Three-Card **Open** Straight Flush, 0 High Cards—345-89T
Suited AK, AQ, AJ
Four-Card **Inside** Straight, Three High Cards—AKJT, AQJT, KQJ9
KQJ
KQT9, QJ98
Suited KT9, QT8, Q98, J97, J87, A23, A35, A45
QJ
A
KQ, KJ
Any Three-Card **Inside** Straight Flush Except Two Gaps 0 High
Suited QT, JT
J, Q, K
Any Three-Card Straight Flush
Any Four-Card Straight
Draw Five New Cards

There you have it—a relatively complex strategy for a relatively complex game.

Short-Pay Super Double Double Bonus Poker

The only change to the short-pay table from the full-pay table is a reduction to 7-for-1 from 8-for-1 for a full house. This one change reduces the return to 98.61 percent. The variance is virtually unchanged at 50.9. Here is the pay table for the 7/5 short-pay version of Super Double Double Bonus Poker:

Super Double Double Bonus Poker 7/5 Short-Pay—Payback: 98.61 Percent, Variance: 50.9					
Hand	*1 Coin*	*2 Coins*	*3 Coins*	*4 Coins*	*5 Coins*
Royal Flush	250	500	750	1,000	4,000
Straight Flush	50	100	150	200	250
Four Aces w/ Any 2, 3, 4	400	800	1,200	1,600	2,000
Four Aces w/ Any J, Q, K	320	640	960	1,280	1,600
Four 2s, 3s, 4s w/ A,2,3,4	160	320	480	640	800
Four Js,Qs,Ks w/ J,Q,K,A	160	320	480	640	800
Four Aces	160	320	480	640	800
Four 2s, 3s, or 4s	80	160	240	320	400
Four 5s through Ks	50	100	150	200	250
Full House	7	14	21	28	35
Flush	5	10	15	20	25
Straight	4	8	12	16	20
Three of a Kind	3	6	9	12	15
Two Pair	1	2	3	4	5
Jacks or Better	1	2	3	4	5

Hand	*Pay 5 Coins*	*Occurs Every*	*% Return*
Royal Flush	4,000	40,238.1	1.99
Straight Flush	250	9,584.7	0.52
Four Aces w/ Any 2,3,4	2,000	16,602.8	2.41
Four Aces w/ Any J,Q,K	1,600	15,784.2	2.03
Four 2s,3s,4s w/ A,2,3,4	800	6,816.5	2.35
Four Js,Qs,Ks w/ J,Q,K,A	800	5,140.9	3.11
Four Aces	800	9,009.2	1.78
Four 2s, 3s, or 4s	400	2,531.2	3.16
Four 5s through Ks	250	718.5	6.96
Full House	35	94.6	7.40
Flush	25	91.7	5.45

Hand	Pay 5 Coins	Occurs Every	% Return
Straight	20	79.3	5.04
Three of a Kind	15	13.2	22.73
Two Pair	5	8.1	12.33
Jacks or Better	5	4.7	21.35
No Win	0	1.8	0

The strategy changes required for the short-pay version are more than can easily be incorporated into a single strategy for both full-pay and short-pay. Here is the strategy for the short-pay version:

Strategy for 7/5 Short-Pay Super Double Double Bonus Poker
Four of a Kind or Better
Four-Card Royal Flush
Three of a Kind, Aces through 4s
Full House
Any Three of a Kind or Better
Any Four-Card Straight Flush
Pair of Aces
Two Pair
High Pair—JJ-KK
Three-Card Royal Flush
Four-Card Flush
KQJT (Straight)
Low Pair—22-44
QJT9, JT98 (Straights)
Low Pair—55-TT
Four-Card **Open** Straight, 0 High Cards—2345-789T
Suited QJ9, JT9
AKQJ (Straight)
Suited KQ9, KJ9, QJ8
Suited QJ, QT9, J98
Three-Card **Open** Straight Flush, 0 High Cards—345-89T
Suited AK, AQ, AJ
Four-Card **Inside** Straight, Two to Three High Cards
KQJ, QJ

Strategy for 7/5 Short-Pay Super Double Double Bonus Poker
Suited KT9, QT8, Q98, J97, J87, A23, A35, A45
A
Any Three-Card **Inside** Straight Flush Except Two Gaps 0 High
KQ, KJ
Suited QT, JT
J, Q, K
Any Three-Card Straight Flush
Any Four-Card Straight
Draw Five New Cards

Like the full-pay version, this game offers many opportunities to score jackpots and mini-jackpots but has a return that is reduced by about 1 percent. The variance is relatively high. If you like the more frequent jackpots and no better-paying games are available, this could be a game for you. Just make sure you bring along enough money to ride through the losing sessions.

CHAPTER 56

Triple Bonus Poker
(Full-Pay, Short-Pay)

Triple Bonus Poker is what the name says. Four-of-a-kind hands are generally paid triple what they would be paid in Bonus Poker. Four aces collect 240-for-1, four 2s, 3s, or 4s collect 120-for-1, and four 5s through kings collect 75-for-1. There are no kickers in this game, so the strategy is somewhat less complex. The full-pay version (11/7) returns 99.59 percent—slightly better than full-pay Jacks or Better.

The higher pays for a full house and flush help favor these two hands a little, getting a bit more of the payback from them as opposed to just the jackpot and mini-jackpots. However, in order to pay for the increased jackpots for quads, full house, and flush, the only cards considered "high" are the king and ace. Its variance is just slightly higher than Double Double Bonus Poker at 45.3.

Full-Pay Triple Bonus Poker

The pay table for 11/7 Triple Bonus Poker follows:

Triple Bonus Poker 11/7 Full-Pay—Payback: 99.59 Percent, Variance: 45.3					
Hand	1 Coin	2 Coins	3 Coins	4 Coins	5 Coins
Royal Flush	250	500	750	1,000	4,000
Straight Flush	50	100	150	200	250
Four Aces	240	480	720	960	1,200
Four 2s, 3s, or 4	120	240	360	480	600
Four 5s through Ks	75	150	225	300	375
Full House	11	22	33	44	55
Flush	7	14	21	28	35
Straight	4	8	12	16	20
Three of a Kind	3	6	9	12	15

Triple Bonus Poker 11/7 Full-Pay—Payback: 99.59 Percent, Variance: 45.3					
Hand	*1 Coin*	*2 Coins*	*3 Coins*	*4 Coins*	*5 Coins*
Two Pair	1	2	3	4	5
Kings or Better	1	2	3	4	5

Hand	*Pay 5 Coins*	*Occurs Every*	*% Return*
Royal Flush	4,000	49,817.1	1.61
Straight Flush	250	8,620.0	0.58
Four Aces	1,200	4,343.5	5.53
Four 2s, 3s, or 4s	600	1,887.8	6.36
Four 5s through Ks	375	623.0	12.04
Full House	55	93.6	11.76
Flush	35	60.7	11.52
Straight	20	80.8	4.95
Three of a Kind	15	13.6	22.10
Two Pair	5	8.3	12.01
Kings or Better	5	9.0	11.13
No Win	0	1.5	0

As mentioned above, the strategy is a little less complex due to the absence of kickers.

Strategy for 11/7 Full-Pay Triple Bonus Poker
Four of a Kind or Better
Four-Card Royal Flush
Any Three of a Kind or Better
Any Four-Card Straight Flush
Pair of Aces
Two Pair
Pair of Kings
Four-Card Flush
Three-Card Royal Flush
Low Pair—22-QQ
Four-Card **Open** Straight, Zero to One High Cards—KQJT, 2345-9TJQ
Three-Card **Open** Straight Flush, 0 High Cards—345-9TJ
Suited A23, A24, A25, A34, A35, A45

Strategy for 11/7 Full-Pay Triple Bonus Poker
Three-Card Flush, Two High Cards—AKx
Suited AK
Any Three-Card **Inside** Straight Flush Except Two Gaps 0 High
Four-Card **Inside** Straight, Two High Cards—AKQJ-AKJT
Three-Card Flush, One High Card
Any Three-Card **Inside** Straight Flush
AK, A
Suited KQ, KJ, KT
Any Four-Card Straight, K High
K
Three-Card Flush, 0 High Cards
Any Four-Card Straight
Suited QJ, QT, JT
Two-Card **Open** Straight Flush
Two-Card **Inside** Straight Flush, One Gap
Draw Five New Cards

Some of the lines in the strategy may look a little different due to the ace and king being the only high cards.

The full-pay version of Triple Bonus Poker pays decently—a little better than full-pay Jacks or Better. It has a more complex strategy than Jacks or Better and higher variance, but the inflated pays for quads, full houses, and flushes can make up for the complexity of the strategy and the higher bankroll requirements demanded by the higher variance.

Short-Pay Triple Bonus Poker

The short-pay version of Triple Bonus Poker is created by reducing the pay for a full house to 10-for-1 from 11-for-1. This drops the return to 98.52 percent—not too bad but not great. Here is the pay table for short-pay Triple Bonus Poker:

Triple Bonus Poker 10/7 Short-Pay—Payback: 98.52 Percent, Variance: 45.3					
Hand	1 Coin	2 Coins	3 Coins	4 Coins	5 Coins
Royal Flush	250	500	750	1,000	4,000
Straight Flush	50	100	150	200	250
Four Aces	240	480	720	960	1,200

Triple Bonus Poker 10/7 Short-Pay—Payback: 98.52 Percent, Variance: 45.3					
Hand	*1 Coin*	*2 Coins*	*3 Coins*	*4 Coins*	*5 Coins*
Four 2s, 3s, or 4s	120	240	360	480	600
Four 5s through Ks	75	150	225	300	375
Full House	10	20	30	40	50
Flush	7	14	21	28	35
Straight	4	8	12	16	20
Three of a Kind	3	6	9	12	15
Two Pair	1	2	3	4	5
Kings or Better	1	2	3	4	5

Hand	*Pay 5 Coins*	*Occurs Every*	*% Return*
Royal Flush	4,000	49,832.8	1.61
Straight Flush	250	8,616.5	0.58
Four Aces	1,200	4,347.2	5.53
Four 2s, 3s, or 4s	600	1,888.2	6.36
Four 5s through Ks	375	623.0	12.04
Full House	50	93.6	11.76
Flush	35	60.8	11.52
Straight	20	80.8	4.95
Three of a Kind	15	13.6	22.10
Two Pair	5	8.3	12.01
Kings or Better	5	9.0	11.13
No Win	0	1.5	0

Even changing the pay for just one hand causes several changes in the strategy for the short-pay version of Triple Bonus Poker, so it is not feasible to combine the two strategies into one. Here is the strategy for short-pay Triple Bonus Poker:

Strategy for 10/7 Short-Pay Triple Bonus Poker
Four of a Kind or Better
Four-Card Royal Flush
Any Three of a Kind or Better
Any Four-Card Straight Flush
Pair of Aces
Two Pair

Strategy for 10/7 Short-Pay Triple Bonus Poker
Pair of Kings
Four-Card Flush
Three-Card Royal Flush
Low Pair—22-QQ
Four-Card **Open** Straight, Zero to One High Cards—KQJT, 2345-9TJQ
Three-Card **Open** Straight Flush, 0 High Cards—345-9TJ
Three-Card Flush, 2 High Cards—AKx
Suited KQ9, KT9, A23, A24, A25, A34, A35, A45
Suited AK
Any Three-Card **Inside** Straight Flush Except Two Gaps 0 High
Four-Card **Inside** Straight, Two High Cards—AKQJ, AKJT
Three-Card Flush, One High Card
AK
Any Three-Card Straight Flush
A
Suited KQ, KJ, KT
Any Four-Card Straight, K High
K
Three-Card Flush, 0 High Cards
Any Four-Card Straight
Suited QJ, QT, JT
Two-Card **Open** Straight Flush
Two-Card **Inside** Straight Flush, One Gap
Draw Five New Cards

There it is—a relatively complex strategy for a game at which you will lose 15¢ for every $10 you play through the machine. If the decent jackpots make this a reasonable price to pay for you, go for it.

CHAPTER 57

Triple Bonus Plus Poker (Full-Pay, Short-Pay)

Triple Bonus Plus Poker has most of the same pays for four of a kinds as Triple Bonus Poker. Four 5s through kings is reduced to 50-for-1 from 75-for-1 as it is in Double Bonus Poker, however.

By lowering the pay, a pair of jacks or better pays 1-for-1 rather than just kings or better as in Triple Bonus Poker. The "plus" is double pay for a straight flush. Normally paying 50-for-1 in almost all other games, in Triple Bonus Plus a straight flush pays 100-for-1. Pays for a full house and flush are also reduced from Triple Bonus Poker.

Full-Pay Triple Bonus Plus Poker

The full-pay version of Triple Bonus Plus Poker returns 99.80 percent—darn close to even—with a variance of 44.3, which is comparable to Triple Bonus Poker. Here is the pay table:

> **Almost Advantage Alert:** *The full-pay version of Triple Bonus Plus Poker returns 99.80 percent—darn close to even.*

Triple Bonus Plus Poker 9/5 Full-Pay—Payback: 99.80 Percent, Variance: 44.3					
Hand	*1 Coin*	*2 Coins*	*3 Coins*	*4 Coins*	*5 Coins*
Royal Flush	250	500	750	1,000	4,000
Straight Flush	100	200	300	400	500
Four Aces	240	480	720	960	1,200
Four 2s, 3s, or 4s	120	240	360	480	600
Four 5s through Ks	50	100	150	200	250
Full House	9	18	27	36	45
Flush	5	10	15	20	25

Triple Bonus Plus Poker 9/5 Full-Pay—Payback: 99.80 Percent, Variance: 44.3					
Hand	1 Coin	2 Coins	3 Coins	4 Coins	5 Coins
Straight	4	8	12	16	20
Three of a Kind	3	6	9	12	15
Two Pair	1	2	3	4	5
Jacks or Better	1	2	3	4	5

Hand	Pay 5 Coins	Occurs Every	% Return
Royal Flush	4,000	38,821.4	2.06
Straight Flush	500	8,448.9	1.18
Four Aces	1,200	4,249.8	5.65
Four 2s, 3s, or 4s	600	1,895.3	6.33
Four 5s through Ks	250	613.8	8.15
Full House	45	92.1	9.77
Flush	25	90.5	5.53
Straight	20	78.5	5.09
Three of a Kind	15	13.3	22.58
Two Pair	5	8.1	12.31
Jacks or Better	5	4.7	21.16
No Win	0	1.8	0

Short-Pay Triple Bonus Plus Poker

The short-pay version of Triple Bonus Plus Poker reduces the pay for a full house to 8-for-1 from 9-for-1. This reduces the return to 98.7 percent. The variance remains unchanged at 44.3.

Triple Bonus Plus Poker 8/5 Short-Pay—Payback: 98.73 Percent, Variance: 44.3					
Hand	1 Coin	2 Coins	3 Coins	4 Coins	5 Coins
Royal Flush	250	500	750	1,000	4,000
Straight Flush	100	200	300	400	500
Four Aces	240	480	720	960	1,200
Four 2s, 3s, or 4s	120	240	360	480	600
Four 5s through Ks	50	100	150	200	250
Full House	8	16	24	32	40
Flush	5	10	15	20	25
Straight	4	8	12	16	20

Triple Bonus Plus Poker 8/5 Short-Pay—Payback: 98.73 Percent, Variance: 44.3					
Hand	*1 Coin*	*2 Coins*	*3 Coins*	*4 Coins*	*5 Coins*
Three of a Kind	3	6	9	12	15
Two Pair	1	2	3	4	5
Jacks or Better	1	2	3	4	5

Hand	*Pay 5 Coins*	*Occurs Every*	*% Return*
Royal Flush	4,000	38,760.2	2.06
Straight Flush	500	8,444.9	1.18
Four Aces	1,200	4,250.5	5.65
Four 2s, 3s, or 4s	600	1,845.8	6.50
Four 5s through Ks	250	613.8	8.15
Full House	40	94.9	8.44
Flush	25	90.5	5.53
Straight	20	78.5	5.10
Three of a Kind	15	13.2	22.66
Two Pair	5	8.1	12.31
Jacks or Better	5	4.7	21.16
No Win	0	1.8	0

The strategy for 9/5 and 8/5 Triple Bonus Poker is very similar, making it possible to combine the two strategies into one list. A combined version is included below. Each strategy line applies to both 9/5 and 8/5 unless specified otherwise.

Strategy for 9/5 (Full-Pay) and 8/5 (Short-Pay) Triple Bonus Plus Poker
Four of a Kind or Better
Four-Card Royal Flush
** 9/5 Only ** Three of a Kind Aces
** 8/5 Only ** Three of a Kind Aces, 2s-4s
Full House
** 9/5 Only ** Any Three of a Kind 2s through Ks
Any Four-Card **Open** Straight Flush
** 8/5 Only ** Any Three of a Kind 5s through Ks
Straight or Better
Any Four-Card **Inside** Straight Flush

Strategy for 9/5 (Full-Pay) and 8/5 (Short-Pay) Triple Bonus Plus Poker
Pair of Aces
Two Pair
Suited KQJ, QJT
High Pair JJ-KK
Any Three-Card Royal Flush
Four-Card Flush
Low Pair—22-44
KQJT, QJT9 (Straights)
Suited JT9, QJ9
JT98
Low Pair 55-TT
Four-Card **Open** Straight, 0 High Cards—2345-789T
Three-Card **Open** Straight Flush, 0 High Cards—345-89T
Three-Card **Inside** Straight Flush, One High Card, One Gap QT9-J98
Three-Card **Inside** Straight Flush, Two High, Two Gaps KhT-QJ8
AKQJ (Straight)
Suited QJ
Three-Card **Inside** Straight Flush, 0 High, One Gap—234, 235-79T
Suited KQ, KJ
AKJT, AQJT, KQJ9 (Straights)
Suited AK, AQ, AJ
Any Three-Card **Inside** Straight Flush except 0 High, Two Gaps
KQJ
KQT9, KJT9, QJ98 (Straights)
QJ, A
Suited JT
KQ, KJ
Suited KT, QT
K, Q, J
Any Three-Card Straight Flush
Any Four-Card Straight
Draw Five New Cards

The added pay for a straight flush and the high pays for four-of-a-kind hands are offset somewhat by the relatively complex strategy. On the plus side, the strategies for the full-pay and short-pay versions are very similar, making it relatively simple to play both games. As with all the triple-bonus variations, Triple Bonus Plus Poker can be fun to play, but make sure you have a large enough bankroll to ride through the losing sessions.

CHAPTER 58

Triple Double Bonus Poker (Full-Pay, Short-Pay)

Triple Double Bonus Poker takes Triple Bonus Poker and Triple Bonus Plus Poker to another level. By introducing kickers into the mix it is possible to get a royal-sized or a half-royal-sized payoff for specific quads with a kicker. To pay for the added bonus hands, the three of a kind pays only 2-for-1.

Kickers make for a more complex strategy. Combine this with the already complex strategy for Triple Bonus Poker variants, and perfect play becomes difficult.

Full-Pay Triple Double Bonus Poker

The full-pay (9/7) version pays 99.58 percent, just slightly better than full-pay Jacks or Better. Variance, however, soars to nearly 100 (98.3), where Jacks or Better is 19.5. This is the highest-variance game yet, with the exception of Royal Aces Bonus Poker with its 180+ variance.

The pay table for the full-pay version of Triple Double Bonus Poker looks like this:

Triple Double Bonus Poker 9/7 Full-Pay—Payback: 99.58 Percent, Variance: 98.3					
Hand	1 Coin	2 Coins	3 Coins	4 Coins	5 Coins
Royal Flush	250	500	750	1,000	4,000
Straight Flush	50	100	150	200	250
Four Aces w/ 2, 3, or 4	800	1,600	2,400	3,200	4,000
Four 2s, 3s, 4s w/ A,2,3,4	400	800	1,200	1,600	2,000
Four Aces	160	320	480	640	800
Four 2s, 3s, or 4s	80	160	240	320	400
Four 5s through Ks	50	100	150	200	250
Full House	9	18	27	36	45

Triple Double Bonus Poker 9/7 Full-Pay—Payback: 99.58 Percent, Variance: 98.3					
Hand	*1 Coin*	*2 Coins*	*3 Coins*	*4 Coins*	*5 Coins*
Flush	7	14	21	28	35
Straight	4	8	12	16	20
Three of a Kind	2	4	6	8	10
Two Pair	1	2	3	4	5
Jacks or Better	1	2	3	4	5

Hand	*Pay 5 Coins*	*Occurs Every*	*% Return*
Royal Flush	4,000	43,358.1	1.76
Straight Flush	250	8,486.8	0.59
Four Aces w/ 2, 3, or 4	4,000	14,214.0	5.63
Four 2s, 3s, 4s w/ A,2,3,4	2,000	5,794.5	6.90
Four Aces	800	6,751.4	2.37
Four 2s, 3s, or 4s	400	3,126.0	2.56
Four 5s through Ks	250	629.3	7.94
Full House	45	96.6	9.32
Flush	35	64.0	10.93
Straight	20	79.0	5.06
Three of a Kind	10	13.6	14.73
Two Pair	5	8.3	11.99
Jacks or Better	5	5.1	19.79
No Win	0	1.8	0

As mentioned earlier, the strategy for this game is quite complex. Here it is.

Strategy for 9/7 Full-Pay Triple Double Bonus Poker
Royal Flush
Four of a Kind with a Kicker
Four of a Kind
Straight Flush
Three Aces with a 2, 3, or 4
Four-Card Royal Flush
Three Aces No Kicker
Three 2s through 4s with A, 2, 3, or 4

Strategy for 9/7 Full-Pay Triple Double Bonus Poker
Three 2s through 4s No Kicker
Any Three of a Kind or Better
Any Four-Card Straight Flush, Including **Inside**
Pair of Aces
Two Pair
Four-Card Flush
Any Three-Card Royal Flush Except A-High-T
High Pair JJ-KK
Three-Card Royal Flush A-High-T
Low Pair 22-44
Any Four-Card **Open** Straight
Suited QJ9, JT9, KQ9, KJ9, QJ8, QT9, J98
Three-Card **Open** Straight Flush, 0 High Cards—345-89T
Low Pair—55-TT
AKQJ (Straight)
Three-Card Flush, Two High Cards
Suited AJ, KQ, KJ, QJ
Three-Card Straight Flush, One High, Two Gaps—KT9-J87, A23-A45
Suited AK, AQ
Any Three-Card Straight Flush, Except 0 High Cards, Two Gaps
AKQT, AKJT, AQJT, KQJ9, KQT9, QJ98 (Straights)
KQJ
A
Three-Card Flush, One High Card
Suited JT
QJT, QJ
Three-Card Straight Flush, 0 High Cards, Two Gaps
Suited QT
KQ, KJ
Suited KT
K, Q, J
Any Three-Card Flush
Any Four-Card Straight
Draw Five New Cards

Short-Pay Triple Double Bonus

The short-pay version of Triple Double Bonus reduces the pay for a flush to 6-for-1 from 7-for-1. This drops the return to 98.15 percent. The variance rises slightly to 100.1.

Triple Double Bonus Poker 9/7 Full-Pay—Payback: 99.58 Percent, Variance: 98.3					
Hand	1 Coin	2 Coins	3 Coins	4 Coins	5 Coins
Royal Flush	250	500	750	1,000	4,000
Straight Flush	50	100	150	200	250
Four Aces w/ 2, 3, or 4	800	1,600	2,400	3,200	4,000
Four 2s, 3s, 4s w/ A,2,3,4	400	800	1,200	1,600	2,000
Four Aces	160	320	480	640	800
Four 2s, 3s, or 4s	80	160	240	320	400
Four 5s through Ks	50	100	150	200	250
Full House	9	18	27	36	45
Flush	6	12	18	24	30
Straight	4	8	12	16	20
Three of a Kind	2	4	6	8	10
Two Pair	1	2	3	4	5
Jacks or Better	1	2	3	4	5

Hand	Pay 5 Coins	Occurs Every	% Return
Royal Flush	4,000	39,709.8	2.01
Straight Flush	250	9,003.9	0.56
Four Aces w/ 2, 3, or 4	4,000	14,205.6	5.63
Four 2s, 3s, 4s w/ A,2,3,4	2,000	5,795.7	6.90
Four Aces	800	6,723.4	2.38
Four 2s, 3s, or 4s	400	3,125.6	2.56
Four 5s through Ks	250	621.5	8.05
Full House	45	95.7	9.41
Flush	30	78.7	7.63
Straight	20	73.9	5.41
Three of a Kind	10	13.4	14.92
Two Pair	5	8.2	12.14
Jacks or Better	5	4.9	20.56
No Win	0	1.8	0

The slight change in the pay table causes several slight tweaks to the strategy, which is shown here.

Strategy for 9/6 Short-Pay Triple Double Bonus Poker
Royal Flush
Four of a Kind with a Kicker
Four of a Kind
Straight Flush
Three Aces with a 2, 3, or 4
Four-Card Royal Flush
Three Aces No Kicker
Three 2s through 4s with A, 2, 3, or 4
Three 2s through 4s No Kicker
Flush or Better
Any Three of a Kind or Better
Straight
Any Four-Card Straight Flush, Including **Inside**
Pair of Aces
Two Pair
Any Three-Card Royal Flush Except A-High-T
High Pair, JJ-KK
Four-Card Flush
Three-Card Royal Flush A-High-T
Low Pair 22-44
Any Four-Card **Open** Straight
Suited QJ9, JT9
Low Pair—55-TT
Suited QJ8
AKQJ (Straight)
Suited KQ9, KJ9, QT9, J98
Three-Card **Open** Straight Flush, 0 High Cards—345-89T
Suited QJ
Four-Card **Inside** Straight, Three High Cards
Suited AK, AQ, AJ, KQ, KJ
Any Three-Card Straight Flush, Except 0 High Cards, Two Gaps
KQJ

Strategy for 9/6 Short-Pay Triple Double Bonus Poker
Four-Card **Inside** Straight, Two High Cards
A
QJT, QJ
Suited JT
KQ, KJ
Suited QT
Three-Card Flush, One High Card
Suited KT
J, Q, K
Any Three-Card Straight Flush
Any Four-Card Straight
Three-Card Flush
Draw Five New Cards

While it is certainly very nice to be able to get a royal flush– or half-royal flush–sized pay every 10,000 hands or so, the complexity of the strategy and the very high variance combine to make Triple Double Bonus Poker a tough choice to play.

But if big pays are what you are looking for and the complexity and variance don't really matter to you, this may be just the game for you.

CHAPTER 59

All American Poker/USA Poker (Full-Pay, Short-Pay)

Alll American Poker, also known as USA Poker, is like Jacks or Better. It has just one payoff for four of a kinds, but it is higher than the Jacks or Better pay of 25-for-1. The amount of the quad payoff varies but is always more than 25-for-1. The straight flush also pays more than virtually any other video-poker game, paying 200-for-1 instead of the standard 50-for-1. In a unique arrangement, a full house, flush, and straight all pay the same at 8-for-1. Because of the high pays on the top end of the pay table, two pairs pay only even money.

The only payoff that changes between full-pay and short-pay games is the reward for a four of a kind.

Full-Pay All American Poker/USA Poker

Advantage Alert: *Full-pay* All American Poker/USA Poker returns 100.72 percent.

The pay table for full-pay All American Poker / USA Poker looks like this:

All American/USA Poker 40/8 Full-Pay—Payback: 100.72 Percent, Variance: 26.8					
Hand	*1 Coin*	*2 Coins*	*3 Coins*	*4 Coins*	*5 Coins*
Royal Flush	250	500	750	1,000	4,000
Straight Flush	200	400	600	800	1,000
Four of a Kind	40	80	120	160	200
Full House	8	16	24	32	40
Flush	8	16	24	32	40
Straight	8	16	24	32	40
Three of a Kind	3	6	9	12	15

All American/USA Poker 40/8 Full-Pay—Payback: 100.72 Percent, Variance: 26.8					
Hand	*1 Coin*	*2 Coins*	*3 Coins*	*4 Coins*	*5 Coins*
Two Pair	1	2	3	4	5
Jacks or Better	1	2	3	4	5

Hand	*Pay 5 Coins*	*Occurs Every*	*% Return*
Royal Flush	4,000	43,401.9	1.84
Straight Flush	1,000	7,050.3	2.84
Four of a Kind	200	444.1	9.01
Full House	40	91.1	8.79
Flush	40	63.7	12.57
Straight	40	54.3	14.74
Three of a Kind	15	14.5	20.65
Two Pair	5	8.4	11.96
Jacks or Better	5	5.5	18.33
No Win	0	1.7	0

The shorthand way of labeling the pays for All American/USA Poker is not the normal full house/flush method, since they are always the same at 8-for-1. Instead the pays for four of a kind and full house/flush/straight is used. The full-pay version pays 40-for-1 for a four of a kind, so it is called a 40/8 game. The full-pay version of All American Poker/USA Poker looks like this:

Strategy for 40/8 Full-Pay All American / USA Poker
Four of a Kind or Better
Four-Card Royal Flush
Any Four-Card **Open** Straight Flush
Straight or Better
Any Four-Card Straight Flush, Including **Inside**
Three of a Kind
Suited KQJ, QJT
Four-Card Flush
Suited KQT, KJT
Two Pair
Suited AKQ, AKJ, AQJ
KQJT, QJT9 (Straights)
High Pair, JJ-AA

Strategy for 40/8 Full-Pay All American / USA Poker
Suited AKT, AQT, AJT
Any Four-Card **Open** Straight
Three-Card **Open** Straight Flush
Three-Card **Inside** Straight Flush, One Gap
AKQJ (Straight)
Four-Card **Inside** Straight, Three High Cards
Suited KQ9, KJ9, QJ8
KQT9, KJT9, QJ98 (Straights)
Three-Card Straight Flush, One High Card, Two Gaps
Four-Card **Inside** Straight, One High Card
Low Pair 22-TT
Any Four-Card **Inside** Straight
Any Three-Card Straight Flush
Suited QJ
QJT-KQJ (Straights)
Three-Card Flush, Two High Cards
Any Two-Card Royal Flush Except AT or KT
JT9, KQT, KJT, QJ9 (Straights)
QJ (Straight)
Three-Card Flush, One High Card
AKQ, AKJ (Straights)
Suited J9, KT
AK, AQ, AJ, KQ, KJ (Straights)
Suited AT
A, K, Q, J
Three-Card **Open** Straight, 0 High Cards—345-89T
Three-Card Flush, 0 High Cards
Two-Card **Open** Straight Flush, 0 High Cards—45-9T
Two-Card **Inside** Straight Flush, 0 High, One Gap—34, 35-8T
Draw Five New Cards

It is interesting that this strategy is so complex. The high pay for a straight flush and the equal pay for a full house, flush, and straight make the strategy a nightmare. Still, the positive return, very high pay for a straight flush, higher than normal (for a non-bonus game) pays for quads, and relatively low variance make this game a favorite among video-poker aficionados.

Short-Pay All American Poker/USA Poker

There are a couple of viable short-pay All American Poker/USA Poker games available. They are 35/8 and 30/8. The 35/8 version returns 99.60 percent, slightly better than full-pay Jacks or Better. Variance remains relatively low at 26.5. Here is the 35/8 pay table:

All American/USA Poker 35/8 Short-Pay—Payback: 99.60 Percent, Variance: 26.5					
Hand	*1 Coin*	*2 Coins*	*3 Coins*	*4 Coins*	*5 Coins*
Royal Flush	250	500	750	1,000	4,000
Straight Flush	200	400	600	800	1,000
Four of a Kind	35	70	105	140	175
Full House	8	16	24	32	40
Flush	8	16	24	32	40
Straight	8	16	24	32	40
Three of a Kind	3	6	9	12	15
Two Pair	1	2	3	4	5
Jacks or Better	1	2	3	4	5

Hand	*Pay 5 Coins*	*Occurs Every*	*% Return*
Royal Flush	4,000	42,323.6	1.89
Straight Flush	1,000	6,928.0	2.89
Four of a Kind	175	446.1	7.85
Full House	40	91.4	8.76
Flush	40	63.1	12.69
Straight	40	54.1	14.80
Three of a Kind	15	14.6	20.53
Two Pair	5	8.4	11.91
Jacks or Better	5	5.5	18.29
No Win	0	1.7	0

The strategy for this short-pay version has several tweaks from the full pay version.

Strategy for 35/8 Short-Pay All American/USA Poker
Four of a Kind or Better
Four-Card Royal Flush
Any Four-Card **Open** Straight Flush
Straight or Better
Any Four-Card Straight Flush, Including **Inside**
Three of a Kind
Suited KQJ, QJT
Four-Card Flush
Suited KQT, KJT
Two Pair
KQJT, QJT9 (Straights)
Suited AKQ, AKJ, AQJ, AKT, AQT, AJT
JT98 (Straight)
High Pair AA-JJ
Any Four-Card **Open** Straight
Three-Card **Open** Straight Flush
Three-Card **Inside** Straight Flush, One Gap
AKQJ (Straight)
Four-Card **Inside** Straight, Three High Cards
Suited KQ9, KJ9, QJ8
KQT9, KJT9, QJ98 (Straights)
Three-Card Straight Flush, One High Card, Two Gaps
Four-Card **Inside** Straight, One High Card
Low Pair 22-TT
Any Four-Card **Inside** Straight
Any Three-Card Straight Flush
Suited QJ
QJT (Straight)
KQJ (Straight)
Three-Card Flush, Two High Cards
Any Two-Card Royal Flush Except AT, KT, or QT
JT9, KQT, KJT, QJ9 (Straights)

Strategy for 35/8 Short-Pay All American/USA Poker
QJ (Straight)
Three-Card Flush, One High Card
Suited QT
AKQ, AKJ (Straights)
Suited J9, KT
AK, AQ, AJ, KQ, KJ (Straights)
Suited AT
A, K, Q, J
Three-Card **Open** Straight, 0 High Cards—345-89T
Three-Card Flush, 0 High Cards
Two-Card **Open** Straight Flush, 0 High Cards—45-9T
Two-Card **Inside** Straight Flush, 0 High, One Gap—34, 35-8T
Draw Five New Cards

The final short-pay All American USA/Poker game worth playing is the 30/8 version, paying 30-for-1 for a four of a kind and 8-for-1 for a full house, flush, or straight. The return for this game is 98.49 percent with a 25.9 variance. Here is the pay table:

All American/USA Poker 30/8 Short-Pay—Payback: 98.49 Percent, Variance: 25.9					
Hand	*1 Coin*	*2 Coins*	*3 Coins*	*4 Coins*	*5 Coins*
Royal Flush	250	500	750	1,000	4,000
Straight Flush	200	400	600	800	1,000
Four of a Kind	30	60	90	120	150
Full House	8	16	24	32	40
Flush	8	16	24	32	40
Straight	8	16	24	32	40
Three of a Kind	3	6	9	12	15
Two Pair	1	2	3	4	5
Jacks or Better	1	2	3	4	5

Hand	Pay 5 Coins	Occurs Every	% Return
Royal Flush	4,000	42,288.9	1.89
Straight Flush	1,000	6,819.9	2.93
Four of a Kind	150	451.6	6.64
Full House	40	92.2	8.68
Flush	40	62.7	12.77
Straight	40	52.2	15.31
Three of a Kind	15	14.9	20.20
Two Pair	5	8.5	11.76
Jacks or Better	5	5.5	18.30
No Win	0	1.7	0

The strategy for this short-pay version has several tweaks from both the full-pay and the 35/8 short-pay versions.

Strategy for 30/8 Short-Pay All American/USA Poker
Four of a Kind or Better
Four-Card Royal Flush
Any Four-Card **Open** Straight Flush
Straight or Better
Any Four-Card Straight Flush, Including **Inside**
Three of a Kind
Suited KQJ, QJT
Four-Card Flush
Suited KQT, KJT
Two Pair
Suited AKQ, AKJ, AQJ
KQJT, QJT9 (Straights)
Suited AKT, AQT, AJT
JT98 (Straight)
High Pair AA-JJ
Any Four-Card **Open** Straight
Three-Card **Open** Straight Flush
Three-Card **Inside** Straight Flush, One Gap
AKQJ (Straight)
Four-Card **Inside** Straight, Three High Cards

Strategy for 30/8 Short-Pay All American/USA Poker
Suited KQ9, KJ9, QJ8
KQT9, KJT9, QJ98 (Straights)
Three-Card Straight Flush, One High Card, Two Gaps
Four-Card **Inside** Straight
Any Three-Card Straight Flush
Low Pair 22-TT
Suited QJ
QJT (Straight)
KQJ (Straight)
Three-Card Flush, Two High Cards
Any Two-Card Royal Flush Except AT, or KT
JT9, KQT, KJT, QJ9 (Straights)
QJ (Straight)
Three-Card Flush, One High Card
AKQ, AKJ (Straights)
Suited J9, KT
AK, AQ, AJ, KQ, KJ (Straights)
Suited AT
A, K, Q, J
Three-Card **Open** Straight, 0 High Cards—345-89T
Three-Card Flush, 0 High Cards
Two-Card **Open** Straight Flush, 0 High Cards—45-9T
Two-Card **Inside** Straight Flush, 0 High, One Gap—34, 35-8T
Draw Five New Cards

Any of the All American Poker/USA Poker games offer very high straight-flush pays, high four-of-a-kind pays, and high straight pays. The variance is in the decent range, although the strategy is fairly complex.

If you like the idea of a large straight-flush pay, this could be the game for you. If you are fortunate enough to locate a full-pay game, can master the strategy, and have a large enough bankroll, this game will make you money in the long run. It has a better return than full-pay Double Bonus Poker and a slightly better variance. If full-pay All American Poker/USA Poker and full-pay Double Bonus Poker are both available, this one might be the best choice for you.

CHAPTER 60

White Hot Aces Poker (Full-Pay, Short-Pay)

White Hot Aces is a Bonus Poker–style game that pays a bonus for four of a kinds. It is similar to Triple Bonus Plus Poker. Four aces pay 240-for-1. Four 2s, 3s, or 4s pay 120-for-1, and four 5s through kings pay 50-for-1. It also pays more than normal for a straight flush (80-for-1 instead of 50-for-1). The variance is moderate at about 43. The strategies are also moderately complex.

Full-Pay White Hot Aces Poker

The pay table for full-pay (9/5) White Hot Aces follows:

White Hot Aces 9/5 Full-Pay—Payback: 99.57 Percent, Variance: 43.7					
Hand	*1 Coin*	*2 Coins*	*3 Coins*	*4 Coins*	*5 Coins*
Royal Flush	250	500	750	1,000	4,000
Straight Flush	80	160	240	320	400
Four Aces	240	480	720	960	1,200
Four 2s, 3s, or 4s	120	240	360	480	600
Four 5s through Ks	50	100	150	200	250
Full House	9	18	27	36	45
Flush	5	10	15	20	25
Straight	4	8	12	16	20
Three of a Kind	3	6	9	12	15
Two Pair	1	2	3	4	5
Jacks or Better	1	2	3	4	5

Hand	Pay 5 Coins	Occurs Every	% Return
Royal Flush	4,000	39,030.3	2.05
Straight Flush	400	8,831.5	0.91
Four Aces	1,200	4,249.2	5.65
Four 2s, 3s, or 4s	600	1,895.3	6.33
Four 5s through Ks	250	613.4	8.15
Full House	45	92.1	9.78
Flush	25	90.1	5.55
Straight	20	78.6	5.09
Three of a Kind	15	13.3	22.59
Two Pair	5	8.1	12.31
Jacks or Better	5	4.7	21.17
No Win	0	1.8	0

Short-Pay White Hot Aces Poker

In the short-pay version of White Hot Aces the full-house pay is reduced to 8-for-1 from 9-for-1. This reduces the return to 98.50 percent. The variance is virtually identical at 43.84. Here is the pay table for short-pay (8/5) White Hot Aces Poker:

White Hot Aces 8/5 Short-Pay—Payback: 98.50 Percent, Variance: 43.8					
Hand	1 Coin	2 Coins	3 Coins	4 Coins	5 Coins
Royal Flush	250	500	750	1,000	4,000
Straight Flush	80	160	240	320	400
Four Aces	240	480	720	960	1,200
Four 2s, 3s, or 4s	120	240	360	480	600
Four 5s through Ks	50	100	150	200	250
Full House	8	16	24	32	40
Flush	5	10	15	20	25
Straight	4	8	12	16	20
Three of a Kind	3	6	9	12	15
Two Pair	1	2	3	4	5
Jacks or Better	1	2	3	4	5

Hand	Pay 5 Coins	Occurs Every	% Return
Royal Flush	4,000	38,834.6	2.06
Straight Flush	400	8,790.4	0.91
Four Aces	1,200	4,249.8	5.65
Four 2s, 3s, or 4s	600	1,845.8	6.50
Four 5s through Ks	250	613.7	8.15
Full House	40	94.8	8.44
Flush	25	90.0	5.55
Straight	20	78.5	5.09
Three of a Kind	15	13.2	22.67
Two Pair	5	8.1	12.31
Jacks or Better	5	4.7	21.17
No Win	0	1.8	0

As mentioned above, the strategy is relatively complex. However, the differences between the full-pay and short-pay strategies are minor, so both strategies are combined in the following strategy chart. Unless otherwise stated, each strategy line applies to both the full-pay and the short-pay games.

Strategy for 9/5 (Full-Pay) and 8/5 (Short-Pay) White Hot Aces
Four of a Kind or Better
Four-Card Royal Flush
** 9/5 Only ** Three of a Kind Aces
** 8/5 Only ** Three of a Kind Aces, 2s-4s
Full House
** 9/5 Only ** Any Three of a Kind 2s through Ks
** 8/5 Only ** Any Three of a Kind 5s through Ks
Flush
Any Four-Card **Open** Straight Flush
Straight
Any Four-Card **Inside** Straight Flush
Pair of Aces
Two Pair
Suited QJT
** 8/5 Only ** Suited KQJ
High Pair JJ-KK

Strategy for 9/5 (Full-Pay) and 8/5 (Short-Pay) White Hot Aces
Any Three-Card Royal Flush
Four-Card Flush
Low Pair—22-44
** 9/5 Only ** Low Pair—77
KQJT, QJT9 (Straights)
** 9/5 Only ** JT98 (Straight)
Suited JT9
** 9/5 Only ** Low Pair 55-66, 88-TT
** 8/5 Only ** Low Pair 88-99
Suited QJ9
** 8/5 Only ** Low Pair 55-77, TT
Four-Card **Open** Straight, 0 High Cards—2345-789T
Three-Card **Open** Straight Flush, 0 High Cards—345-89T
Three-Card **Inside** Straight Flush, One High Card, One Gap QT9-J98
Suited QJ8
AKQJ (Straight)
Suited KQ9, KJ9
Suited KQ, KJ, QJ
AKJT, AQJT, KQJ9 (Straights)
Suited AK, AQ, AJ
Any Three-Card **Inside** Straight Flush Except 0 High, Two Gaps
KQJ
KQT9, KJT9, QJ98 (Straights)
QJ, A
Suited JT
KQ, KJ
Suited KT, QT
K, Q, J
Any Three-Card Straight Flush
Any Four-Card Straight
Draw Five New Cards

Anyone who would like to play Triple Bonus Plus Poker will also like White Hot Aces. The two games are nearly identical, with similar paybacks, variances, and strategies. Consider playing White Hot Aces Poker in locations that don't have Triple Double Bonus Plus Poker.

CHAPTER 61

Aces and Faces Poker
(Full-Pay, Short-Pay)

Aces and Faces Poker pays a bonus for four aces or four faces just as the name implies. Four aces pays 80-for-1. Four faces consisting of jacks, queens, and kings pays 40-for-1. Four 2s through 10s pays the standard 25-for-1. Since the jackpots are not extremely high, the variance is low at about 21 and the strategy is relatively straightforward.

Full-Pay Aces and Faces Poker

Here is the pay table for full-pay (8/5) Aces and Faces Poker:

Aces and Faces Poker (8/5) Full-Pay—Payback: 99.26 Percent, Variance: 21.0					
Hand	1 Coin	2 Coins	3 Coins	4 Coins	5 Coins
Royal Flush	250	500	750	1,000	4,000
Straight Flush	50	100	150	200	250
Four Aces	80	160	240	320	400
Four Js, Qs, Ks	40	80	120	160	200
Four 2s through Ts	25	50	75	100	125
Full House	8	16	24	32	40
Flush	5	10	15	20	25
Straight	4	8	12	16	20
Three of a Kind	3	6	9	12	15
Two Pair	2	4	6	8	10
Jacks or Better	1	2	3	4	5

Hand	Pay 5 Coins	Occurs Every	% Return
Royal Flush	4,000	40,249.3	1.99
Straight Flush	250	9,433.2	0.53
Four Aces	400	5,106.1	1.57
Four Js, Qs, Ks	200	1,703.7	2.35
Four 2s through Ts	125	623.8	3.95
Full House	40	86.8	9.21
Flush	25	92.1	5.43
Straight	20	89.2	4.48
Three of a Kind	15	13.4	22.34
Two Pair	10	7.7	25.86
Jacks or Better	5	4.6	21.54
No Win	0	1.8	0

Short-Pay Aces and Faces Poker

The short-pay version reduces the pay for the full house to 7-for-1 from 8-for-1. This reduces the return to 98.1 percent with the variance slightly reduced to 20.8. A 98 percent return is the absolute minimum that should be played. The pay table for the short-pay version of Aces and Faces Poker looks like this:

Aces and Faces Poker (7/5) Short-Pay—Payback: 98.10 Percent, Variance: 20.8					
Hand	1 Coin	2 Coins	3 Coins	4 Coins	5 Coins
Royal Flush	250	500	750	1,000	4,000
Straight Flush	50	100	150	200	250
Four Aces	80	160	240	320	400
Four Js, Qs, Ks	40	80	120	160	200
Four 2s through Ts	25	50	75	100	125
Full House	7	14	21	28	35
Flush	5	10	15	20	25
Straight	4	8	12	16	20
Three of a Kind	3	6	9	12	15
Two Pair	2	4	6	8	10
Jacks or Better	1	2	3	4	5

Hand	Pay 5 Coins	Occurs Every	% Return
Royal Flush	4,000	40,259.9	1.99
Straight Flush	250	9,379.8	0.53
Four Aces	400	5,106.3	1.57
Four Js, Qs, Ks	200	1,703.8	2.35
Four 2s through Ts	125	633.1	3.95
Full House	35	86.8	8.06
Flush	25	92.0	5.44
Straight	20	88.8	4.51
Three of a Kind	15	13.4	22.33
Two Pair	10	7.7	25.85
Jacks or Better	5	4.6	21.53
No Win	0	1.8	0

The strategy for both versions of Aces and Faces Poker is fairly straight-forward. There also are not a lot of differences between strategies for the full-pay and the short-pay versions, so both strategies are combined in the chart below. Unless otherwise stated, each strategy line applies to both versions of the game.

Strategy for 8/5 (Full-Pay) and 7/5 (Short-Pay) Aces and Faces Poker
Four of a Kind or Better
Four Cards of a Royal Flush
Three of a Kind or Better
** 8/5 Only ** Two Pair
Any Four-Card Straight Flush, Including Inside
** 7/5 Only ** Two Pair
High Pair (JJ-AA)
Three Cards of a Royal Flush
Four Cards of a Flush
KQJT (Straight)
** 7/5 Only ** QJT9 (Straight)
Low Pair (22-TT)
** 8/5 Only ** QJT9 (Straight)
JT98 (Straight)
Four Cards of an **Open** Straight (0 High Cards)—2345-789T
Suited QJ9, JT9, QJ8

Strategy for 8/5 (Full-Pay) and 7/5 (Short-Pay) Aces and Faces Poker
AKQJ (Straight)
Suited KQ9, KJ9
** 7/5 Only ** Suited QT9, J98
Suited KQ, KJ, QJ
** 8/5 Only ** Suited QT9, J98
Three-Card **Open** Straight Flush—Suited 345-89T
Suited AK, AQ, AJ
Four-Card **Inside** Straight—Three High Cards
KQJ, QJ
Three-Card **Inside** Straight Flush Two Gaps One High Card
KJ
Suited JT
Three-Card **Inside** Straight Flush Except 0 High Cards, Two Gaps
AK, AQ, AJ, KQ
Suited QT
J, Q, K, A
Any Three-Card Straight Flush
Draw Five New Cards

Aces and Faces Poker is a decent game to play if you can find the full-pay (8/5) version. It has a decent payback, reasonable variance, and a straight-forward strategy. It also has some higher paybacks for quads to spice up play. If you cannot find the full-pay version, the author would recommend looking for a totally different game.

CHAPTER 62

Double Aces and Faces Poker (Full-Pay, Short-Pay)

Double Aces and Faces Poker is just what its name says. Four-of-a-kind hands pay double what they pay in Aces and Faces Poker—four aces pays 160-for-1 rather than 80-for-1, four faces (jacks, queens, or kings) pays 80-for-1 instead of 40-for-1, and four 2s through 10s pays 50-for-1, not the standard 25-for-1.

Full-Pay Double Aces and Faces Poker

In the full-pay version a full house pays 9-for-1 and a flush pays 7-for-1. To fund the increased pays, two pair pays only even money rather than 2-for-1. It never fails to surprise me how much this minor change affects the return of a video-poker game. The full-pay (9/7) version of the game returns 99.24 percent, which is decent. Variance is also decent at 28.5.

The pay table for full-pay Double Aces and Faces follows:

Double Aces and Faces Poker (9/7) Full-Pay—Payback: 99.24 Percent, Variance: 28.5					
Hand	*1 Coin*	*2 Coins*	*3 Coins*	*4 Coins*	*5 Coins*
Royal Flush	250	500	750	1,000	4,000
Straight Flush	50	100	150	200	250
Four Aces	160	320	480	640	800
Four Js, Qs, Ks	80	160	240	320	400
Four 2s through Ts	50	100	150	200	250
Full House	9	18	27	36	45
Flush	7	14	21	28	35
Straight	5	10	15	20	25
Three of a Kind	3	6	9	12	15
Two Pair	1	2	3	4	5
Jacks or Better	1	2	3	4	5

Hand	Pay 5 Coins	Occurs Every	% Return
Royal Flush	4,000	48,642.2	1.64
Straight Flush	250	8,889.4	0.56
Four Aces	800	4,577.1	3.50
Four Js, Qs, Ks	400	1,758.5	4.55
Four 2s through Ts	250	638.9	7.83
Full House	45	93.9	9.59
Flush	35	67.3	10.41
Straight	25	66.7	7.50
Three of a Kind	15	13.7	21.93
Two Pair	5	8.4	11.93
Jacks or Better	5	5.1	19.81
No Win	0	1.8	0

Strategy for this game is more complex than the standard Aces and Faces Poker due to the various higher-paying hands.

Strategy for 9/7 (Full-Pay) Double Aces and Faces Poker
Straight Flush or Better
Four Cards of a Royal Flush
Three of a Kind or Better
Any Four-Card Straight Flush Including Inside
Pair of Aces
Two Pair
High Pair (JJ-KK)
Four Cards of a Flush—3 High Cards
Suited KQJ, QJT
Any Four Cards of a Flush
Suited AKQ, AKJ, AQJ, AKT, AQT, AJT, KQT, KJT
Any Four-Card **Open** Straight
Suited JT9, QJ9
Low Pair (22-TT)
AKQJ (Straight)
Three Cards of an **Open** Straight Flush (345-89T)
Suited QT9, JT8, KQ9, KJ9, QJ8
Four-Card **Inside** Straight—Three High Cards (AhhT, KQJ9)

Strategy for 9/7 (Full-Pay) Double Aces and Faces Poker
Suited QJ
Three-Card Flush, Two High Cards
Suited KQ, KJ
Three-Card **Inside** Straight Flush Except Two Gaps 0 High Cards
Suited AK, AQ, AJ
KQT9, QJ98, KQJ, QJT (Straights)
Four-Card **Inside** Straight, One High—A234-A345, QT98, J987
Suited JT
Suited QTx (Flush)
Suited QT
QJ
Three-Card Flush, One High Card
Any Three-Card Straight Flush
KQ, KJ, A, J
Suited KT
K, Q
Four-Card **Inside** Straight, 0 High Cards—2346-689T
Any Three-Card Flush
Draw Five New Cards

Short-Pay Double Aces and Faces Poker

The short-pay version of Double Aces and Faces Poker reduces the pay for a flush to 6-for-1 from 7-for-1. This small change drops the return for this game to 97.97 percent. This return is under the acceptable minimum of 98 percent but close enough to sneak in under the wire. The variance is up slightly to 30.4.

Here is the pay table:

Double Aces and Faces Poker (9/6) Short-Pay—Payback: 97.97 Percent, Variance: 30.4					
Hand	1 Coin	2 Coins	3 Coins	4 Coins	5 Coins
Royal Flush	250	500	750	1,000	4,000
Straight Flush	50	100	150	200	250
Four Aces	160	320	480	640	800
Four Js, Qs, Ks	80	160	240	320	400
Four 2s through Ts	50	100	150	200	250

Double Aces and Faces Poker (9/6) Short-Pay—Payback: 97.97 Percent, Variance: 30.4					
Hand	1 Coin	2 Coins	3 Coins	4 Coins	5 Coins
Full House	9	18	27	36	45
Flush	6	12	18	24	30
Straight	5	10	15	20	25
Three of a Kind	3	6	9	12	15
Two Pair	1	2	3	4	5
Jacks or Better	1	2	3	4	5

Hand	Pay 5 Coins	Occurs Every	% Return
Royal Flush	4,000	42,469.0	1.88
Straight Flush	250	9,310.8	0.54
Four Aces	800	4,506.1	3.55
Four Js, Qs, Ks	400	1,721.5	4.65
Four 2s through Ts	250	638.2	7.83
Full House	45	92.9	9.69
Flush	35	90.8	6.61
Straight	25	64.6	7.73
Three of a Kind	15	13.5	22.24
Two Pair	5	8.3	12.12
Jacks or Better	5	4.7	21.13
No Win	0	1.8	0

The strategy is only slightly less complex.

Strategy for 9/6 (Short-Pay) Double Aces and Faces Poker
Four of a Kind or Better
Four Cards of a Royal Flush
Three of a Kind or Better
Any Four-Card Straight Flush, Including **Inside**
Pair of Aces
Two Pair
High Pair (JJ-KK)
Any Three-Card Royal Flush Except AhT
Any Four-Card Flush
Suited AKT, AQT, AJT (Three-Card Royal Flush—AhT)

Strategy for 9/6 (Short-Pay) Double Aces and Faces Poker
Any Four-Card **Open** Straight
Low Pair—77
Suited JT9
Low Pair (88-TT)
Suited QJ9
Low Pair (22-66)
AKQJ (Straight)
Three Cards of an **Open** Straight Flush (345-89T)
Suited QT9, J98
Four-Card **Inside** Straight—Three High Cards (AhhT, KQJ9)
Suited KQ9, KJ9, QJ8
Suited KQ, KJ, QJ
KQT9, QJ98 (Straights)
Suited AK, AQ, AJ
Any Three-Card Straight Flush Except Two Gaps, 0 High Cards
KQJ (Straight)
Suited QJT
Any Four-Card **Inside** Straight, One High—QT98, J987, A234-A345
Suited JT
KQ, KJ, QJ
Suited QT
AK, AQ, AJ
Suited KT
J, Q, K, A
Four-Card **Inside** Straight, 0 High Cards—2346-689T
Any Three-Card Straight Flush
Draw Five New Cards

As stated above, the short-pay version of Double Aces and Faces Poker falls just under the limit of 98 percent return. It does have relatively low variance, however, and a moderately complex strategy. If you can find a better (higher return, lower variance, simpler strategy) game, you would be well advised to play it rather than this game.

CHAPTER 63

Double Double Aces and Faces Poker (Full-Pay, Short-Pay)

Double Double Aces and Faces Poker adds kickers into the mix in order to bump pays into the half-royal-flush category. Four aces with a kicker of a jack, queen, or king pays 400-for-1. Four kings, queens, or jacks pays 160-for-1, the same as four aces without a kicker in both this game and Double Aces and Faces Poker. Four face cards (kings, queens, or jacks) and four 2s through 10s pay the same as in Double Aces and Faces Poker. With the fewer higher pays, the variance increases to 42.

Full-Pay Double Double Aces and Faces Poker

The full-pay (9/6) version pays 9-for-1 for a full house and 6-for-1 for a flush. Here is the complete pay table:

Double Double Aces and Faces Poker (9/6) Full-Pay—Payback: 99.46 Percent, Variance: 42.2					
Hand	*1 Coin*	*2 Coins*	*3 Coins*	*4 Coins*	*5 Coins*
Royal Flush	250	500	750	1,000	4,000
Straight Flush	50	100	150	200	250
Four Aces w/ any J,Q,K	400	800	1,200	1,600	2,000
Four Js,Qs,Ks w/ J,Q,K,A	160	320	480	640	800
Four Aces	160	320	480	640	800
Four Js, Qs, Ks	80	160	240	320	400
Four 2s through Ts	50	100	150	200	250
Full House	9	18	27	36	45
Flush	6	12	18	24	30
Straight	4	8	12	16	20
Three of a Kind	3	6	9	12	15

Double Double Aces and Faces Poker (9/6) Full-Pay—Payback: 99.46 Percent, Variance: 42.2					
Hand	*1 Coin*	*2 Coins*	*3 Coins*	*4 Coins*	*5 Coins*
Two Pair	1	2	3	4	5
Jacks or Better	1	2	3	4	5

Hand	*Pay 5 Coins*	*Occurs Every*	*% Return*
Royal Flush	4,000	42,442.1	1.88
Straight Flush	250	9,224.6	0.54
Four Aces w/ any J,Q,K	2,000	15,564.1	2.57
Four Js,Qs,Ks w/ J,Q,K,A	800	5,785.6	2.77
Four Aces	800	6,325.2	2.53
Four Js, Qs, Ks	400	2,427.1	3.30
Four 2s through Ts	250	634.1	7.89
Full House	45	92.3	9.75
Flush	30	90.1	6.66
Straight	20	78.9	5.07
Three of a Kind	15	13.3	22.51
Two Pair	5	8.1	12.29
Jacks or Better	5	4.6	21.70
No Win	0	1.8	0

The strategy is moderately complex.

Strategy for 9/6 (Full-Pay) Double Double Aces and Faces Poker
Four of a Kind or Better
Four Cards of a Royal Flush
Three Aces
Any Three of a Kind or Better
Any Four-Card Straight Flush, Including **Inside**
Pair of Aces
Two Pair
High Pair (JJ-KK)
Any Three-Card Royal Flush Except AhT
Any Four-Card Flush, Two High Cards
Suited AKT, AQT, AJT (Three-Card Royal Flush—AhT)
Any Four-Card Flush

Strategy for 9/6 (Full-Pay) Double Double Aces and Faces Poker
KQJT, QJT9, JT98 (Straights)
Low Pair (22-TT)
Suited QJ9, JT9
Four-Card **Open** Straight—2345-789T
Suited KQ9, KJ9, QJ8, QT9, J98
Any Three-Card **Open** Straight Flush, 0 High Cards—345-89T
AKQJ (Straight)
Suited AK, AQ, AJ, KQ, KJ, QJ
Four-Card **Inside** Straight—Three High Cards (AhhT, KQJ9)
Any Three-Card Straight Flush Except 0 High Cards, Two Gaps
KQJ, QJ
KQT9, KJT9, QJ98 Straights
AK, AQ, AJ, KQ, KJ
A
Suited QT, JT
J, Q, K
Any Three-Card Straight Flush
Any Four-Card Straight
Draw Five New Cards

With its 99.46 percent return and moderate variance, Double Double Aces and Faces Poker is a reasonable game for those who like more high-paying wins. Just make sure you have the bankroll to last through the losing streaks.

Short-Pay Double Double Aces and Faces Poker

The short-pay version of Double Double Aces and Faces Poker is formed by reducing the pay for a flush to 5-for-1 from 6-for-1. This reduces the return to 98.37. Variance changes slightly to 42.7. Here is the complete pay table information.

Double Double Aces and Faces Poker (9/5) Short-Pay—Payback: 98.37 Percent, Variance: 42.7					
Hand	1 Coin	2 Coins	3 Coins	4 Coins	5 Coins
Royal Flush	250	500	750	1,000	4,000
Straight Flush	50	100	150	200	250
Four Aces w/ any J,Q,K	400	800	1,200	1,600	2,000

Double Double Aces and Faces Poker (9/5) Short-Pay—Payback: 98.37 Percent, Variance: 42.7					
Hand	1 Coin	2 Coins	3 Coins	4 Coins	5 Coins
Four Js, Qs, Ks w/ J,Q,K,A	160	320	480	640	800
Four Aces	160	320	480	640	800
Four Js, Qs, Ks	80	160	240	320	400
Four 2s through Ts	50	100	150	200	250
Full House	9	18	27	36	45
Flush	5	10	15	20	25
Straight	4	8	12	16	20
Three of a Kind	3	6	9	12	15
Two Pair	1	2	3	4	5
Jacks or Better	1	2	3	4	5

Hand	Pay 5 Coins	Occurs Every	% Return
Royal Flush	4,000	40,895.1	1.96
Straight Flush	250	9,642.2	0.52
Four Aces w/ any J,Q,K	2,000	15,518.7	2.58
Four Js ,Qs, Ks w/ J,Q,K,A	800	5,756.3	2.78
Four Aces	800	6,383.6	2.51
Four Js, Qs, Ks	400	2,425.6	3.30
Four 2s through Ts	250	634.1	7.88
Full House	45	92.3	9.76
Flush	25	93.2	5.36
Straight	20	78.9	5.07
Three of a Kind	15	13.3	22.51
Two Pair	5	8.1	12.30
Jacks or Better	5	4.6	21.86
No Win	0	1.8	0

The strategy is similar to full-pay Double Double Aces and Faces Poker but has several little tweaks.

Strategy for 9/5 (Short-Pay) Double Double Aces and Faces Poker
Four of a Kind or Better
Four Cards of a Royal Flush
Three Aces

Strategy for 9/5 (Short-Pay) Double Double Aces and Faces Poker
Any Three of a Kind or Better
Any Four-Card Straight Flush, Including **Inside**
Pair of Aces
Two Pair
High Pair (JJ-KK)
Any Three-Card Royal Flush
Any Four-Card Flush
KQJT, QJT9, JT98 (Straights)
Low Pair (22-TT)
Four-Card **Open** Straight—2345-789T
Suited QJ9, JT9
AKQJ (Straight)
Suited KQ9, KJ9, QJ8, QJ, QT9, J98
Any Three-Card **Open** Straight Flush, 0 High Cards—345-89T
Suited AK, AQ, AJ, KQ, KJ
Four-Card **Inside** Straight—Three High Cards (AhhT, KQJ9)
KQJ, QJ
Any Three-Card Straight Flush, A low—A23-A45
KQT9, QJ98 (Straights)
Three-Card Straight Flush, One High Card, Two Gaps—KT9-J87
AK, AQ, AJ
A
Any Three-Card Straight Flush Except 0 High Cards, Two Gaps
KQ, KJ
Suited QT, JT
J, Q, K
Any Three-Card Straight Flush
Four-Card Straight
Draw Five New Cards

While not giving the return of the full-pay version, 9/5 Double Double Aces and Faces Poker provides a decent game for those who want some larger pays.

CHAPTER 64

Video Poker with Wild Cards

We now introduce a different type of video-poker game—wild-card video poker. In all the games covered so far, each card had only one value (with the exception of aces, which could be either the highest or the lowest card in a straight or straight flush). A wild card, however, can be used as *any card value* and be *any suit*. In Deuces Wild, each deuce (2) is wild. It can be used as any other card in the deck when it is advantageous to do so.

Because of the power of a wild card, the pays for standard hands are much lower than non–wild card versions of the game. In fact, some of the lower-paying hands, such as two pair and high pair, are eliminated from the pay tables.

There is also a new category of hand—the "wild" hand. A wild hand is any hand that contains a wild card. For example, in a deuces-wild game a wild royal flush would have one or more 2s in the hand. Many times the pay table does not differentiate between wild and non-wild hands. In those cases, the pay is the same whether or not the hand contains a wild card.

Because wild cards can substitute for any other card, it is possible to have more than four of a kind. Since there are five cards in a hand, five-of-a-kind hands are possible if they contain one or more wild cards.

Having a wild card dramatically changes the dynamics of the game from a Jacks or Better game. There are just so many more possibilities with wild cards. Also, the strategy dramatically changes. Since the wild card is the most important card, it takes precedent in determining play strategy. Rather than simply listing hands from best to least, the plays are grouped by the number of wild cards dealt. This can simplify the strategy, since the more wild cards, the less other things matter. Only when you are dealt no wild cards does the strategy become a little complex.

Most wild-card video-poker games have at least one other jackpot-type hand—usually four deuces. Because there are two high-paying hands, variance is a bit higher in wild-card games.

In a Jacks or Better class of games the inside straights and inside straight flushes are easy to distinguish. A four-card inside straight with one gap can be anything as low or high as an ace. For example, A234 is a one-gap inside straight, as is JQKA. However, because wild cards can be any number, the number of gaps changes.

Here is an example: With one deuce dealt, the lowest open four-card straight flush is 567. Since the deuce is a wild card, it cannot be the lowest, meaning 3 will be the lowest possible card when determining whether a sequence is open. To complete the above straight flush, you need a 3, 4, 8, or 9. In a wild-card game the chance of completing an open straight or straight flush doubles.

CHAPTER 65

Deuces Wild–Class Video Poker

O f all wild-card video-pokers games, the Deuces Wild category is by far
the largest. Countless variations of pay tables provide a nearly limitless
selection of deuces-wild games for the video-poker player. Helping to add to
the popularity of Deuces Wild games are dozens of different cool-sounding
names such as Loose Deuces, Downtown Deuces, Big Split Poker Deuces Wild,
Colorado Deuces, Airport Deuces, and Illinois Deuces.

Even the term *deuce* is given the colloquial moniker of "duck." Rather
than just call a short-pay schedule "a short-pay schedule" they have been
given catchy nicknames: Not So Ugly Ducks and Ugly Ducks are examples.

When playing a Deuces Wild game, there are four possible wild cards—the
four 2s. One-thirteenth of the deck is wild cards. That makes lots of normally
higher-paying hands than in a Jacks or Better game. Because of that, pays
are dramatically lower than Jacks or Better. In fact the lowest-paying hand
in most Deuces Wild games is three-of-a-kind.

Four-of-a-kind hands are much easier to get in a Deuces Wild game since
one or more deuces can help form the quad. All four-of-a-kind hands are
easier to get except one—four deuces. For that reason, a hand of four deuces
is paid very high. Other quads are paid significantly less than in Jacks or
Better.

There are also two new hands on the pay table. The first is a royal flush
with a deuce or a "wild royal flush," as it is commonly called. This is a royal
flush that is composed of one or more deuces. The second new paying hand is
five of a kind. It is formed by one or more deuces with the remainder of the
hand being cards of the same rank. Examples are: 22266, 22444, and 29999.

The strategy charts for Deuces Wild games are broken into five categories
based on the number of deuces dealt: four deuces dealt, three deuces dealt,
two deuces dealt, one deuce dealt, and no deuces dealt. The hold strategy
gets more complex as fewer deuces are dealt, but the overall strategy tends
to be easier to master because of the categories and the fact that there are
fewer paying hands with no deuces than in Jacks or Better.

Deuces Wild video-poker games are exciting and easy to learn with low variance available in many of the available games. The strategy is relatively simple to learn, and the player has two big hits to play for—the royal and four deuces.

The reader should seriously consider learning and playing at least one Deuces Wild game. Now let's move on to some specific games.

CHAPTER 66

Deuces Wild Poker
(Full-Pay, Short-Pay)

The first wild-card game we will examine is Deuces Wild. This wildly (pardon the pun) popular video-poker game has been around for decades. There are numerous versions and pay schedules scattered throughout almost every casino.

Advantage Alert: *The full-pay version of this game returns more than 100 percent—100.76 percent to be precise.*

This game was quite prevalent years ago, but a combination of better-informed and trained players and casino greed have lowered the inventory. They still can be found, however.

One of the hardest things to get used to when playing Deuces Wild Poker is that high cards are virtually meaningless. There is no such thing as a high pair. The lowest pay is three of a kind. If the player is used to the strategy for a Jacks or Better–style game, it will take a while to get the new strategy down—all pairs are equal, and single high cards are meaningless.

Unlike the Jacks or Better–based games where only one or two pays are changed to reduce the return, several different pays are regularly changed to modify the return on Deuces Wild. There are arguably more different pay tables of Deuces Wild than any other video-poker game. Because of this, the shortcut name for full-pay and various short-pay games requires more than just two numbers. Also, because there are so many different pay tables available, it is even more important to check all the lines on the pay table to make sure you are playing the game you think you are playing.

With dozens of different pay schedules available, it is beyond the scope of this book to cover all of them. Three of the best and most common versions will be covered: Full-Pay, Not So Ugly Deuces, and Ugly Deuces. The returns vary from 100.76 percent down to 98.91 percent. Even this lowest return is still better than a lot of Jacks or Better–based games available in today's casinos.

Full-Pay Deuces Wild Poker

Full-pay Deuces Wild Poker is commonly referred to as 25/15/9/5. These numbers correspond to the pays for wild royal flush (25-for-1), five-of-a-kind (15-for-1), straight flush (9-for-1), and four of a kind (5-for-1).

Here is the complete pay table information for full-pay Deuces Wild Poker:

Deuces Wild Poker (25/15/9/5) Full-Pay—Payback: 100.76 Percent, Variance: 25.8					
Hand	*1 Coin*	*2 Coins*	*3 Coins*	*4 Coins*	*5 Coins*
Royal Flush no 2s	250	500	750	1,000	4,000
Four Deuces	200	400	600	800	1,000
Wild Royal Flush	25	50	75	100	125
Five of a Kind	15	30	45	60	75
Straight Flush	9	18	27	36	45
Four of a Kind	5	10	15	20	25
Full House	3	6	9	12	15
Flush	2	4	6	8	10
Straight	2	4	6	8	10
Three of a Kind	1	2	3	4	5

Hand	*Pay 5 Coins*	*Occurs Every*	*% Return*
Royal Flush no 2s	4,000	45,281.9	1.77
Four Deuces	1,000	4,909.1	4.07
Wild Royal Flush	125	556.8	4.49
Five of a Kind	75	312.3	4.80
Straight Flush	45	242.7	3.71
Four of a Kind	25	15.4	32.47
Full House	15	47.1	6.37
Flush	10	60.5	3.30
Straight	10	17.7	11.32
Three of a Kind	5	3.5	28.45
No Win	0	1.8	0

Deuces Wild Poker has two jackpot-sized pays—the royal flush with no deuces and four deuces. Because there are only two and the lower one is only 200-for-1, the variance is fairly low.

The strategy for Deuces Wild is arranged quite differently from what has been shown so far. The primary factor in determining what to hold is the number of wild cards dealt in the initial hand. The strategy is arranged starting with four wild cards, then three, then two, then one, and then none.

Strategy For 25/15/9/5 (Full-Pay) Deuces Wild Poker
Four Deuces Dealt
All Four Deuces
Three Deuces Dealt
Wild Royal Flush
Five of a Kind
Three Deuces
Two Deuces Dealt
Four of a Kind or Better
Four-Card Wild Royal Flush
Four-Card **Open** Straight Flush—67-9T
Two Deuces
One Deuce Dealt
Four of a Kind or Better
Four-Card Wild Royal Flush
Full House
Four-Card **Open** Straight Flush—567-9TJ
Three of a Kind or Better
Any Four-Card Straight Flush
Three-Card Wild Royal Flush Kh, Qh, JT only
Three-Card **Open** Straight Flush—67-9T
One Deuce
No Deuce Dealt
Royal Flush
Four Cards of a Royal Flush
Three of a Kind or Better
Four-Card **Open** Straight Flush—4567-9TJQ
Suited QJT
Four-Card **Inside** Straight Flush, One Gap—3456, 3457-9JQK, A345

Strategy For 25/15/9/5 (Full-Pay) Deuces Wild Poker
Three-Card Royal Flush, AKQ, AKJ, AQJ, KQJ
One Pair (Discard Either Pair If Dealt Two Pair)
Four-Card Flush
Four-Card **Open** Straight—4567-10JQK
Three-Card **Open** Straight Flush—567-9TJ, 345-456
Three-Card **Inside** Straight Flush, 1 Gap—457-9JQ
Suited JT
Three-Card **Inside** Straight Flush—346-356, 347-69T, 78J-79J, 89Q-9QK
Four-Card **Inside** Straight—89TQ-10QKA, JQKA
Suited QJ, QT
Four-Card **Inside** Straight—3456, 3457-79TJ
Draw Five New Cards

As might be expected, the fewer wild cards you are dealt, the more complex the strategy. With the arrangement of the strategy, it is fairly easy to master perfect play. Combine that with a low variance and a positive player expectation with the 100.76 percent return, and full-pay Deuces Wild Poker is a favorite among serious and novice players alike.

Short-Pay Deuces Wild—Not So Ugly Deuces or Not So Ugly Ducks (NSUD)

The first short-pay version of Deuces Wild Poker that we will look at is commonly referred to as Not So Ugly Deuces or sometimes as Not So Ugly Ducks. Although not a full-pay game, it is close to 100 percent return at 99.73 percent.

The shortcut way to label this game is 25/16/10. The full-pay game is a 25/15/9/5 game. Notice that on the short-pay schedule, the pays for both the five of a kind and straight flush are one *higher* than the full-pay version. This shows how much of a game's return is tied up in lower-paying hands. Here is the complete pay table information for Not So Ugly Deuces:

Deuces Wild Poker (25/16/10) Short-Pay (NSUD)—Payback: 99.73 Percent, Variance: 25.8					
Hand	*1 Coin*	*2 Coins*	*3 Coins*	*4 Coins*	*5 Coins*
Royal Flush no 2s	250	500	750	1,000	4,000
Four Deuces	200	400	600	800	1,000
Wild Royal Flush	25	50	75	100	125

Deuces Wild Poker (25/16/10) Short-Pay (NSUD)—Payback: 99.73 Percent, Variance: 25.8					
Hand	1 Coin	2 Coins	3 Coins	4 Coins	5 Coins
Five of a Kind	16	32	48	64	80
Straight Flush	10	20	30	40	50
Four of a Kind	4	8	12	16	20
Full House	4	8	12	16	20
Flush	3	6	9	12	15
Straight	2	4	6	8	10
Three of a Kind	1	2	3	4	5

Hand	Pay 5 Coins	Occurs Every	% Return
Royal Flush no 2s	4,000	43,436.3	1.84
Four Deuces	1,000	5,355.9	3.73
Wild Royal Flush	125	524.5	4.77
Five of a Kind	80	321.7	4.97
Straight Flush	50	194.7	5.14
Four of a Kind	20	16.4	24.42
Full House	20	38.3	10.45
Flush	15	48.2	6.23
Straight	10	17.4	11.47
Three of a Kind	5	3.7	26.72
No Win	0	1.8	0

In addition to the five-of-a-kind and straight-flush pays increasing by one, so do the pays for a full house and a flush. In fact, the only pay lowered from the full-pay version is the four of a kind to 4-for-1 from 5-for-1. Lowering that one pay counteracts the other four increases and reduces the return by just more than 1 percent. Logic doesn't really help in trying to determine the return of some games. You really need to have some software or a good reference to know what to expect.

The strategy doesn't change much for hands initially containing two or more wild cards. However, because of all the changes farther down the pay table, there are several changes if dealt zero or one wild cards on the initial hand. Here is the strategy chart for Not So Ugly Deuces Poker:

Strategy For 25/16/10 (Short-Pay) Not So Ugly Deuces Wild Poker
Four Deuces Dealt
All Four Deuces
Three Deuces Dealt
Five of a Kind or Better
Three Deuces
Two Deuces Dealt
Four of a Kind or Better
Four-Card Wild Royal Flush
Any Four-Card Straight Flush—67-9T, 45-56, 57-9J
Two Deuces
One Deuce Dealt
Full House or Better
Four-Card Wild Royal Flush
Flush
Any Four-Card Straight Flush, zero to One Gap—567-9TJ, 345-456, 457-9JQ
Straight
Any Four-Card Straight Flush Except A Low—346, 356, 347-9QK
Three of a Kind
Any Four-Card Straight Flush, A Low—A34, A45
Any Three-Card Royal Flush Except A High
Three-Card **Open** Straight Flush—67-9T
Three-Card Royal Flush, A High
Any Three-Card Straight Flush—57-9J, 45, 56
Any Four-Card **Open** Straight—789-10JQ
One Deuce
No Deuce Dealt
Royal Flush
Four Cards of a Royal Flush
Any Paying Hand—Three of a Kind or Better
Any Four-Card Straight Flush
Any Three-Card Royal Flush
Four-Card Flush
Two Pair
Three-Card **Open** Straight Flush—567-9TJ
One Pair

Strategy For 25/16/10 (Short-Pay) Not So Ugly Deuces Wild Poker
Four-Card **Open** Straight—4567-10JQK
Any Three-Card **Inside** Straight Flush Except A Low
Suited QJ, QT, JT
Four-Card **Inside** Straight—3456, 3567
Three-Card **Inside** Straight Flush A Low—A34, A35, A45
Four-Card **Inside** Straight—4568-10QKA, JQKA
Suited KQ, KJ, KT
Draw Five New Cards

Again, because the strategy for Deuces Wild Poker is broken into groups based on the number of wild cards initially dealt, it is fairly easy to learn. The variance of Not So Ugly Deuces is the same as full-pay, and the return is a very good 99.73 percent—even more than full-pay Jacks or Better. Although Not So Ugly Deuces is not as readily available as it once was, it is still available, but you will have to look around for it. Your search could pay decent dividends.

Short-Pay Deuces Wild Poker—Ugly Deuces

The last Deuces Wild game to be reviewed is a 25/15/9/4/4/3 version sometimes called Ugly Deuces or Ugly Ducks.

This game starts with the Not So Ugly Deuces pay table and reduces the pays for five of a kind and straight flush by one each to the level they are paid in the full-pay version. The remainder of the pay table remains the same as in Not So Ugly Deuces. This reduces the return to 98.91 percent. This is still almost 99 percent—better than probably 50 to 75 percent of the returns in any given casino's inventory of video-poker games.

The variance is also slightly less than Not So Ugly Deuces at 25.6. This makes Ugly Deuces—the lowest-paying Deuces Wild Game being reviewed here—a decent game to play.

Here is the complete pay table information for Ugly Deuces Poker:

Deuces Wild Poker (25/15/9/4/4/3) Short-Pay (UD)—Payback: 98.91 Percent, Variance: 25.8					
Hand	*1 Coin*	*2 Coins*	*3 Coins*	*4 Coins*	*5 Coins*
Royal Flush no 2s	250	500	750	1,000	4,000
Four Deuces	200	400	600	800	1,000
Wild Royal Flush	25	50	75	100	125

Deng Deuces Wild Poker (25/15/9/4/4/3) Short-Pay (UD)—Payback: 98.91 Percent, Variance: 25.8					
Hand	*1 Coin*	*2 Coins*	*3 Coins*	*4 Coins*	*5 Coins*
Five of a Kind	15	30	45	60	75
Straight Flush	9	18	27	36	45
Four of a Kind	4	8	12	16	20
Full House	4	8	12	16	20
Flush	3	6	9	12	15
Straight	2	4	6	8	10
Three of a Kind	1	2	3	4	5

Hand	*Pay 5 Coins*	*Occurs Every*	*% Return*
Royal Flush no 2s	4,000	43,410.0	1.84
Four Deuces	1,000	5,348.0	3.74
Wild Royal Flush	125	523.7	4.77
Five of a Kind	75	320.2	4.68
Straight Flush	45	202.7	4.44
Four of a Kind	20	16.3	24.53
Full House	20	38.2	10.48
Flush	15	48.9	6.13
Straight	10	17.4	11.49
Three of a Kind	5	3.7	26.80
No Win	0	1.8	0

The strategy for Ugly Deuces is similar to Not So Ugly Deuces, but there are a few changes.

Strategy for 25/15/9/4/4/3 (Short-Pay) Ugly Deuces Wild Poker
Four Deuces Dealt
All Four Deuces
Three Deuces Dealt
Five of a Kind or Better
Three Deuces
Two Deuces Dealt
Straight Flush or Better
Four-Card Wild Royal Flush—JT Only
Four of a Kind

Strategy for 25/15/9/4/4/3 (Short-Pay) Ugly Deuces Wild Poker
Four-Card Wild Royal Flush
Any Four-Card Straight Flush—67-9T, 45-56, 57-9J
Two Deuces
One Deuce Dealt
Full House or Better
Four-Card Wild Royal Flush
Flush
Any Four-Card Straight Flush, Zero to One Gaps—567-9TJ, 345-456, 457-9JQ
Straight
Three of a Kind
Any Four-Card Straight Flush
Any Three-Card Royal Flush Except A High
Three-Card **Open** Straight Flush—67-9T
Three-Card Royal Flush, A High
Any Three-Card Straight Flush—57-9J, 56
Any Four-Card **Open** Straight—567-10JQ
One Deuce
No Deuce Dealt
Royal Flush
Four Cards of a Royal Flush
Any Paying Hand—Three of a Kind or Better
Any Four-Card Straight Flush
Any Three-Card Royal Flush
Four-Card Flush
Two Pair
Three-Card **Open** Straight Flush—567-9TJ
One Pair
Four-Card **Open** Straight—4567-10JQK
Any Three-Card **Inside** Straight Flush Except A Low
Suited QJ, QT, JT
Four-Card **Inside** Straight—3456, 3457-10QKA, JQKA
Suited KQ, KJ, KT
Three-Card **Inside** Straight Flush A Low—A34, A35, A45
Draw Five New Cards

As stated, there are dozens of different pay tables for Deuces Wild Poker. The three versions explored in this chapter are all decent versions to play. They have decent returns, fairly low variance, and the strategies is straightforward.

When searching for a Deuces Wild game, you must look at virtually the entire pay table as changes can—*and usually are*—made to almost all of the pays. Some versions may have a high return but also a high variance if they concentrate the returns in a few very high-paying hands. Just be careful that you select a proper game to play, and make sure you have the strategy for the game you select. Deuces Wild Poker can be a lot of fun and profitable if played correctly.

CHAPTER 67

Loose Deuces Poker (Full-Pay, Short-Pay)

One particular form of Deuces Wild Poker is called Loose Deuces Poker. This variation is characterized by a slightly different pay for a natural royal flush and a very large pay for four deuces. Most video poker games pay 250-for-1 for a royal flush when the maximum of five credits are not inserted. Loose Deuces Poker pays 300-for-1.

For the purposes of this book it will not matter, as all the strategy is based on the maximum five coins being played. The other major change for Loose Deuces Poker is the 500-for-1 pay rather than the standard 200-for-1 pay for four deuces. The variance is very high, topping at 70 from the normal 26 or so.

Full-Pay Loose Deuces Poker

Advantage Alert: *The return on Loose Deuces Poker is 100.97 percent.*

Loose Deuces Poker (25/15/10) Full-Pay—Payback: 100.97 Percent, Variance: 70.3

Hand	1 Coin	2 Coins	3 Coins	4 Coins	5 Coins
Royal Flush no 2s	300	600	900	1,200	4,000
Four Deuces	500	1,000	1,500	2,000	2,500
Wild Royal Flush	25	50	75	100	125
Five of a Kind	15	30	45	60	75
Straight Flush	10	20	30	40	50
Four of a Kind	4	8	12	16	20
Full House	3	6	9	12	15
Flush	2	4	6	8	10
Straight	2	4	6	8	10
Three of a Kind	1	2	3	4	5

Hand	Pay 5 Coins	Occurs Every	% Return
Royal Flush no 2s	4,000	45,235.6	1.77
Four Deuces	2,500	4,702.6	10.63
Wild Royal Flush	125	588.7	4.25
Five of a Kind	75	315.3	4.76
Straight Flush	50	229.7	4.35
Four of a Kind	20	15.4	26.04
Full House	15	47.3	6.34
Flush	10	61.0	3.27
Straight	10	18.0	11.09
Three of a Kind	5	3.5	28.46
No Win	0	1.8	0

Strategy for 25/15/10 (Full-Pay) Loose Deuces Poker
Four Deuces Dealt
All Four Deuces
Three Deuces Dealt
Three Deuces
Two Deuces Dealt
Four of a Kind or Better
Four-Card Wild Royal Flush
Two Deuces
One Deuce Dealt
Four of a Kind or Better
Four-Card Wild Royal Flush
Full House
Any Four-Card Straight Flush, Zero to One Gaps—567-9TJ, 345-456, 457-9JQ
Three of a Kind or Better
Any Four-Card Straight Flush
Any Three-Card Royal Flush Except A High
Three-Card **Open** Straight Flush—67-9T
One Deuce
No Deuce Dealt
Royal Flush
Four-Cards Royal Flush
Any Paying Hand—Three of a Kind or Better

Strategy for 25/15/10 (Full-Pay) Loose Deuces Poker
Any Four-Card Straight Flush
Any Three-Card Royal Flush
Three-Card **Open** Straight Flush—567-9TJ
One Pair (Discard Either Pair If Dealt Two Pair)
Four-Card Flush
Four-Card **Open** Straight—4567-TJQK
Three-Card **Inside** Straight Flush, One to Two Gaps—345-456, 457-9J, 67T-9QK
Suited JT
Three-Card **Inside** Straight Flush, Two Gaps—346, 356, 347-478, 569, 589
Four-Card **Inside** Straight—789J-10QKA. JQKA
Suited QJ, QT
Four-Card **Inside** Straight—3456, 3457-689T
Draw Five New Cards

This strategy is manageable due to the classes of holds based on number of deuces dealt. The return of higher than 100 percent makes this an interesting game to play; however, the variance of 70 is very high. Care must be taken to have an adequate bankroll to ride through the loss cycle and cash in on the winning cycle before losing all your funds. Please proceed with caution. Variance can be a killer if your bankroll is too small.

Short-Pay Loose Deuces Poker

There are several short-pay versions of Loose Deuces Poker available. I will only present two of these. The first is called 25/15/8 after the pays for the wild royal flush, five of a kind, and straight flush.

25/15/8 Loose Deuces Poker

Advantage Alert: *A smidgen higher than 100 percent at 100.15 percent.*

The variance stays around 70. Here is the complete pay table information for the 25/15/8 version of Loose Deuces Poker:

Loose Deuces Poker (25/15/8) Short-Pay—Payback: 100.15 Percent, Variance: 70.7					
Hand	*1 Coin*	*2 Coins*	*3 Coins*	*4 Coins*	*5 Coins*
Royal Flush no 2s	300	600	900	1,200	4,000
Four Deuces	500	1,000	1,500	2,000	2,500

Loose Deuces Poker (25/15/8) Short-Pay—Payback: 100.15 Percent, Variance: 70.7					
Hand	*1 Coin*	*2 Coins*	*3 Coins*	*4 Coins*	*5 Coins*
Wild Royal Flush	25	50	75	100	125
Five of a Kind	15	30	45	60	75
Straight Flush	8	16	24	32	40
Four of a Kind	4	8	12	16	20
Full House	3	6	9	12	15
Flush	2	4	6	8	10
Straight	2	4	6	8	10
Three of a Kind	1	2	3	4	5

Hand	*Pay 5 Coins*	*Occurs Every*	*% Return*
Royal Flush no 2s	4,000	44,890.5	1.78
Four Deuces	2,500	4,664.4	10.72
Wild Royal Flush	125	585.0	4.27
Five of a Kind	75	314.0	4.78
Straight Flush	40	257.8	3.10
Four of a Kind	20	15.3	26.17
Full House	15	47.2	6.36
Flush	10	61.7	3.24
Straight	10	17.8	11.21
Three of a Kind	5	3.5	28.51
No Win	0	1.8	0

The changes to the pay table are very minor, but they are enough to cause several changes to the strategy, which follows.

Strategy for 25/15/8 (Short-Pay) Loose Deuces Poker
Four Deuces Dealt
All Four Deuces
Three Deuces Dealt
Three Deuces
Two Deuces Dealt
Four of a Kind or Better
Four-Card Wild Royal Flush
Two Deuces
One Deuce Dealt

Strategy for 25/15/8 (Short-Pay) Loose Deuces Poker
Four of a Kind or Better
Four-Card Wild Royal Flush
Full House
Four-Card **Open** Straight Flush—567-9TJ
Straight or Better
Four-Card **Inside** Straight Flush, One Gap—345-456, 457-9JQ
Three of a Kind or Better
Any Four-Card Straight Flush
Any Three-Card Royal Flush Except A High
One Deuce
No Deuce Dealt
Royal Flush
Four Cards of a Royal Flush
Any Paying Hand—Three of a Kind or Better
Any Four-Card **Open** Straight Flush—4567-9TJQ
Any Three-Card Royal Flush
Any Four-Card Straight Flush
One Pair (Discard Either Pair If Dealt Two Pair)
Four-Card Flush
Four-Card **Open** Straight—4567-10JQK
Three-Card Straight Flush, Zero to One Gaps—567-9TJ, 345-456, 457-9JQ
Suited JT
Four-Card **Inside** Straight, Two-Plus High Cards—9TJK-10JQA, JQKA
Three-Card **Inside** Straight Flush, Two Gaps—9TK-9QK
Four-Card **Inside** Straight—3456, 3457-79TJ
Three-Card **Inside** Straight Flush, Two Gaps, T or J High—67T-69T, 78J-79J
Four-Card **Inside** Straight, Q High—89TQ-89JQ
Three-Card **Inside** Straight Flush, Two Gaps, Q High—89Q-8JQ
Two-Card Royal Flush, Q High—QJ, QT
Any Three-Card Straight Flush
Draw Five New Cards

The strategy gets a little complex with no deuce dealt but can still be workable. As with the full-pay version of Loose Deuces Poker, the high variance means a large bankroll is required to be able to emerge victorious after riding out the downswings.

25/12/8 Loose Deuces Poker

The last Loose Deuces Poker game included in this book is the 25/12/8 version. The game returns 99.20 percent with perfect play but still has the 70+ variance. The complete pay table information looks like this:

Loose Deuces Poker (25/12/8) Short-Pay—Payback: 99.20 Percent, Variance: 70.4					
Hand	*1 Coin*	*2 Coins*	*3 Coins*	*4 Coins*	*5 Coins*
Royal Flush no 2s	300	600	900	1,200	4,000
Four Deuces	500	1,000	1,500	2,000	2,500
Wild Royal Flush	25	50	75	100	125
Five of a Kind	12	24	36	48	60
Straight Flush	8	16	24	32	40
Four of a Kind	4	8	12	16	20
Full House	3	6	9	12	15
Flush	2	4	6	8	10
Straight	2	4	6	8	10
Three of a Kind	1	2	3	4	5

Hand	*Pay 5 Coins*	*Occurs Every*	*% Return*
Royal Flush no 2s	4,000	44,763.3	1.79
Four Deuces	2,500	4,673.9	10.70
Wild Royal Flush	125	583.0	4.29
Five of a Kind	60	314.7	3.81
Straight Flush	40	255.1	3.14
Four of a Kind	20	15.3	26.13
Full House	15	47.2	6.36
Flush	10	61.5	3.25
Straight	10	17.8	11.25
Three of a Kind	5	3.5	28.49
No Win	0	1.8	0

The minor change in the pay table causes several changes in the strategy, especially when no deuce is dealt.

Strategy for 25/12/8 (Short-Pay) Loose Deuces Poker
Four Deuces Dealt
All Four Deuces
Three Deuces Dealt
Three Deuces
Two Deuces Dealt
Straight Flush or Better
Four-Card Wild Royal Flush—JT
Four of a Kind
Four-Card Wild Royal Flush
Two Deuces
One Deuce Dealt
Four of a Kind or Better
Four-Card Wild Royal Flush
Full House
Four-Card **Open** Straight Flush—567-9TJ
Straight or Better
Four-Card **Inside** Straight Flush, One Gap—345-456, 457-9JQ
Three of a Kind or Better
Any Four-Card Straight Flush
Any Three-Card Royal Flush Except A High
Suited 9T
One Deuce
No Deuce Dealt
Royal Flush
Four Cards of a Royal Flush
Any Paying Hand—Three of a Kind or Better
Any Four-Card **Open** Straight Flush—4567-9TJQ
Any Three-Card Royal Flush
Any Four-Card Straight Flush
One Pair (Discard Either Pair If Dealt Two Pair)
Four-Card Flush
Four-Card **Open** Straight—4567-10JQK
Three-Card Straight Flush, Zero to One Gaps—567-9TJ, 345-456, 457-9JQ
Suited JT
Four-Card **Inside** Straight—TQKA, 89TQ-9JQK

Strategy for 25/12/8 (Short-Pay) Loose Deuces Poker
Three-Card **Inside** Straight Flush, Two Gaps—89Q-8JQ
AKQJ (Straight)
Three-Card **Inside** Straight Flush, Two Gaps K High—9TK-9QK
Four-Card **Inside** Straight—678T-79TJ
Three-Card **Inside** Straight Flush, Two Gaps, T, J High—67T-69T, 78J-79J
Four-Card **Inside** Straight—3456, 3457-5789
Suited QJ, QT
Any Three-Card Straight Flush
Draw Five New Cards

While the return for this game is higher than 99 percent, it is not much higher. The variance is higher than 70. All things considered, I would prefer to play a different game with a return of greater than 99 percent and much less variance.

Still, if deuces are your thing and you like the shot at a 500-for-1 pay for four deuces every 5,000 hands or so *and* you have the necessary bankroll to handle the wide swings inherent in this game, then by all means, have at it.

CHAPTER 68

Double Deuces Poker (Full-Pay, Short-Pay)

The name tells it all. Double Deuces Poker pays double for four deuces—400-for-1 instead of 200-for-1. That is the only change from the standard Deuces Wild Poker. That change, however, roughly doubles the variance to about 50 from about 25.

Full-Pay Double Deuces Poker

The full-pay version returns 99.62 percent, however, so it is a decent-paying game.

Double Deuces Poker (16/11) Full-Pay—Payback: 99.62 Percent, Variance: 51.0					
Hand	1 Coin	2 Coins	3 Coins	4 Coins	5 Coins
Royal Flush no 2s	250	500	750	1,000	4,000
Four Deuces	400	800	1,200	1,600	2,000
Wild Royal Flush	25	50	75	100	125
Five of a Kind	16	32	46	64	80
Straight Flush	11	22	33	44	55
Four of a Kind	4	8	12	16	20
Full House	3	6	9	12	15
Flush	2	4	6	8	10
Straight	2	4	6	8	10
Three of a Kind	1	2	3	4	5

Hand	Pay 5 Coins	Occurs Every	% Return
Royal Flush no 2s	4,000	44,913.2	1.78
Four Deuces	2,000	4,779.5	8.37
Wild Royal Flush	125	568.7	4.40
Five of a Kind	80	317.6	5.04
Straight Flush	55	218.6	5.03
Four of a Kind	20	15.5	25.85
Full House	15	47.5	6.31
Flush	10	59.9	3.34
Straight	10	17.9	11.18
Three of a Kind	5	3.5	28.32
No Win	0	1.8	0

The game is called 16/11 after the pays for five of a kind and straight flush, which are the only two pays normally changed when modifying the return. This game returns 99.62 percent with perfect play and has a variance of about 51.

Strategy for 16/11 (Full-Pay) Double Deuces Poker
Four Deuces Dealt
All Four Deuces
Three Deuces Dealt
Wild Royal Flush
Three Deuces
Two Deuces Dealt
Four of a Kind or Better
Four-Card Wild Royal Flush
Two Deuces
One Deuce Dealt
Four of a Kind or Better
Four-Card Wild Royal Flush
Full House
Any Four-Card Straight Flush, Zero to One Gaps—567-9TJ, 345-456, 457-9JQ
Straight or Better
Four-Card **Inside** Straight Flush, Two Gaps—346-356, 347-9QK
Three of a Kind or Better
Any Four-Card Straight Flush

Strategy for 16/11 (Full-Pay) Double Deuces Poker
Three-Card Royal Flush Q, J High
Suited 89, 9T, KT, 67, KJ, 78, KQ
One Deuce
No Deuce Dealt
Royal Flush
Four Cards of a Royal Flush
Any Paying Hand—Three of a Kind or Better
Any Four-Card Straight Flush
Any Three-Card Royal Flush
Three-Card **Open** Straight Flush—567-9TJ
One Pair (Discard Either Pair If Dealt Two Pair)
Four-Card Flush
Four-Card **Open** Straight—4567-TJQK
Any Three-Card Straight Flush, Except Two Gaps and 3 Low
Suited JT
Three-Card Straight Flush, Two Gaps and 3 Low—346-356, 347-367
Four-Card **Inside** Straight—678T-10QKA, JQKA
Suited QJ, QT
Four-Card **Inside** Straight—3456, 3457-5789
Draw Five New Cards

The strategy is somewhat less complex than Loose Deuces Poker. With a return of better than 99.6 percent and a variance of 51, this is a decent game to play if you have a large enough bankroll to weather the fairly sizable losses that will certainly happen in a game with such strong variance.

Short-Pay Double Deuces Poker

The only short-pay version of Double Deuces Poker to be included in this book is the 15/10 (a five of a kind pays 15-for-1, a straight flush pays 10-for-1) version. It returns 98.86 percent and has a 51 variance like the full-pay version.

Double Deuces Poker (15/10) Short-Pay—Payback: 98.86 Percent, Variance: 50.9					
Hand	*1 Coin*	*2 Coins*	*3 Coins*	*4 Coins*	*5 Coins*
Royal Flush no 2s	250	500	750	1,000	4,000
Four Deuces	400	800	1,200	1,600	2,000
Wild Royal Flush	25	50	75	100	125

Double Deuces Poker (15/10) Short-Pay—Payback: 98.86 Percent, Variance: 50.9					
Hand	1 Coin	2 Coins	3 Coins	4 Coins	5 Coins
Five of a Kind	15	30	45	60	75
Straight Flush	10	20	30	40	50
Four of a Kind	4	8	12	16	20
Full House	3	6	9	12	15
Flush	2	4	6	8	10
Straight	2	4	6	8	10
Three of a Kind	1	2	3	4	5

Hand	Pay 5 Coins	Occurs Every	% Return
Royal Flush no 2s	4,000	44,828.0	1.78
Four Deuces	2,000	4,766.2	8.39
Wild Royal Flush	125	564.8	4.43
Five of a Kind	75	315.9	4.75
Straight Flush	50	230.1	4.35
Four of a Kind	20	15.4	26.00
Full House	15	47.3	6.34
Flush	10	60.8	3.29
Straight	10	18.0	11.10
Three of a Kind	5	3.5	28.43
No Win	0	1.8	0

The strategy is slightly less complex than the full-pay version and is listed here:

Strategy for 15/10 (Short-Pay) Double Deuces Poker
Four Deuces Dealt
All Four Deuces
Three Deuces Dealt
Wild Royal Flush
Three Deuces
Two Deuces Dealt
Four of a Kind or Better
Four-Card Wild Royal Flush
Two Deuces
One Deuce Dealt

Strategy for 15/10 (Short-Pay) Double Deuces Poker
Four of a Kind or Better
Four-Card Wild Royal Flush
Full House
Any Four-Card Straight Flush, Zero to One Gaps—567-9TJ, 345-456, 457-9JQ
Three of a Kind or Better
Any Four-Card Straight Flush
Any Three-Card Royal Flush Except A High
Three-Card **Open** Straight Flush—67-9T
One Deuce
No Deuce Dealt
Royal Flush
Four-Card Royal Flush
Any Paying Hand—Three of a Kind or Better
Any Four-Card Straight Flush
Any Three-Card Royal Flush
Three-Card **Open** Straight Flush—567-9TJ
One Pair (Discard Either Pair If Dealt Two Pair)
Four-Card Flush
Four-Card **Open** Straight—4567-TJQK
Any Three-Card Straight Flush
Suited JT
Four-Card **Inside** Straight—789T-TQKA, JQKA
Suited QJ, QT
Four-Card **Inside** Straight—3456, 3457-689T
Draw Five New Cards

As stated, the strategy is slightly less complex. With a return of 98.86 percent and a variance of nearly 51, I would not recommend playing this version of Double Deuces Poker. The reason? There is too little return for the complexity and variance. It is a close call, however, so if you like getting a 400-for-1 pay or more every 5,000 hands or so and if the 1.2 percent house edge and variance don't bother you, then please, be my guest. I'll skip it.

CHAPTER 69

Triple Deuces Poker

As with Double Deuces Poker, the name tells it all. Triple Deuces Poker pays triple the Deuces Wild pay for four deuces—600-for-1 instead of 200-for-1. Along with some changes to lesser-paying hands, the only version of Triple Deuces Poker in this book is the full-pay version, returning 99.92 percent with perfect play. The reason for no short-pay versions is the variance. With so much of the return concentrated in two rare hands, the variance soars to 96.5—very, very high. Getting anything less than nearly 100 percent just is not worth the bankroll swings.

> **Almost Advantage Alert:** *The full-pay version of Triple Deuces Poker returns 99.92 percent.*

Triple Deuces Poker (20/10/8) Full-Pay—Payback: 99.92 Percent, Variance: 96.5					
Hand	*1 Coin*	*2 Coins*	*3 Coins*	*4 Coins*	*5 Coins*
Royal Flush No 2s	250	500	750	1,000	4,000
Four Deuces	600	1,200	1,800	2,400	3,000
Wild Royal Flush	20	40	60	80	100
Five of a Kind	10	20	30	40	50
Straight Flush	8	16	24	32	40
Four of a Kind	4	8	12	16	20
Full House	3	6	9	12	15
Flush	2	4	6	8	10
Straight	2	4	6	8	10
Three of a Kind	1	2	3	4	5

Hand	Pay 5 Coins	Occurs Every	% Return
Royal Flush No 2s	4,000	45,764.3	1.75
Four Deuces	3,000	4,466.0	13.44
Wild Royal Flush	100	746.2	2.68
Five of a Kind	50	309.6	3.23
Straight Flush	40	257.3	3.11
Four of a Kind	20	15.1	26.49
Full House	15	47.1	6.36
Flush	10	64.3	3.11
Straight	10	18.0	11.13
Three of a Kind	5	3.5	28.63
No Win	0	1.8	0

By looking at the % Return column, it is easy to see why the variance is so high. More than 15 percent of the return is tied up in the natural royal flush and four deuces. That means while you are playing and not getting these high-impact hands, you are playing at a 15 percent house edge—which means $15 of every $100 you run through this game is not returned until you hit a royal flush or four deuces. If you play at a fairly slow 400 hands per hour on quarter games, you will lose $75 an hour.

With that in mind, here's the strategy:

Strategy for 20/10/8 (Full-Pay) Triple Deuces Poker
Four Deuces Dealt
All Four Deuces
Three Deuces Dealt
Three Deuces
Two Deuces Dealt
Four of a Kind or Better
Four-Card Wild Royal Flush, Q or J High Only
Two Deuces
One Deuce Dealt
Full House or Better
Four-Card Wild Royal Flush
Four-Card **Open** Straight Flush—567-9TJ
Straight or Better
Four-Card **Inside** Straight Flush, One Gap—345-456, 457-9JQ

Strategy for 20/10/8 (Full-Pay) Triple Deuces Poker
Three of a Kind or Better
Any Four-Card Straight Flush
Three-Card Royal Flush Q, J High
One Deuce
No Deuce Dealt
Royal Flush
Four-Card Royal Flush
Any Paying Hand—Three of a Kind or Better
Any Four-Card **Open** Straight Flush
Suited QJT
Any Four-Card Straight Flush
Any Three-Card Royal Flush, A or K High
One Pair (Discard Either Pair If Dealt Two Pair)
Four-Card Flush
Four-Card **Open** Straight—4567-10JQK
Any Three-Card Straight Flush, Except Two Gaps
Suited JT
Any Four-Card Straight
Three-Card Straight Flush
Suited QJ, QT
Draw Five New Cards

With much more return centered on just two hands, the strategy becomes simplified. If this were a positive-expectation game (more than 100 percent return), it would be a decent game to play. As it is, however, I consider it marginal because of the high variance.

If that doesn't bother you, then this is a great game to play. It is even better if you get slot-club points for play, as even a 0.1 (one-tenth) percent slot-club bonus puts this game in positive territory.

CHAPTER 70

Deuces Wild Bonus Poker (Full-Pay, Short-Pay)

Deuces Wild Bonus Poker adds a bonus for four deuces with an ace kicker and five of a kinds. A hand of four deuces with an ace kicker pays double the normal four deuces at 400-for-1 rather than 200-for-1. Rather than one pay rate for any five of a kind, the pay varies by rank.

Five aces pays 80-for-1, five 3s, 4s, or 5s pays 40-for-1, and five 6s through kings pays 20-for-1. The higher pays for certain hands comes with a price. Pays for lower hands such as flush and straight are reduced. Variance increases to about 32 from about 25, and the strategy becomes more complex since there are more combinations that win.

Two different Deuces Wild Bonus variations will be reviewed in this chapter—the full-pay (99.45 percent) and a short-pay (98.80 percent).

Full-Pay Deuces Wild Bonus Poker

The full-pay table's complete information follows.

Notice that the pay table is represented by 25/9/4/4, using the pays for the wild royal flush, straight flush, four of a kind, and full house. This is because the pays for five of a kinds do not normally change, although it is always a good practice to verify every line of the pay table before considering play on the chosen game.

Deuces Wild Bonus Poker (25/9/4/4) Full-Pay—Payback: 99.45 Percent, Variance: 32.7					
Hand	*1 Coin*	*2 Coins*	*3 Coins*	*4 Coins*	*5 Coins*
Royal Flush No 2s	250	500	750	1,000	4,000
Four Deuces w/ Ace	400	800	1,200	1,600	2,000
Four Deuces	200	400	600	800	1,000
Wild Royal Flush	25	50	75	100	125

Deap Poker (25/9/4/4) Full-Pay—Payback: 99.45 Percent, Variance: 32.7					
Hand	1 Coin	2 Coins	3 Coins	4 Coins	5 Coins
Five Aces	80	160	240	320	400
Five 3s, 4s, 5s	40	80	120	160	200
Five 6s through Ks	20	40	60	80	100
Straight Flush	9	18	27	36	45
Four of a Kind	4	8	12	16	20
Full House	4	8	12	16	20
Flush	3	6	9	12	15
Straight	1	2	3	4	5
Three of a Kind	1	2	3	4	5

Hand	Pay 5 Coins	Occurs Every	% Return
Royal Flush No 2s	4,000	42,670.0	1.90
Four Deuces w/ Ace	2,000	36,210.4	1.1
Four Deuces	1,000	6,416.1	3.12
Wild Royal Flush	125	481.8	5.19
Five Aces	400	3,004.1	2.66
Five 2s, 3s, 4s	200	1,283.3	3.12
Five 6s through Ks	100	481.6	4.15
Straight Flush	45	251.7	3.58
Four of a Kind	20	15.9	25.14
Full House	20	37.8	10.59
Flush	15	42.5	7.06
Straight	10	25.0	4.01
Three of a Kind	5	3.6	27.84
No Win	0	1.8	0

As I mentioned, strategy for this game becomes more complex because of the additional higher pays, and the variance goes up for the same reason.

Strategy for 25/9/4/4 (Full-Pay) Deuces Wild Bonus Poker
Four Deuces Dealt
Four Deuces with Ace
Four Deuces
Three Deuces Dealt

Strategy for 25/9/4/4 (Full-Pay) Deuces Wild Bonus Poker
Five of a Kind
Wild Royal Flush
Four Aces
Three Deuces with Ace
Three Deuces
Two Deuces Dealt
Four of a Kind or Better
Four-Card Wild Royal Flush
Two Deuces with Ace
Two Deuces
One Deuce Dealt
Full House or Better
Four-Card Wild Royal Flush
Flush
Three of a Kind—Aces, 3s through 5s
Four-Card **Open** Straight Flush—567-9TJ
Three of a Kind—6s through Ks
Any Four-Card Straight Flush
Three-Card Royal Flush—JT, Q High, K High, A High
Straight
Four-Card Flush
Three-Card **Open** Straight Flush—67-9T
One Deuce
No Deuce Dealt
Royal Flush
Four Cards of a Royal Flush
Four Aces
Straight Flush
Four 3s through Ks
Flush or Better
Any Three of a Kind
Any Four-Card Straight Flush
Any Three-Card Royal Flush
Straight
Four-Card Flush

Strategy for 25/9/4/4 (Full-Pay) Deuces Wild Bonus Poker
Two Pair
One Pair
Three-Card **Open** Straight Flush—567-9TJ
Any Three-Card **Inside** Straight Flush Except A Low
Suited JT, QJ, QT
Three-Card **Inside** Straight Flush A Low—A34, A35, A45
Suited KQ, KJ, KT
Draw Five New Cards

Short-Pay Deuces Wild Bonus Poker

The common short-pay version of Deuces Wild Bonus Poker has a 25/13/4/3 pay table. Notice that the pay for a straight flush improves considerably to 13-for-1 from 9-for-1, but the pay for a full house is reduced to 3-for-1 from 4-for-1. The reduction of one credit for the full house is more than enough to offset the increased pay for the straight flush, reducing the overall return to 98.80 percent. The variance is slightly reduced to 32.1 from 32.7. Here is the complete information about the short-pay version of Deuces Wild Bonus Poker:

Deuces Wild Bonus Poker (25/13/4/3) Short-Pay—Payback: 98.80 Percent, Variance: 32.1					
Hand	1 Coin	2 Coins	3 Coins	4 Coins	5 Coins
Royal Flush No 2s	250	500	750	1,000	4,000
Four Deuces w/ Ace	400	800	1,200	1,600	2,000
Four Deuces	200	400	600	800	1,000
Wild Royal Flush	25	50	75	100	125
Five Aces	80	160	240	320	400
Five 3s, 4s, 5s	40	80	120	160	200
Five 6s through Ks	20	40	60	80	100
Straight Flush	13	26	39	52	65
Four of a Kind	4	8	12	16	20
Full House	3	6	9	12	15
Flush	3	6	9	12	15
Straight	1	2	3	4	5
Three of a Kind	1	2	3	4	5

Hand	Pay 5 Coins	Occurs Every	% Return
Royal Flush No 2s	4,000	42,369.5	1.89
Four Deuces w/ Ace	2,000	38,514.9	1.04
Four Deuces	1,000	7,018.6	2.85
Wild Royal Flush	125	495.3	5.05
Five Aces	400	3,018.2	2.65
Five 2s, 3s, 4s	200	1,284.9	3.11
Five 6s through Ks	100	490.1	4.08
Straight Flush	65	184.8	7.03
Four of a Kind	20	15.8	25.27
Full House	15	47.3	6.34
Flush	15	45.8	6.56
Straight	10	23.8	4.20
Three of a Kind	5	3.5	28.74
No Win	0	1.8	0

The strategy for the short-pay (25/13/4/3) version of Deuces Wild Bonus Poker is just slightly more complex than the full-pay version.

Strategy for 25/13/4/3 (Short-Pay) Deuces Wild Bonus Poker
Four Deuces Dealt
Four Deuces with Ace
Four Deuces
Three Deuces Dealt
Five of a Kind
Wild Royal Flush
Three Deuces with Ace
Three Deuces
Two Deuces Dealt
Four of a Kind or Better
Four-Card Wild Royal Flush
Four-Card Straight Flush, Zero to One Gaps—56-9T, 45-9J
Three Aces
Two Deuces
One Deuce Dealt
Four of a Kind or Better

Strategy for 25/13/4/3 (Short-Pay) Deuces Wild Bonus Poker
Four-Card Wild Royal Flush
Flush or Better
Any Four-Card Straight Flush Except Ace Low
Three of a Kind
Four-Card Straight Flush, Ace Low—A34-A45
Three-Card Royal Flush—JT, Q High, K High
Three-Card **Open** Straight Flush—67-9T
Three-Card Royal Flush—A High
Straight
Three-Card **Inside** Straight Flush, One Gap—57-9J
Suited 56
One Deuce
No Deuce Dealt
Royal Flush
Four Cards of a Royal Flush
Flush or Better
Three of a Kind
Four-Card Straight Flush
Three-Card Royal Flush
Straight
Four-Card Flush
Pair of Aces
Three-Card **Open** Straight Flush—567-9TJ
One Pair (When dealt two pair hold 33-55, then 66-KK)
Any Three-Card **Inside** Straight Flush
Suited JT, QJ, QT, KQ, KJ, KT
Draw Five New Cards

Deuces Wild Bonus Poker can give the thrill of additional big pays with decent returns. The strategy, while moderately complex, can still be mastered. If you have a large enough bankroll to last through the losing streaks, this can be a fun game to play and should be considered if other higher-paying or less-complex games are not available.

CHAPTER 71

Deuces Wild Double Bonus Poker (Full-Pay, Short-Pay)

Deuces Wild Double Bonus Poker sweetens the jackpot by doubling the pay for five aces to 160-for-1 from 80-for one. The pay for five 3s through 5s is also bumped to 50-for-1 from 40-for-1. Some lower pays are reduced to make up the difference. With more money concentrated in fewer higher-paying hands, the variance increases by around 10 points. Strategy is roughly comparable to Deuces Wild Bonus Poker.

Full-Pay Deuces Wild Double Bonus Poker

The full-pay version is referred to as 25/12. For the purposes of this book, there are only two versions worth playing, and the only pay that changes is for the straight flush. The full-pay version pays 12-for-1.

Almost Advantage Alert: *The return is 99.81 percent—almost an even game.*

Deuces Wild Double Bonus Poker (25/12) Full-Pay—Payback: 99.81 Percent, Variance: 40.4

Hand	1 Coin	2 Coins	3 Coins	4 Coins	5 Coins
Royal Flush No 2s	250	500	750	1,000	4,000
Four Deuces w/ Ace	400	800	1,200	1,600	2,000
Four Deuces	200	400	600	800	1,000
Wild Royal Flush	25	50	75	100	125
Five Aces	160	320	480	640	800
Five 3s, 4s, 5s	50	100	150	200	250
Five 6s through Ks	20	40	60	80	100
Straight Flush	12	24	36	48	60
Four of a Kind	4	8	12	16	20

Deuces Wild Double Bonus Poker (25/12) Full-Pay—Payback: 99.81 Percent, Variance: 40.4					
Hand	*1 Coin*	*2 Coins*	*3 Coins*	*4 Coins*	*5 Coins*
Full House	3	6	9	12	15
Flush	2	4	6	8	10
Straight	1	2	3	4	5
Three of a Kind	1	2	3	4	5

Hand	*Pay 5 Coins*	*Occurs Every*	*% Return*
Royal Flush No 2s	4,000	44,210.9	1.81
Four Deuces w/ Ace	2,000	34,088.0	1.17
Four Deuces	1,000	6,755.8	2.96
Wild Royal Flush	125	499.9	5.00
Five Aces	800	2,565.0	6.24
Five 2s, 3s, 4s	250	1,271.6	3.93
Five 6s through Ks	100	486.6	4.11
Straight Flush	60	222.7	5.39
Four of a Kind	20	15.5	25.89
Full House	15	48.1	6.24
Flush	10	55.9	3.58
Straight	5	24.3	4.12
Three of a Kind	5	3.4	29.37
No Win	0	1.8	0

Since not a lot of pay lines changed, the strategy remains relatively simple.

Strategy for 25/12 (Full-Pay) Deuces Wild Double Bonus Poker
Four Deuces Dealt
Four Deuces with Ace
Four Deuces
Three Deuces Dealt
Five of a Kind
Wild Royal Flush
Three Deuces with Ace
Three Deuces
Two Deuces Dealt

Strategy for 25/12 (Full-Pay) Deuces Wild Double Bonus Poker
Four of a Kind or Better
Four-Card Wild Royal Flush
Two Deuces with Ace
Four-Card **Open** Straight Flush—67-9T
Two Deuces
One Deuce Dealt
Four of a Kind or Better
Four-Card Wild Royal Flush
Three Aces
Full House
Any Four-Card Straight Flush, Zero to One Gaps—567-9TJ, 345-456, 457-9JQ
Three of a Kind—33-55
Flush
Any Four-Card Straight Flush
Three of a Kind—66-KK
Three-Card Royal Flush—JT, Q High, K High
Straight
Three-Card **Open** Straight Flush—67-9T
Three-Card Royal Flush—Ace High
Pair of Aces
One Deuce
No Deuce Dealt
Royal Flush
Four-Card Royal Flush
Four of a Kind or Better
Three Aces
Flush or Better
Three of a Kind 333-KKK
Four-Card Straight Flush
Three-Card Royal Flush
Straight
One Pair (When dealt two pair hold AA, then 33-55, then 66-KK)
Four-Card Flush
Three-Card **Open** Straight Flush—567-9TJ
Any Three-Card **Inside** Straight Flush

Strategy for 25/12 (Full-Pay) Deuces Wild Double Bonus Poker
Suited JT, QJ, QT
Draw Five New Cards

There you have it. Not too complex for a nearly 100 percent return.

Short-Pay Deuces Wild Double Bonus Poker

The only short-pay version of Deuces Wild Double Bonus Poker to be reviewed in this book is the 25/9 version, where a wild royal flush is paid at 25-for-1 and a straight flush is paid at 9-for-1. The variance is virtually unchanged at 40.6.

Deuces Wild Double Bonus Poker (25/9) Short-Pay—Payback: 98.61 Percent, Variance: 40.6					
Hand	1 Coin	2 Coins	3 Coins	4 Coins	5 Coins
Royal Flush No 2s	250	500	750	1,000	4,000
Four Deuces w/ Ace	400	800	1,200	1,600	2,000
Four Deuces	200	400	600	800	1,000
Wild Royal Flush	25	50	75	100	125
Five Aces	160	320	480	640	800
Five 3s, 4s, 5s	50	100	150	200	250
Five 6s through Ks	20	40	60	80	100
Straight Flush	9	18	27	36	45
Four of a Kind	4	8	12	16	20
Full House	3	6	9	12	15
Flush	2	4	6	8	10
Straight	1	2	3	4	5
Three of a Kind	1	2	3	4	5

Hand	Pay 5 Coins	Occurs Every	% Return
Royal Flush No 2s	4,000	44,184.6	1.81
Four Deuces w/ Ace	2,000	33,325.3	1.20
Four Deuces	1,000	6,621.4	3.02
Wild Royal Flush	125	484.5	5.16
Five Aces	800	2,511.0	6.37
Five 2s, 3s, 4s	250	1,262.7	3.96
Five 6s through Ks	100	481.4	4.15

Hand	Pay 5 Coins	Occurs Every	% Return
Straight Flush	45	266.5	3.38
Four of a Kind	20	15.3	26.15
Full House	15	47.9	6.27
Flush	10	55.7	3.59
Straight	5	24.9	4.01
Three of a Kind	5	3.4	29.53
No Win	0	1.8	0

Though very similar, the strategy for the 12/9 short-pay version of Deuces Wild Double Bonus Poker has several minor changes.

Strategy for 25/9 (Short-Pay) Deuces Wild Double Bonus Poker
Four Deuces Dealt
Four Deuces with Ace
Four Deuces
Three Deuces Dealt
Five of a Kind
Wild Royal Flush
Three Deuces with Ace
Three Deuces
Two Deuces Dealt
Four of a Kind or Better
Four-Card Wild Royal Flush
Two Deuces with Ace
Two Deuces
One Deuce Dealt
Four of a Kind or Better
Four-Card Wild Royal Flush
Three Aces
Full House
Three of a Kind—33-55
Flush
Any Four-Card **Open** Straight Flush—567-9TJ
Three of a Kind—66-KK
Any Four-Card Straight Flush

Strategy for 25/9 (Short-Pay) Deuces Wild Double Bonus Poker
Three-Card Royal Flush—JT, Q High
Straight
Three-Card Royal Flush—K High, A High
Pair of Aces
One Deuce
No Deuce Dealt
Royal Flush
Four-Card Royal Flush
Four of a Kind or Better
Three Aces
Flush or Better
Three of a Kind 333-KKK
Four-Card Straight Flush
Three-Card Royal Flush
Straight
One Pair (When dealt two pair hold AA, then 33-55, then 66-KK)
Four-Card Flush
Three-Card **Open** Straight Flush—567-9TJ
Three-Card **Inside** Straight Flush—345-456, 457-9JQ, 569-9QK
Suited JT
Three-Card **Inside** Straight Flush—346, 356, 347-478
Suited QJ, QT
Draw Five New Cards

Deuces Wild Double Bonus Poker, while having a fairly high variance and somewhat complex strategy, also has decent returns and multiple opportunities for large payoffs. The key, as always, is having a large enough bankroll to weather the losses.

CHAPTER 72

Super Bonus Deuces Wild Poker (Full-Pay, Short-Pay)

Super Bonus Deuces Wild Poker has the bonus for four deuces with an ace kicker, but the five-of-a-kind pays are different from Deuces Wild Bonus Poker or Deuces Wild Double Bonus Poker. This game pays extra for any five of a kind with only one deuce—in other words, this game pays a bonus for a natural four of a kind with a deuce kicker. Because there are only two pay lines for five of a kind rather than the three pay lines in the Bonus/Double Bonus Deuces Wild games, the variance is slightly reduced. The strategy, however, is as complex as the Deuces Wild Bonus games.

Full-Pay Super Bonus Deuces Wild Poker

Advantage Alert: *Full-pay Super Bonus Deuces Wild Poker's payback is 100.13 percent.*

Super Bonus Deuces Wild Poker (25/15/10) Full-Pay—Payback: 100.13 Percent, Variance: 36.4					
Hand	*1 Coin*	*2 Coins*	*3 Coins*	*4 Coins*	*5 Coins*
Royal Flush No 2s	250	500	750	1,000	4,000
Four Deuces w/ Ace	400	800	1,200	1,600	2,000
Four Deuces	200	400	600	800	1,000
Wild Royal Flush	25	50	75	100	125
Five of a Kind w/ One Deuce	160	320	480	640	800
Five of a Kind	15	30	45	60	75
Straight Flush	10	20	30	40	50
Four of a Kind	4	8	12	16	20
Full House	3	6	9	12	15
Flush	2	4	6	8	10

Super Bonus Deuces Wild Poker (25/15/10) Full-Pay—Payback: 100.13 Percent, Variance: 36.4					
Hand	*1 Coin*	*2 Coins*	*3 Coins*	*4 Coins*	*5 Coins*
Straight	2	4	6	8	10
Three of a Kind	1	2	3	4	5

Hand	*Pay 5 Coins*	*Occurs Every*	*% Return*
Royal Flush No 2s	4,000	44,488.0	1.80
Four Deuces w/ Ace	2,000	44,902.9	0.89
Four Deuces	1,000	6,050.1	3.31
Wild Royal Flush	125	527.9	4.74
Five of a Kind w/ One Deuce	800	2,925.2	5.47
Five of a Kind	75	364.6	4.11
Straight Flush	50	205.1	4.88
Four of a Kind	20	15.8	26.33
Full House	15	47.4	6.33
Flush	10	57.8	3.46
Straight	10	17.1	11.70
Three of a Kind	5	3.6	28.12
No Win	0	1.8	0

The full-pay version of Super Bonus Deuces Wild Poker returns more than 100 percent—a rarity in the newer games. The strategy, while fairly complex, can be learned by number of deuces dealt, which makes it somewhat simpler to master.

Strategy for 25/15/10 (Full-Pay) Super Bonus Deuces Wild Poker
Four Deuces Dealt
Four Deuces with Ace
Four Deuces
Three Deuces Dealt
Five of a Kind
Three Deuces with Ace
Three Deuces
Two Deuces Dealt
Four of a Kind or Better
Four-Card Wild Royal Flush
Four-Card Straight Flush—67-9T, 45, 56, 57-9J

Strategy for 25/15/10 (Full-Pay) Super Bonus Deuces Wild Poker
Two Deuces
One Deuce Dealt
Four of a Kind or Better
Four-Card Wild Royal Flush
Full House
Four-Card Straight Flush, Zero to One Gaps—567-9TJ, 345-456, 457-9JQ
Three of a Kind or Better
Any Four-Card Straight Flush
Any Three-Card Royal Flush Except A High
Any Three-Card **Open** Straight Flush—67-9T
Three-Card Royal Flush—A High
Four-Card **Open** Straight—567-10JQ
Three-Card Straight Flush—57-9J, 56
One Deuce
No Deuce Dealt
Royal Flush
Four Cards of a Royal Flush
Any Paying Hand
Four-Card Straight Flush
Three-Card Royal Flush
One Pair (When dealt two pair hold either)
Three-Card **Open** Straight Flush—567-9TJ
Four-Card Flush
Four-Card **Open** Straight—4567-10JQK
Three-Card Straight Flush—345-456, 457-9JQ, 78J-7TJ
Suited JT
Three-Card **Inside** Straight Flush—346, 356, 347-69T, 89Q-9QK
Four-Card **Inside** Straight—5679-10QKA, JQKA
Suited QJ, QT
Four-Card **Inside** Straight—3456, 3457-79TJ
Suited KJ, KT
Draw Five New Cards

Playing this strategy on a full-pay machine will make money for you in the long run. You will have large upswings and downswings, but ultimately you will make money on this game with this strategy.

Short-Pay Super Bonus Deuces Wild Poker
There are two short-pay games that are worth playing.

25/15/9 Super Bonus Deuces Wild Poker
The first short-pay version we will cover is a 25/15/9 game that returns nearly 100 percent—99.67, more precisely. The variance increases slightly to 36.6. Here is the complete pay table information for 25/15/9 short-pay Super Bonus Deuces Wild Poker:

Super Bonus Deuces Wild Poker (25/15/9) Short-Pay—Payback: 99.67 Percent, Variance: 36.6					
Hand	1 Coin	2 Coins	3 Coins	4 Coins	5 Coins
Royal Flush No 2s	250	500	750	1,000	4,000
Four Deuces w/ Ace	400	800	1,200	1,600	2,000
Four Deuces	200	400	600	800	1,000
Wild Royal Flush	25	50	75	100	125
Five of a Kind w/ One Deuce	160	320	480	640	800
Five of a Kind	15	30	45	60	75
Straight Flush	9	18	27	36	45
Four of a Kind	4	8	12	16	20
Full House	3	6	9	12	15
Flush	2	4	6	8	10
Straight	2	4	6	8	10
Three of a Kind	1	2	3	4	5

Hand	Pay 5 Coins	Occurs Every	% Return
Royal Flush No 2s	4,000	44,457.3	1.80
Four Deuces w/ Ace	2,000	44,196.4	0.91
Four Deuces	1,000	5,844.2	3.42
Wild Royal Flush	125	519.8	4.81
Five of a Kind w/ One Deuce	800	2,916.3	5.49
Five of a Kind	75	353.8	4.24
Straight Flush	45	244.3	3.68
Four of a Kind	20	15.6	25.60
Full House	15	47.3	6.34
Flush	10	59.0	3.39

Hand	Pay 5 Coins	Occurs Every	% Return
Straight	10	17.0	11.78
Three of a Kind	5	3.5	28.21
No Win	0	1.8	0

The strategy is similar to the full-pay version with just a few changes.

Strategy for 25/15/9 (Short-Pay) Super Bonus Deuces Wild Poker
Four Deuces Dealt
Four Deuces with Ace
Four Deuces
Three Deuces Dealt
Wild Royal Flush
Five of a Kind—TT–AA
Four Aces
Three Deuces
Two Deuces Dealt
Four of a Kind or Better
Four-Card Wild Royal Flush
Four-Card **Open** Straight Flush—67–9T
Two Deuces
One Deuce Dealt
Four of a Kind or Better
Four-Card Wild Royal Flush
Full House
Four-Card **Open** Straight Flush—567–9TJ
Straight or Better
Four-Card **Inside** Straight Flush, One Gap—345–456, 457–9JQ
Three of a Kind
Any Four-Card Straight Flush
Any Three-Card Royal Flush Except A High
Any Three-Card **Open** Straight Flush—67–9T
Three-Card Royal Flush—A High
Four-Card **Open** Straight—567–10JQ
One Deuce
No Deuce Dealt

Strategy for 25/15/9 (Short-Pay) Super Bonus Deuces Wild Poker
Royal Flush
Four-Card Royal Flush
Any Paying Hand
Four-Card Straight Flush—4567-9TJQ, 89TQ, 9JQK
Suited QJT
Any Four-Card Straight Flush
Three-Card Royal Flush—K High or A High
One Pair (When dealt two pair hold either)
Four-Card Flush
Four-Card **Open** Straight—4567-TJQK
Three-Card Straight Flush—567-9TJ, 345-456, 457-9JQ
Suited JT
Three-Card **Inside** Straight Flush—346, 356, 347-9QK
Four-Card **Inside** Straight—3456, 3457-TQKA, JQKA
Suited KJ, KT, QJ, QT
Draw Five New Cards

25/12/9 Super Bonus Deuces Wild Poker

The second short-pay version of Super Bonus Deuces Wild Poker is the 25/12/9 version. By dropping the pay for a five of a kind with other than one deuce to 12-for-1, the return drops to 98.87 percent. This is not bad, but it is not what the other versions of this game pay. Variance is approximately the same as other versions of this game, as is the strategy.

Super Bonus Deuces Wild Poker (25/12/9) Short-Pay—Payback: 98.84 Percent, Variance: 36.5					
Hand	*1 Coin*	*2 Coins*	*3 Coins*	*4 Coins*	*5 Coins*
Royal Flush No 2s	250	500	750	1,000	4,000
Four Deuces w/ Ace	400	800	1,200	1,600	2,000
Four Deuces	200	400	600	800	1,000
Wild Royal Flush	25	50	75	100	125
Five of a Kind w/ One Deuce	160	320	480	640	800
Five of a Kind	12	24	36	48	60
Straight Flush	9	18	27	36	45
Four of a Kind	4	8	12	16	20
Full House	3	6	9	12	15

Super Bonus Deuces Wild Poker (25/12/9) Short-Pay—Payback: 98.84 Percent, Variance: 36.5					
Hand	**1 Coin**	**2 Coins**	**3 Coins**	**4 Coins**	**5 Coins**
Flush	2	4	6	8	10
Straight	2	4	6	8	10
Three of a Kind	1	2	3	4	5

Hand	**Pay 5 Coins**	**Occurs Every**	**% Return**
Royal Flush No 2s	4,000	44,457.3	1.80
Four Deuces w/ Ace	2,000	44,196.4	0.91
Four Deuces	1,000	5,844.2	3.42
Wild Royal Flush	125	519.8	4.81
Five of a Kind w/ One Deuce	800	2,916.3	5.49
Five of a Kind	60	353.8	4.24
Straight Flush	45	244.3	3.68
Four of a Kind	20	15.6	25.60
Full House	15	47.3	6.34
Flush	10	59.0	3.39
Straight	10	17.0	11.78
Three of a Kind	5	3.5	28.21
No Win	0	1.8	0

Here is the strategy for the 25/12/9 short-pay version of Super Bonus Deuces Wild Poker:

Strategy for 25/12/9 (Short-Pay) Super Bonus Deuces Wild Poker
Four Deuces Dealt
Four Deuces with Ace
Four Deuces
Three Deuces Dealt
Wild Royal Flush
Three Deuces with Ace
Three Deuces
Two Deuces Dealt
Straight Flush or Better
Suited JT
Four of a Kind

Strategy for 25/12/9 (Short-Pay) Super Bonus Deuces Wild Poker
Four-Card Royal Flush
Four-Card **Open** Straight Flush—67-9T
Two Deuces
One Deuce Dealt
Four of a Kind or Better
Four-Card Wild Royal Flush
Full House
Four-Card **Open** Straight Flush—567-9TJ
Straight or Better
Four-Card **Inside** Straight Flush, One Gap—345-456, 457-9JQ
Three of a Kind
Any Four-Card Straight Flush
Any Three-Card Royal Flush Except A High
Any Three-Card **Open** Straight Flush—67-9T
Three-Card Royal Flush—A High
Four-Card **Open** Straight—567-10JQ
Suited 8T
One Deuce
No Deuce Dealt
Royal Flush
Four-Card Royal Flush
Any Paying Hand
Four-Card **Open** Straight Flush—4567-9TJQ
Suited QJT
Any Four-Card Straight Flush
Three-Card Royal Flush—K High or A High
One Pair (When dealt two pair hold either)
Four-Card Flush
Four-Card **Open** Straight—4567-10JQK
Three-Card Straight Flush—567-9TJ, 345-456, 457-9JQ
Suited JT
Three-Card **Inside** Straight Flush—346, 356, 347-9QK
Four-Card **Inside** Straight—3456, 3457-10QKA, JQKA
Suited KJ, KT, QJ, QT
Draw Five New Cards

Any of the versions of Super Bonus Deuces Wild Poker presented in this book are suitable to play—depending on your tolerance for house edge and bankroll fluctuations. If you can find the full-pay version, that is definitely what you should play, as it will return more than you put in over the long run. By breaking down the strategy into sections based on the number of deuces dealt, it is easier to learn and play.

CHAPTER 73

Joker Poker–Class Video Poker

Joker Poker is another wild-card video-poker game, but it is different than Deuces Wild. Rather than having any of four cards of a particular rank (such as deuces) as wild, a single extra card (joker) is used. This means that rather than a 52-card deck, there is a 53-card deck. It also means that determining gaps for inside straights is more normal, since no rank of cards is wild. This somewhat simplifies the strategy.

In Joker Poker, five of a kinds get paid a bonus. As with other wild-card video-poker games, the pays for normal hands such as four of a kind, full house, flush, and so forth are reduced since they are easier to make. Because Joker Poker has only one wild card rather than the four wild cards in Deuces Wild, the pay table includes pays for a pair of kings or better as the lowest pay rather than the three of a kind. A straight flush pays 50-for-1 like most Jacks or Better games. Also, two pair is a paying hand in Joker Poker

There are several varieties of Joker Poker. I will cover Kings or Better, Two Pairs or Better, and Aces or Better.

Let's get right to it.

CHAPTER 74

Kings or Better Joker Poker (Full-Pay, Short-Pay)

Full-Pay Kings or Better Joker Poker

There are two different Kings or Better Joker Poker pay schedules that are considered full-pay. They are referred to as 20/7 games, paying 20-for-1 for a four of a kind and 7-for-1 for a full house.

4,700 Royal Kings or Better Joker Poker

The best full-pay game available pays 4,700-for-5 for a natural royal flush. Its variance of 33.6, while moderate, can be handled with a large enough bankroll.

Advantage Alert: *The full-pay Kings or Better Joker Poker returns 101 percent.*

Kings or Better Joker Poker (20/7) 4,700 Royal (Full-Pay)—Payback: 101.00 Percent, Variance: 33.6					
Hand	*1 Coin*	*2 Coins*	*3 Coins*	*4 Coins*	*5 Coins*
Royal Flush No Joker	250	500	750	1,000	4,700
Five of a Kind	200	400	600	800	1,000
Wild Royal Flush	100	200	300	400	500
Straight Flush	50	100	150	200	250
Four of a Kind	20	40	60	80	100
Full House	7	14	21	28	35
Flush	5	10	15	20	25
Straight	3	6	9	12	15
Three of a Kind	2	4	6	8	10
Two Pair	1	2	3	4	5
Kings or Better	1	2	3	4	5

Hand	Pay 5 Coins	Occurs Every	% Return
Royal Flush No Joker	4,700	38,614.5	2.43
Five of a Kind	1,000	10,724.9	1.86
Wild Royal Flush	500	9,245.7	1.08
Straight Flush	250	1,739.0	2.88
Four of a Kind	100	117.1	17.08
Full House	35	63.9	10.96
Flush	25	63.5	7.88
Straight	15	60.1	4.99
Three of a Kind	10	7.5	26.73
Two Pair	5	9.0	11.07
Kings or Better	5	7.1	14.03
No Win	0	1.8	0

4,000 Royal Kings or Better Joker Poker

The other full-pay version of Kings or Better Joker Poker is the same as the last version except a five-credit royal flush pays only 4,000 credits. The variance drops to about 26, which is reasonable. The complete pay table information is below.

Advantage Alert: *The second full-pay Kings or Better Joker Poker returns 100.65 percent.*

Kings or Better Joker Poker (20/7) 4,000 Royal (Full-Pay)—Payback: 100.65 Percent, Variance: 26.2					
Hand	1 Coin	2 Coins	3 Coins	4 Coins	5 Coins
Royal Flush No Joker	250	500	750	1,000	4,000
Five of a Kind	200	400	600	800	1,000
Wild Royal Flush	100	200	300	400	500
Straight Flush	50	100	150	200	250
Four of a Kind	20	40	60	80	100
Full House	7	14	21	28	35
Flush	5	10	15	20	25
Straight	3	6	9	12	15
Three of a Kind	2	4	6	8	10
Two Pair	1	2	3	4	5
Kings or Better	1	2	3	4	5

Hand	Pay 5 Coins	Occurs Every	% Return
Royal Flush No Joker	4,000	41,213.8	1.94
Five of a Kind	1,000	10,713.0	1.87
Wild Royal Flush	500	9,611.0	1.04
Straight Flush	250	1,739.6	2.87
Four of a Kind	100	116.9	17.11
Full House	35	63.8	10.98
Flush	25	64.2	7.79
Straight	15	60.3	4.98
Three of a Kind	10	7.5	26.79
Two Pair	5	9.0	11.09
Kings or Better	5	7.0	14.20
No Win	0	1.8	0

Short Pay Kings-or-Better Joker Poker

Two versions of short-pay Kings or Better Joker Poker are included in the book—18/7 and 17/7, where the first number refers to the pay for a four of a kind and the second number refers to the pay for a full house. Both of these games are playable, though the 17/7 game is reaching the lower limit of my tolerance with a house edge of 99.29 percent.

18/7 Short-Pay Kings or Better Joker Poker

The complete pay table information for the 18/7 short-pay version of Kings or Better Joker Poker is presented here:

Kings or Better Joker Poker (18/7) Short-Pay—Payback: 99.29 Percent, Variance: 33.1					
Hand	1 Coin	2 Coins	3 Coins	4 Coins	5 Coins
Royal Flush No Joker	250	500	750	1,000	4,700
Five of a Kind	200	400	600	800	1,000
Wild Royal Flush	100	200	300	400	500
Straight Flush	50	100	150	200	250
Four of a Kind	18	36	54	72	90
Full House	7	14	21	28	35
Flush	5	10	15	20	25
Straight	3	6	9	12	15
Three of a Kind	2	4	6	8	10
Two Pair	1	2	3	4	5
Kings or Better	1	2	3	4	5

Hand	Pay 5 Coins	Occurs Every	% Return
Royal Flush No Joker	4,700	38,477.1	2.44
Five of a Kind	1,000	10,736.8	1.86
Wild Royal Flush	500	9,286.8	1.08
Straight Flush	250	1,722.7	2.90
Four of a Kind	90	117.3	15.35
Full House	35	63.9	10.95
Flush	25	63.2	7.91
Straight	15	59.4	5.05
Three of a Kind	10	7.5	26.69
Two Pair	5	9.0	11.06
Kings or Better	5	7.1	14.01
No Win	0	1.8	0

17/7 Short-Pay Kings or Better Joker Poker

The final short-pay version of Kings or Better Joker Poker to be included is the 17/7 version, with a payback of 98.44 percent. Here are the complete pay table details for this game:

Kings or Better Joker Poker (17/7) Short-Pay—Payback: 98.44 Percent, Variance: 32.8					
Hand	1 Coin	2 Coins	3 Coins	4 Coins	5 Coins
Royal Flush No Joker	250	500	750	1,000	4,700
Five of a Kind	200	400	600	800	1,000
Wild Royal Flush	100	200	300	400	500
Straight Flush	50	100	150	200	250
Four of a Kind	17	34	51	68	85
Full House	7	14	21	28	35
Flush	5	10	15	20	25
Straight	3	6	9	12	15
Three of a Kind	2	4	6	8	10
Two Pair	1	2	3	4	5
Kings or Better	1	2	3	4	5

Hand	Pay 5 Coins	Occurs Every	% Return
Royal Flush No Joker	4,700	38,477.6	2.44
Five of a Kind	1,000	10,769.0	1.86
Wild Royal Flush	500	9,330.1	1.07
Straight Flush	250	1,683.5	2.97
Four of a Kind	85	117.7	14.44
Full House	35	64.1	10.93
Flush	25	62.6	7.99
Straight	15	59.3	5.06
Three of a Kind	10	7.5	26.62
Two Pair	5	9.1	11.05
Kings or Better	5	7.1	14.00
No Win	0	1.8	0

Strategy for Kings or Better Joker Poker

The Joker Poker pay table looks a lot closer to Jacks or Better rather than Deuces Wild. The strategy will also look closer to Jacks or Better games than to Deuces Wild games. The strategy for both the 4,700 royal flush and the 4,000 royal flush are identical.

The strategies for the short-pay games are very close to each other and to the full-pay versions, so the strategy chart will include strategy for all the Kings or Better Joker Poker games. Here is the simplified strategy for all of the Kings or Better Joker Poker games included in this book—full-pay 4,700-for-5 and 4,000-for-5 royal flush and short-pay 18/7 and 17/7 Joker Poker. Unless otherwise noted, each strategy line covers all versions of Kings or Better Joker Poker.

Strategy for 20/7 4,700 and 4,000 Royal (Full-Pay) plus 18/7 and 17/7 (Short-Pay) Kings or Better Joker Poker
Joker Dealt
Four of a Kind or Better
Four-Card Royal Flush
Full House
Four-Card **Open** Straight Flush—345-9TJ
Flush
Four-Card **Inside** Straight Flush, 0 High Cards—234, 236-9JQ
Four-Card **Inside** Straight Flush, K High, A Low—9TK-9QK, A23-A45

Strategy for 20/7 4,700 and 4,000 Royal (Full-Pay) plus 18/7 and 17/7 (Short-Pay) Kings or Better Joker Poker
17/7 Only Any Four-Card Straight Flush
Three of a Kind
Any Four-Card Straight Flush
Straight
Suited KQ, KJ, KT, JT
Four-Card Flush, One High Card
Suited AK, AQ, AJ, AT
Three-Card **Open** Straight Flush—45-9T
Three-Card **Inside** Straight Flush, K High or A Low
Suited QJ, QT
Pair of AA
18/7, 17/7 Only ** Four-Card **Inside Straight, One High—TJK, TQK, JQK
Pair of KK
Three-Card **Inside** Straight Flush, One Gap—34, 35-9J
Four-Card Flush, 0 High Cards
Any Three-Card Straight Flush
Four-Card **Open** Straight—345-9TJ
Low Pair—(pick in sequence) 6-8, T, 5, 9
Joker Only
No Joker Dealt
Four of a Kind or Better
Four Cards of a Royal Flush
Flush or Better
Any Four-Card Straight Flush
Two Pair or Better
Any Three-Card Royal Flush
High Pair—AA, KK
Four-Card Flush
18/7, 17/7 Only Three-Card **Open** Straight Flush—345-9TJ
Low Pair—22-QQ
20/7 Only Three-Card **Open** Straight Flush—345-9TJ
TJQK
Any Three-Card Straight Flush, Except Two Gaps, 0 High Cards
Suited AK

Strategy for 20/7 4,700 and 4,000 Royal (Full-Pay) plus 18/7 and 17/7 (Short-Pay) Kings or Better Joker Poker
Any Four-Card **Open** Straight
Three-Card **Inside** Straight Flush, Two Gaps, 0 High Cards—236-9QK
Suited KQ, KJ, KT
AK
Suited AQ, AJ, AT
A, K
Suited QJ, QT, JT
Draw Five New Cards

In Joker Poker, being dealt a wild card (joker) does not simplify the strategy. In fact, it is more complex than with no joker. The nice thing about the strategy for Kings or Better Joker Poker is the strategy changes very little with different pay tables, making it easy to play different versions accurately. If the reader can find a full-pay game and has an adequate bankroll to weather the inevitable losses, Kings or Better Joker Poker is a good game.

CHAPTER 75

Two Pair or Better Joker Poker

Another version of Joker Poker that is relatively common is Two Pair or Better Joker Poker. In this version the lowest-paying hand is two pair. There are also several changes to the pays on other hands. The natural royal flush pays 1,000-for-1 instead of 800-for-1. The five of a kind pays 100-for-1 instead of 200-for-1. A wild royal flush pays 50-for-1 instead of 100-for-1. Some of the lower-paying hands have increased pays. Overall, the return and variance is close to the 18/7 Kings or Better Joker Poker game.

Almost Advantage Alert: *Two Pair or Better Joker Poker returns 99.92 percent, close to an even game.*

Two Pair or Better Joker Poker—Payback: 99.92 Percent, Variance: 31.3					
Hand	*1 Coin*	*2 Coins*	*3 Coins*	*4 Coins*	*5 Coins*
Royal Flush No Joker	500	1,000	1,500	2,000	5,000
Five of a Kind	100	200	300	400	500
Wild Royal Flush	50	100	150	200	250
Straight Flush	50	100	150	200	250
Four of a Kind	20	40	60	80	100
Full House	10	20	30	40	50
Flush	6	12	18	24	30
Straight	5	10	15	20	25
Three of a Kind	2	4	6	8	10
Two Pair	1	2	3	4	5

Hand	*Pay 5 Coins*	*Occurs Every*	*% Return*
Royal Flush No Joker	5,000	43,617.3	2.29
Five of a Kind	500	11,001.3	0.91
Wild Royal Flush	250	12,542.3	0.40

Hand	Pay 5 Coins	Occurs Every	% Return
Straight Flush	250	1,708.9	2.93
Four of a Kind	100	122.9	16.28
Full House	50	66.6	15.01
Flush	30	48.6	12.34
Straight	25	34.5	14.49
Three of a Kind	10	8.1	24.81
Two Pair	5	9.6	10.47
No Win	0	1.4	0

This is the only version of Two Pair or Better Joker Poker presented in this book. If the reader cannot find this pay table, the game probably is not worth playing. This version has a nearly 100 percent return with a moderate variance. Notice that a wild royal flush and a straight flush pay the same. Because of that, the following strategy chart will use the term "RS Flush" to mean any straight flush including a royal flush. This term is *only used* in this strategy chart. Here is the simplified strategy for Two Pair or Better Joker Poker.

Strategy for Two Pair or Better Joker Poker
Joker Dealt
Full House or Better
Four-Card **Open** RS Flush—345-TJQ
Flush
Four-Card **Inside** RS Flush, One Gap—234, 235-10QK, JQK
Straight
Four-Card RS **Inside** Flush, Two Gaps—A34-A45, 236-9QK, A High
Three of a Kind
Four-Card **Open** Straight—345-TJQ
Three-Card **Open** RS Flush—45-TJ
Three-Card **Inside** RS Flush, One Gap—34, 35-9J, Q High
Four-Card Flush
Four-Card **Inside** Straight—234, 235-9JQ, K High
Three-Card RS Flush, Two Gaps—23, 24, 25-9Q, K High
Three-Card **Open** Straight—45-TJ
Low Pair—(pick in sequence) 5-T, 4, J
Four-Card **Inside** Straight, Two Gaps—A23, QKA

Strategy for Two Pair or Better Joker Poker
Joker Only
No Joker Dealt
Straight Flush or Better
Four Cards of a Royal Flush
Straight or Better
Any Four-Card Straight Flush
Two Pair
Any Three-Card Royal Flush
Four-Card Flush
Any Four-Card **Open** Straight—2345-TJQK
Three-Card **Open** Straight Flush—345-9TJ
One Pair
Three-Card **Inside** Straight Flush—234, 235-9JQ, A23-A45, 236-9QK
Four-Card **Inside** Straight—2346-TQKA, A234-A345, JQKA
Suited JT, QJ, QT
Three-Card Flush
Three-Card **Open** Straight—345-TJQ
Two-Card **Open** Flush—45-9T
Suited KQ, KJ, KT
Two-Card **Inside** Straight Flush, One Gap—34, 35-9J
Suited AQ, AJ, AT
Two-Card **Inside** Straight Flush, Two Gaps—23, 24, 25-9Q
Hold Single Card in Sequence Shown—T, 5-9, J
Draw Five New Cards

The strategy gets pretty complex if there is no joker to the point of holding single middle-rank cards. The high return and moderate variance could make a viable game for the reader if there is a sufficiently sized bankroll to ride out the losses.

CHAPTER 76

Pick 'Em Poker/Pick-a-Pair Poker (Full-Pay, Short-Pay)

The original game was called Pick 'Em Poker. It enjoyed a reasonable run for several years and then slowly faded. Today there are only a few places where you can find Pick 'Em Poker. However, in recent years a game called Pick-a-Pair Poker has started appearing on the scene. It may be called by a different name, but it is the same game.

Please note that from here on I will use the name Pick 'Em Poker to refer to both Pick 'Em Poker and Pick-a-Pair Poker.

Pick 'Em Poker is played differently from other video-poker games. Rather than dealing five cards and then allowing the player to hold or discard each card, Pick 'Em Poker deals two cards plus two piles of three cards each, where you can see only the top card. You must pick one of the two piles of three cards to complete the five-card hand. So you can see four cards, and you must discard one out of two of those cards—three of the dealt cards must remain in your hand. This can be particularly annoying when your visible cards make a great hand, such as a four of a kind—you *must* break it up.

On the plus side, Pick 'Em Poker has a decent pay table, a good return, and low variance.

Full-Pay Pick 'Em Poker/Pick-a-Pair Poker
Here is the complete pay table information for the full-pay version of Pick 'Em Poker/Pick-a-Pair Poker:

Almost Advantage Alert: *Full-pay Pick 'Em Poker/Pick-a-Pair Poker has a 99.95 percent return—an almost even game.*

Pick 'Em Poker/Pick-a-Pair Poker—Full-Pay—Payback: 99.95 Percent, Variance: 15.0					
Hand	*1 Coin*	*2 Coins*	*3 Coins*	*4 Coins*	*5 Coins*
Royal Flush	1,000	2,000	3,000	4,000	6,000
Straight Flush	200	400	600	800	1,199
Four of a Kind	100	200	300	400	600
Full House	18	36	54	72	90
Flush	15	30	45	60	75
Straight	11	22	33	44	55
Three of a Kind	5	10	15	20	25
Two Pair	3	6	9	12	15
9s or Better	2	4	6	8	10

Hand	*Pay 5 Coins*	*Occurs Every*	*% Return*
Royal Flush	6,000	351,817.7	0.34
Straight Flush	1,199	38,451.0	0.62
Four of a Kind	600	2,360.8	5.08
Full House	90	424.4	4.24
Flush	75	313.6	4.78
Straight	55	197.4	5.57
Three of a Kind	25	33.3	15.01
Two Pair	15	16.1	18.63
9s or Better	10	4.4	45.68
No Win	0	1.5	0

The royal flush is paid 50 percent higher than standard pays, but it is also approximately 10 times less likely to happen. Another interesting feature of this pay table is the even-money pay for 9s or better rather than the normal jacks or better.

The strategy for Pick 'Em Poker is different from others because you must always save exactly three cards that you can see. For that reason there are no four-card or five-card hands listed in the strategy.

The variance is among the very lowest available in any video-poker game, meaning you don't need as large a bankroll to play for a certain period of time. Not only that, but the strategy is not too complex, making this game a good one for the more casual player.

The strategy for the full-pay version of Pick 'Em Poker/Pick-a-Pair poker is shown below. Since the maximum (or minimum, for that matter) number of cards that can be saved are three, "Three-Card" is assumed ahead of the described hand (royal, straight flush, flush, etc.).

Strategy for Full-Pay Pick 'Em Poker/Pick-a-Pair Poker
Three of a Kind
Royal Flush, Q or K High
High Pair—99-AA
Royal Flush, A High
Any Straight Flush Except Two Gaps, Zero to One High Cards
Flush, Three High Cards
9TJ, TJQ (Straights)
Inside Straight Flush, Two Gaps, One High Card
Flush, Two High Cards
Low Pair—22-88
Any Straight Flush
Inside Straight, One Gap, Three High Cards
89T (Straight)
Flush, One High Card
Inside Straight, Two Gaps Three High, or One Gap Two High
789 (Straight)
Flush, 0 High Cards
Three High Cards
Inside Straight, Two Gaps, Two High Cards
T87, 986, 976
Open Straight, 0 High Cards—345-678
Two High Cards
Any Straight Except 2 Gaps, 0 High Cards
One High Card
Any Straight
0 High Cards

It certainly is a different-looking strategy table. The lowest line is to keep three low cards since you cannot discard everything. Once this strategy is learned, the game is a lot of fun to play. Your money tends to last a while, and it is nice to get 2-for-1 on a pair of 9s or better. Who knows, you might even get lucky and hit a royal flush!

Short-Pay Pick 'Em Poker/Pick-a-Pair Poker

There are a few different pay tables that pay less than the full-pay version shown above. The book will only explore one of them. It returns 99.24 percent with a variance of 20.9. Here is the pay table:

Pick 'Em Poker/Pick-a-Pair Poker—Short-Pay—Payback: 99.24 Percent, Variance: 20.9					
Hand	1 Coin	2 Coins	3 Coins	4 Coins	5 Coins
Royal Flush	1,000	2,000	3,000	4,000	10,000
Straight Flush	200	400	600	800	1,000
Four of a Kind	100	200	300	400	500
Full House	18	36	54	72	90
Flush	15	30	45	60	75
Straight	11	22	33	44	55
Three of a Kind	5	10	15	20	25
Two Pair	3	6	9	12	15
9s or Better	2	4	6	8	10

Hand	Pay 5 Coins	Occurs Every	% Return
Royal Flush	10,000	351,817.7	0.34
Straight Flush	1,000	38,451.0	0.62
Four of a Kind	500	2,360.8	5.08
Full House	90	424.4	4.24
Flush	75	313.6	4.78
Straight	55	197.4	5.57
Three of a Kind	25	33.3	15.01
Two Pair	15	16.1	18.63
9s or Better	10	4.4	45.68
No Win	0	1.5	0

Only three pay lines are changed—the royal flush pay is raised to 10,000 from 6,000, the straight flush is lowered to 1,000 from 1,199, and the four of a kind is lowered to 500 from 600. This combines to lower the return seven-tenths of a percentage point and raise the variance to about 21. These few changes are enough to cause several tweaks to the strategy, which is listed here:

Strategy for Short-Pay Pick 'Em Poker/Pick-a-Pair Poker
Three of a Kind
Any Royal Flush
High Pair—99-AA
Open Straight Flush—345-9TJ
Inside Straight Flush, One Gap—235-9TQ, plus 234
Flush, Three High Cards
Inside Straight Flush, Two Gaps, Two to Three High Cards
9TJ, TJQ (Straights)
Flush, Two High Cards
Inside Straight Flush, Two Gaps, One High Card
Low Pair—22-88
Any Straight Flush
Inside Straight, One Gap, Three High Cards
89T (Straight)
Flush, One High Card
Inside Straight, Two Gaps Three High, or One Gap Two High
789 (Straight)
Flush, 0 High Cards
Three High Cards
Inside Straight, Two Gaps, Two High Cards
T87, 986, 976
Open Straight, 0 High Cards—345-678
Two High Cards
Any Straight Except 2 Gaps, 0 High Cards
One High Card
Any Straight
0 High Cards

Even with the slightly lower return and the higher variance, this is still a good game—if you can find it. Look around. Check the multi-game machines. You just may run across this very good game.

CHAPTER 77

Shockwave Poker
(Full-Pay, Short-Pay)

Shockwave video poker is a unique style of Jacks or Better video poker. There are two different modes of play. The "normal mode" accounts for much more than 90 percent of play. The game operates in normal mode until a four of a kind hits. It then switches to "Shockwave" mode for ten plays or until another four of a kind, whichever happens first.

In Shockwave mode a four of a kind pays the same as a royal flush.

Full-Pay Shockwave Poker

The complete pay table information for the 12/8/5 (12-for-1 for a full house, 8-for-1 for a flush, and 5-for-1 for a straight) full-pay version follows.

Shockwave Poker—Full-Pay—(Normal Mode) Payback: 95.24 Percent, Variance: 19.8					
Hand	*1 Coin*	*2 Coins*	*3 Coins*	*4 Coins*	*5 Coins*
Royal Flush	250	500	750	1,000	4,000
Straight Flush	100	200	300	400	500
Four of a Kind	25	50	75	100	125
Full House	12	24	36	48	60
Flush	8	16	24	32	40
Straight	5	10	15	20	25
Three of a Kind	3	6	9	12	15
Two Pair	1	2	3	4	5
Jacks or Better	1	2	3	4	5

Hand	Pay 5 Coins	Occurs Every	% Return
Royal Flush	4,000	45,814.0	1.75
Straight Flush	500	7,468.8	1.34
Four of a Kind	125	438.1	5.71
Full House	60	89.9	13.35
Flush	40	58.7	13.63
Straight	25	67.9	7.36
Three of a Kind	15	14.2	21.12
Two Pair	5	8.2	12.23
Jacks or Better	5	5.3	18.75
No Win	0	1.7	0

Shockwave Poker—Full-Pay—(Shockwave Mode) Payback: 290.00 Percent, Variance: 1,683.1

Hand	1 Coin	2 Coins	3 Coins	4 Coins	5 Coins
Royal Flush	250	500	750	1,000	4,000
Straight Flush	100	200	300	400	500
Four of a Kind	250	500	750	1,000	4,000
Full House	12	24	36	48	60
Flush	8	16	24	32	40
Straight	5	10	15	20	25
Three of a Kind	3	6	9	12	15
Two Pair	1	2	3	4	5
Jacks or Better	1	2	3	4	5

Hand	Pay 5 Coins	Occurs Every	% Return
Royal Flush	4,000	49,854.6	1.60
Straight Flush	500	9,253.2	1.08
Four of a Kind	4,000	382.3	209.33
Full House	60	146.6	8.18
Flush	40	100.2	7.98
Straight	25	98.9	5.06
Three of a Kind	15	12.0	25.05
Two Pair	5	10.4	9.64
Jacks or Better	5	4.5	22.07
No Win	0	1.8	0

Shockwave Poker—Full-Pay—(Combined) Payback: 99.59 Percent, Variance: 22.6					
Hand	*1 Coin*	*2 Coins*	*3 Coins*	*4 Coins*	*5 Coins*
Royal Flush	250	500	750	1,000	4,000
Straight Flush	100	200	300	400	500
Four of a Kind	44	88	132	176	220
Full House	12	24	36	48	60
Flush	8	16	24	32	40
Straight	5	10	15	20	25
Three of a Kind	3	6	9	12	15
Two Pair	1	2	3	4	5
Jacks or Better	1	2	3	4	5

Hand	*Pay 5 Coins*	*Occurs Every*	*% Return*
Royal Flush	4,000	46,237.4	1.73
Straight Flush	500	7,909.5	1.26
Four of a Kind	125	435.6	10.10
Full House	60	89.5	13.41
Flush	40	59.3	13.49
Straight	25	68.6	7.29
Three of a Kind	15	14.1	21.27
Two Pair	5	8.1	12.30
Jacks or Better	5	5.3	18.74
No Win	0	1.7	0

There are three different pay tables—one for normal mode, one for Shockwave mode, and a combined pay table. Notice the very high return and astronomical variance for Shockwave mode. However, the game is only in Shockwave mode for about 9.8 plays, so the impact on the combined pay table is minor.

There are only two versions of Shockwave Poker that I recommend playing—the full-Pay (12/8/5) with a combined return of 99.59 percent and the short-pay (11/8/5) with a combined return of 98.48 percent.

Short-Pay Shockwave Poker

Here is the pay table information for the short pay 11/8/5 version:

Shockwave Poker—Short-Pay 11/8/5—(Normal Mode) Payback: 94.13 Percent, Variance: 19.6					
Hand	1 Coin	2 Coins	3 Coins	4 Coins	5 Coins
Royal Flush	250	500	750	1,000	4,000
Straight Flush	100	200	300	400	500
Four of a Kind	25	50	75	100	125
Full House	11	22	33	44	55
Flush	8	16	24	32	40
Straight	5	10	15	20	25
Three of a Kind	3	6	9	12	15
Two Pair	1	2	3	4	5
Jacks or Better	1	2	3	4	5

Hand	Pay 5 Coins	Occurs Every	% Return
Royal Flush	4,000	45,844.0	1.75
Straight Flush	500	7,382.2	1.35
Four of a Kind	125	438.6	5.70
Full House	55	90.0	12.23
Flush	40	58.6	13.65
Straight	25	67.8	7.37
Three of a Kind	15	14.2	21.08
Two Pair	5	8.2	12.22
Jacks or Better	5	5.3	18.76
No Win	0	1.7	0

Shockwave Poker—Short-Pay 11/8/5—(Shockwave Mode) Payback: 289.31 Percent, Variance: 1,682.9					
Hand	1 Coin	2 Coins	3 Coins	4 Coins	5 Coins
Royal Flush	250	500	750	1,000	4,000
Straight Flush	100	200	300	400	500
Four of a Kind	250	500	750	1,000	4,000
Full House	11	22	33	44	55
Flush	8	16	24	32	40
Straight	5	10	15	20	25

Shockwave Poker—Short-Pay 11/8/5—(Shockwave Mode) Payback: 289.31 Percent, Variance: 1,682.9

Hand	1 Coin	2 Coins	3 Coins	4 Coins	5 Coins
Three of a Kind	3	6	9	12	15
Two Pair	1	2	3	4	5
Jacks or Better	1	2	3	4	5

Hand	Pay 5 Coins	Occurs Every	% Return
Royal Flush	4,000	49,839.7	1.61
Straight Flush	500	9,234.6	1.08
Four of a Kind	4,000	382.2	209.32
Full House	55	146.6	7.50
Flush	40	100.1	7.99
Straight	25	98.8	5.06
Three of a Kind	15	12.0	25.04
Two Pair	5	10.4	9.64
Jacks or Better	5	4.5	22.07
No Win	0	1.8	0

Shockwave Poker—Short-Pay 11/8/5—(Combined) Payback: 98.48 Percent, Variance: 22.3

Hand	1 Coin	2 Coins	3 Coins	4 Coins	5 Coins
Royal Flush	250	500	750	1,000	4,000
Straight Flush	100	200	300	400	500
Four of a Kind	44	88	132	176	220
Full House	11	22	33	44	55
Flush	8	16	24	32	40
Straight	5	10	15	20	25
Three of a Kind	3	6	9	12	15
Two Pair	1	2	3	4	5
Jacks or Better	1	2	3	4	5

Hand	Pay 5 Coins	Occurs Every	% Return
Royal Flush	4,000	46,242.6	1.73
Straight Flush	500	7,910.0	1.26
Four of a Kind	125	435.6	10.10
Full House	55	89.5	12.29

Hand	Pay 5 Coins	Occurs Every	% Return
Flush	40	59.3	13.49
Straight	25	68.6	7.29
Three of a Kind	15	14.1	21.26
Two Pair	5	8.1	12.30
Jacks or Better	5	5.3	18.74
No Win	0	1.7	0

To properly play Shockwave Poker, we want to be aggressive chasing four of a kinds, since that starts Shockwave mode. In Shockwave mode we are also very aggressive chasing four of a kinds, as they pay as much as royal flushes.

The strategy is identical for either the full-pay (12/8/5) or the short-pay (11/8/5) versions of the game covered in this book.

Strategy for Normal Mode Full-Pay (12/8/5) and Short-Pay (11/8/5) Shockwave Poker
Four of a Kind or Better
Four-Card Royal Flush
Flush or Better
Four-Card **Open** Straight Flush—Suited 2345-9TJQ
Three of a Kind or Better
Any Four-Card Straight Flush, Incl. **Inside**
Two Pair
Four-Card Flush—Three High Cards
Suited QJT
Four-Card Flush—Two High Cards
Suited KQJ
Any Four-Card Flush
Any Three-Card Royal Flush except AhT
High Pair—JJ-AA
Any Three-Card Royal Flush
KQJT, QJT9 (Straights)
Suited JT9
JT98 (Straight)
Suited QJ9

Strategy for Normal Mode Full-Pay (12/8/5) and Short-Pay (11/8/5) Shockwave Poker
Three-Card **Open** Straight Flush—Suited 345-89T
Any Four-Card **Open** Straight, 0 High Cards—2345-789T
Three-Card **Inside** Straight Flush One Gap One High/Two Gap Two High
Low Pair 22-TT
Three-Card **Inside** Straight Flush, One Gap 0 High Cards
AKQJ (Straight)
Any Three-Card **Inside** Straight Flush
Any Four-Card **Inside** Straight, One Gap, Three High Cards
89T (Straight)
Any Three-Card Flush, Two High Cards
Any Two-Card Royal Flush, Two High cards
Any Four-Card **Inside** Straight, Two High Cards
Any Three-Card **Inside** Straight Flush
KQJ (Not Suited)
Three-Card Flush, One High Card
Suited JT
QJT
Any Four-Card **Inside** Straight except 0 High Cards
Suited QT
QJ (Not Suited)
Suited KT
KQ, KJ (Not Suited)
Suited J9
AJ, J, AQ
Suited AT
Q, AK, K, A
Any Four-Card **Inside** Straight
Three-Card Flush, 0 High Cards
Any Two-Card **Open** Straight Flush, 0 High Cards—45-9T

That is quite a complex strategy. The strategy for Shockwave mode is simpler, as presented here:

Strategy for Shockwave Mode Full-Pay (12/8/5) and Short-Pay (11/8/5) Shockwave Poker
Four of a Kind or Better
Three of a Kind
Four-Card Royal Flush
Flush or Better
Four-Card **Open** Straight Flush—Suited 2345-9TJQ
Straight or Better
Any Four-Card Straight Flush, Incl. **Inside**
High Pair—JJ-AA
Low Pair—22-TT
Two Pair
Suited QJT, KQJ
Any Four-Card Flush
Any Three-Card Royal Flush
KQJT, QJT9 (Straights)
Suited JT9
89TJ (Straight)
Suited QJ9
Any Three-Card **Open** Straight Flush—Suited 345-89T
Any Four-Card **Open** Straight—2345-789T
Any Three-Card Straight Flush Except two gaps, Zero to One High Cards
Suited QJ
AKQJ (Straight)
Suited KQ, KJ
J, Q
Suited AK, AQ, AJ
K, A
Three-Card **Inside** Straight Flush, Two Gaps, One High Card
Any Four-Card **Inside** Straight, Three High Cards
Any Three-Card **Inside** Straight Flush
Any Four-Card **Inside** Straight, Two High Cards
KQJ (Straight)

The relatively low variance for the combined mode and the relatively high returns for the full-pay version make Shockwave Poker a decent game to play if you can switch strategy during the Shockwave mode.

Keep in mind, however, that nearly 3 percent of the return comes from Shockwave mode, and hitting a quad in Shockwave mode is rare (approximately once every 40–45 times).

Your bankroll will be drawn down fairly quickly at this rate. So if you want to play Shockwave Poker, make sure you have the bankroll and can handle the emotional aspect of losing fairly quickly until you hit that quad in Shockwave mode.

CHAPTER 78

Progressive Video Poker

If the wide selection of games types and the endless variety of pay tables are not enough, there are other variations of video-poker games to consider. One of the most popular is progressive video poker.

In standard video poker each line of the pay table has one value, and it never changes: a high pair always pays 1-for-1, a four of a kind always pays 25-for-1 or some other fixed number, and a royal flush always pays 800-for-1 with five credits played.

Progressive video poker changes this. Progressive video poker games typically add money to a jackpot as players play the machine. Usually the jackpot is for hitting a royal flush, but some progressive games have running jackpots for straight flushes or certain four-of-a-kind hands.

Normally progressive games have reduced payouts for the full house and flush hands. For example, a Jacks or Better game that would normally pay 9-for-1 for a full house and 6-for-1 for a flush will only pay 8-for-1 for a full house (sometimes only 7-for-1 for a full house) and 5-for-1 for a flush when it is a progressive game.

The good news is that as the progressive jackpots climb, the house edge decreases and can eventually become favorable for the player. For a Jacks or Better game, the house edge moves toward the player by about 0.5 to 0.6 percent for each additional 1,000 credits in the jackpot. For example, an 8/5 game (8-for-1 paid for a full house and 5-for-1 paid for a flush) has a 97.30 percent payback when the royal flush progressive jackpot is at the reset value of 4,000 credits. When the jackpot climbs to 5,000 credits, the payback improves to 97.81 percent. Should the jackpot climb to double the reset value of 4,000 to 8,000 credits, the payback is approximately the same as a full-pay 9/6 Jacks or Better game (99.59 percent).

What this means is that when the jackpot of an 8/5 Jacks or Better progressive game is at 8,000 credits, a player can play the game with the same payback expectation as the increasingly harder to find full-pay game.

However, just because the payback is the same doesn't mean everything about the game is the same. Because more of the payback is concentrated in the royal flush, the variance of the game will increase—and increase dramatically from 19.32 to more than four times that amount, or 81.75.

What this means for the player is additional money is required for the bankroll. It also means that the play strategy will have to change. Since the royal is worth so much more, saving for the royal will become more common. When the jackpot is at 4,000 credits, expert strategy says to save four of a kind before four to a royal. But when the jackpot is 8,000 credits, save four to a royal before four of a kind. Actually a player would never have to make this decision in live play because he would never be dealt a hand that would have four of a kind *and* four of a royal flush.

But the following play change will happen with some regularity. With the royal flush jackpot at 4,000, the strategy says to save a high pair (pair of jacks through a pair of aces) before saving three of a royal. When the jackpot reaches 8,000, the strategy reverses to saving three of a royal before saving a high pair.

This means the strategy must change depending on the size of the jackpot. As the jackpot increases, the player will increasingly choose saving for a royal over other plays that would make some smaller amount of money. This means the player's bankroll will be drained faster than normal until a jackpot is won, so he must have adequate money to handle this.

Saving for a royal more often causes the frequency of hitting a royal to actually increase. At 4,000 credits for a royal on an 8/5 Jacks or Better game, playing expert strategy will have a royal hit every 40,170 hands, on average. At 8,000 credits on the same game, a royal will be hit every 32,644 hands—a 20 percent increase. The percentage of overall payback for hitting a royal flush also increases as the jackpot climbs, to 4.90 percent at 8,000 credits from 1.99 percent at 4,000 credits—almost two and a half times more.

Is playing progressive video poker for you? If you have an adequate bankroll and the software to change your strategy basically on the fly, it may be. Also, if all that is available are poor-paying nonprogressive games, waiting for a sufficiently high jackpot to make the game worth playing may be the best strategy for the serious recreational player. However, only you can determine if you are willing to do what is required to be a winner at progressive video-poker play.

CHAPTER 79

Yikes! 3/5/10/50/100 Times Poker

The standard video-poker machines are called "single-play" because the player plays only one game at a time. However, these are not the only types of video-poker games. Also available are games that play three, five, 10, 50, and even 100 games at a time. These multiple-play (or multiplay) games deal the exact same hand to three, five, 10, 50, or 100 hands. The player then decides which cards to save for *all* the hands dealt. The strategy for playing a multiplay game is exactly the same as when playing a single-play game.

If you are dealt a good initial hand you can make a lot of money. Imagine your delight at being dealt four of a kind! However, if you are dealt a poor hand, you stand to lose a lot of money. Over half of all hands in video poker end up being losers. Because of this, the variance for multiple-play games is higher than for single-play games. You need a bigger bankroll to play multi-play games of the same denomination.

In a single-play game, variance is higher when more money is paid out on high-paying hands. For example, 9/6 Jacks or Better (where a full house is paid at 9-for-1 and a flush is paid at 6-for-1) has only one very-high-paying hand—the royal flush. The variance on this game is 19.5.

Bonus Poker is different than Jacks or Better because it pays a bonus for four aces (80-for-1 instead of 25-for-1) and four 2s, 3s, or 4s (40-for-1). Payoffs for a full house and a flush are reduced to make up for the higher payoffs on the quads. The variance for Bonus Poker is 20.9—a 7 percent increase over Jacks or Better.

Double Bonus Poker increases the bonus on four aces to 160-for-1, the bonus on four 2s, 3s, or 4s to 80-for-1, and the bonus on 5s through kings to 50-for-1. Two-pair payoffs are reduced to 1-for-1 to compensate for the increased quad payoffs. By concentrating much more of the payoff money in fewer, large payoffs and reducing the more frequent lower payoffs, variance

314

on Double Bonus Poker soars to nearly 28.3—a 48 percent increase from Jacks or Better.

In multiple-play games, variance increases as the number of plays increases—not because more money is concentrated in fewer high-paying hands but because the strength of each multiple-play game is determined by the initial five cards that are dealt. If it is a strong hand, each play will have a strong hand. If it is a weak hand, each play will be weak. For example, if the initial hand contains three aces, the minimum each play will return is 3-for-1. If, however, the initial hand contains nothing and needs to be completely discarded, the chances for a positive outcome for this hand are small.

Now let's look at some specific games, plays, and variances.

As stated, variance for single-play Jacks or Better is 19.5. A three-play Jacks or Better game has a variance of 23.4—a 20 percent increase. In the five-play version of Jacks or Better the variance becomes 27.3—40 percent greater than single-play. The 50-play Jacks or Better has a variance of 115.8, and the 100-play version has a variance of 214—a whopping 997 percent greater than the single-play version of the game. That is quite an increase for a game that initially has a relatively low variance.

What about a game with a higher single-play variance? Double Bonus Poker has a single-play variance of 28.3—48 percent higher than single-play Jacks or Better. The three-play version of Double Bonus Poker has a variance of 35.0—a 24 percent increase from the single-play version. The five-play Double Bonus Poker has a variance of 41.8—48 percent higher. The variance on 10-play is 58.5—108 percent higher, while 50-play variance is 194.4—588 percent higher. And 100-play variance is 364—1,188 percent higher!

Those are some pretty big numbers. But what do they mean to you, the average video-poker player?

The more knowledge you have about the game you are playing, the better prepared you are to enjoy the game. If you are planning to play multiple-play video poker you will need to bring a larger bankroll in order to play as long as you would on a single-play game. Even on the relatively low-variance Jacks or Better, the variance of the 100-play game is 10 times that of the single-play game. This means that even if you were to play a lower-denomination multiple-play version of the game, you still may need a larger bankroll.

For example, if you normally play single-play Jacks or Better at the $1 level, it may seem logical that you could play 100-play Jacks or Better at the 1¢ level. After all, at maximum coin-in you wager $5 on each hand in either game. But by looking at the increased variance for 100-play (10 times that of single-play), it is easy to see that the same bankroll will not nearly be enough.

316 EVERYTHING CASINO POKER

Keep in mind that variance can be good or bad. When riding the wave of positive variance, life is very good indeed. However, when wallowing in the pit of negative variance, life is tough. It is always a good idea to make sure you have a large enough bankroll when you gamble. Keep your casino experiences enjoyable. Make sure you bring a large enough bankroll with you if you are planning to play multiple-play video poker.

CHAPTER 80
Multi-Strike Poker

Including detailed strategies for various versions of Multi-Strike Poker is beyond the scope of this book. Since it is a fun game to play and has a very distinctive sound when played, I am including some general information about the game. There is enough information in this chapter to play a full-pay Jacks or Better version of Multi-Strike Poker. If you are serious about playing it, however, the author recommends researching and practicing strategies before playing.

Multi-Strike Poker is a variation of standard video poker. It is a four-line game where you play the bottom line first. If you get a winning hand (or a randomly appearing Free Ride card) you advance to the next line. Each successive line pays twice the previous line. The second line pays twice the first line, the third line pays four times, the first line, and the fourth line pays eight times the first line.

As you can see there is a decent level of excitement as you progress through the four levels.

The general rules of play are as follows: The player can select one to four lines (levels) to play and one to five credits per line—although five credits per line should always be chosen. The player is dealt five cards on the bottom (or level one) line. Sometimes a Free Ride card will be dealt, which is replaced with a regular card after a short pause. The player then selects the cards to save and hits the *draw* button, just as in regular video poker. If the resulting hand is a winner or if there is a Free Ride card, the player advances to level two.

The process is repeated, except the level-two winning hands are now paid double the normal amount. The player advances to level three (paying four times normal) and level four (paying eight times normal) in the same fashion as advancing from level one to level two. The round is over after level four has been played or when there is no Free Ride card or winning hand on a lower level. All accumulated winnings are collected at that time.

318   EVERYTHING CASINO POKER

The increased return for Multi-Strike Poker versus the standard version of the game varies between about 0.1 percent and 0.67 percent depending on the game. Unfortunately, the better bumps in return are for truly awful original returns of less than 95 percent. With proper play a full-pay Jacks or Better game will return 99.69 percent—a 0.25 percent improvement.

When playing Multi-Strike Poker, always play the maximum of five credits and four lines. You are risking 20 credits per round. You will regularly play more than one hand per round when you advance to higher levels. Because you are risking more per round, the variance increases. You will need a larger bankroll for Multi-Strike Poker than for standard video-poker games.

Since the goal of lower-level play is geared toward advancing to the next level, generating a paying hand has priority over getting the highest return for the hand. In other words, frequency of hit is more important than the return. Strategy changes have to be made to implement this goal. These cannot be done in the head. A strategy-generating software program will need to be used. The strategy will change on each level. When you practice, you should practice each level separately.

One simple way to handle full-pay Jacks or Better is to add six credits to each winning hand amount for level one. Add four credits for level two and two credits for level three. Level four uses standard strategy. With these pay-table changes entered into your strategy-generating software, generate a separate strategy for levels one, two, and three. You already have the strategy for level four.

As you can see, playing Multi-Strike Poker means a lot of work, but the game can be very exciting. Is it for everyone? Absolutely not. But it might be for you.

CHAPTER 81

Get An Edge When the Percentages Favor the House

O nce upon a time the casinos were filled with all kinds of video-poker games that returned more than 100 percent with proper play. A knowledgeable player using the proper playing strategy could expect to make money from his play. Sadly the commonness of these positive-payback machines has been dramatically reduced.

So how is a savvy player supposed to make money on machines that pay back less than 100 percent? How can you be a winner if you are always playing games returning less than 100 percent? Well, you can't—that is, unless you have something to increase your return to more than 100 percent.

Fortunately, such things do exist! Here are the areas that will take certain games in the 99 percent range into positive territory for smart players:

- Slot clubs
- Casino promos
- Comps

All of these add payback for your casino play!

Originally player's clubs were invented as marketing tools to track play and build loyalty to a casino or brand of casino. Most player's clubs now offer cash back, meals, rooms, and more.

Casinos typically offer 0.1 to 0.33 percent of video-poker play as cash back. Full-pay Jacks or Better returns 99.54 percent with perfect play, so adding 0.33 percent for cash back raises the return to 99.87 percent. Okay, this is still not greater than 100 percent.

However, by playing four hours on a $1 machine at an average speed of 600 hands per hour, the player will play $12,000 through the game. The theoretical loss (including cash back) for this amount of play is $15.60. This level of play will also get a meal or two and a room. This pushes the return well into positive territory. So you make more than you lose!

How can the casinos do this?

Casinos know from past experience that the average player, who does not play the proper strategy, will lose between $250 and $300 rather than $15.60 for this amount of play. The casino normally will give back $60 to $80 in cash and comps to keep the players coming back. By playing perfect strategy, you will lose only $15.60 but still get $60 to $80 in freebies. Not too bad. You are now in the driver's seat!

Casinos also offer promotions such as multiple points on certain days. By taking advantage of multiple-point promotions you are multiplying the cash back. If a casino is offering even a low 0.1 percent cash-back rate and offering 5X points, the effective cash-back rate is 0.5 percent. Adding 0.5 percent to the 99.54 percent return of full-pay Jacks or Better yields 100.04 percent return. Yes, again, the game now becomes a long-term winner!

Many casinos offer "bounce-back" cash—vouchers or free play credit on the player's club card that can be used like cash if presented during the proper time period. Even if the bounce-back cash can only be used for free play, it is effectively as good as cash because it is *free play!*

Some casinos even offer special promotions such as scratch-off cards paying $2 to $5,000 for getting any four-of-a-kind or card-of-the-day bonuses for getting four of a kind of a particular card. They may even offer gifts at various times during the year for regular players.

Player's club promotions offer real value that adds to your normal return. By playing the best games and best strategies, a savvy player who takes advantage of player's club promotions can achieve significant profits over time. It only makes sense to take advantage of player's club benefits.

Advantage Alert: *It pays to use a player's club card for all video-poker play.*

So play the best games, use your slot-club card, take advantage of everything the casino offers you, and there's an excellent chance you have turned the tables (and the machines!) on the house!

Glossary

401(g): A money-market or other savings account for a player's gambling bank-roll. This money is to be used only for gambling.

Action: Any betting, calling, raising, or other act made by a player can be referred to as "action." If a player calls your bet, you are getting action.

Active Player: A player who has money in the pot and has not folded their hand.

All In: Placing all of your remaining chips into the pot.

Backdoor Flush or Straight: A flush or straight made by catching the last two cards to make the hand.

Bad Beat: When you have a good hand that is a favorite to win beaten by a better hand.

Banker: Each player in the Pai Gow Poker game is playing head-to-head against the banker (who may be the casino dealer or one of the other players at the table).

Bankroll: A sum of money used to finance some type of activity. In this book, bankroll is the money used to finance one or more casino-play sessions.

Bet: To voluntarily put money into the pot.

Blinds: The large and small blinds are forced bets made before the first cards are dealt.

Board: The community cards turned faceup in the middle of the table.

Bonus: An extra payment. Used in the name of a video-poker game, it refers to certain hands being paid more than in the standard game.

Call: To place money in the pot equal to the previous bet.

Calling Station: A player who will not fold his hand and will call all the pots to the river. This is a weak, passive player who rarely raises the pot. You will make a lot of money from this type of player.

Carousel: A raised, circular area having several slot machines. Sometimes the carousel revolves, but it does not have to.

Case Card: This is the fourth card of a certain rank. If you held two kings and a third was showing on the board, the fourth king would be the "case king."

Chop: When no players have called the blind bets and the two players in the blinds choose to take their bets back rather than play out the hand.

Coins/Coin-In: The number of credits in the game's denomination that are played in one hand.

Cold Call: To call a raise without having already called a bet.

Commission: The amount that the house takes on a winning Pai Gow Poker hand. This is usually 5 percent of the player's winnings.

Copy Hand: If both the player and the banker get the same or identical hands, then this is called a "copy." In the event of an exact match between hands, the tie goes to the banker.

Counterfeited: The board pairs one or more of your hole cards that you were using to make the low hand, rendering your hand worthless.

Credits: When used to define the amount played per hand, "credits" means the same as "coins/coin-in." Credits can also refer to the total amount of money residing in the machine.

***Deal* Button:** The button on a video poker game that causes the first five cards of a video-poker hand to be dealt. On most video-poker machines the *draw* button will also deal the first five cards of a video-poker hand.

Denomination: The amount of money that defines one credit on a video-poker or slot machine. Common denominations for video poker include 1¢, 5¢, 25¢, 50¢, $1, $2, $5, $10, $25, $100, $500, and $1,000.

Deuce: Deuce is another name for a two (2) in a video-poker hand. A two is sometimes also called a "duck."

Discard: To throw away or not keep. Video-poker players select the cards they want to keep. The cards they do not select are discarded when they hit the *draw* button.

Dragon Hand: At some Pai Gow Poker games, all players have the option to play a second hand, which is called a "dragon." A dragon is considered in this game as a bonus bet. A dragon can be offered in turn to every player on the table as an added option. It can also work as a community hand.

***Draw* Button:** The button on a video-poker game that, when hit, completes a video-poker hand. Pressing the *draw* button will eliminate (discard) any of the five originally dealt cards that are not held and replace them with different random cards. The *draw* button will not deal a new video-poker hand.

Drawing Dead: Drawing to a hand that has no chance of winning.

Drowning on the River: Getting beat by a player who makes his drawing hand with the river card to beat you.

Duck: A colloquial term for a deuce or card with a rank of 2.

Edge: The percentage amount that the casino or player will take from the other over a long period of play. A video-poker machine that returns 99.54 percent of the money played has a casino (or house) edge of 0.46 percent. A video-poker game that returns 100.17 percent of money played has a player edge of 0.17 percent.

Even Money: Winning a hand and getting the money you originally bet back as the winning amount. It can also be called 1-for-1.

Five of a Kind: Five cards of the same rank. This can only be formed by using one or more wild cards.

Flop: The first three community cards that are turned over at the same time.

Flush: A video-poker hand that contains cards of the same suit, such as diamonds or spades.

Fold: To cease play by throwing in your hand.

Fortune Pai Gow Poker: A side bet in Pai Gow Poker that pays based on the value of the player's seven cards. It doesn't matter how the player sets his hand. The typical minimum for the fortune bonus is $1. In addition, if another player has a four of a kind or better, the player making the fortune bet will get an "envy bonus." In most casinos there is usually a $5 minimum required to qualify for the envy bonus.

Four of a Kind: Four cards of the same rank, such as four kings or four 3s.

Free Ride: Randomly shows up for a short period in place of a card in Multi-Strike Poker. It then is replaced by a regular card. When this happens, this hand gets a "free ride" to the next level of play for twice the return of the current level.

Full House: A five-card hand having both a three of a kind and a pair.

Full-Pay: The highest-paying and normally original version of a video-poker game. Most full-pay video-poker games return at least 99 percent with some returning more than 100 percent.

Gap: Used with straights and straight flushes, a gap is a "hole" in the sequence. The sequence 3, 4, 6, 7 has one gap—the 5. The sequence 3, 5, 7 has two gaps—the 4 and 6.

Hand: Five cards played until they win or lose. In video poker the player normally is dealt five cards and can then select which cards to save and replace the rest, leaving the final set of five cards. This is considered one hand.

High Card: A high card is a card of any rank that, when combined with another of the same rank, would make a pair high enough to win. In Jacks or Better, high cards are jacks through aces. In Kings or Better, they are kings or aces. In Nines or Better, the high cards are 9s through aces.

High Pair: A high pair is any pair that is high enough to win some money—usually it is even money (getting back what you bet). In a Jacks or Better game, it is a pair with the rank of jacks or higher. A pair of jacks, queens, kings, or aces would all be considered high pairs in a Jacks or Better game. In a Kings or Better game only a pair of kings or aces would be considered high pairs. In a Nines or Better game, a pair of 9s, 10s, jacks, queens, kings, or aces would be high pairs.

Hold **Button:** In video poker it is the button that is pressed to keep the associated card. Hitting this button once holds a card. Hitting it again releases the hold.

House Edge: The amount expressed as a percentage of total money played that the casino keeps over the long term.

House Way: The dealer in Pai Gow Poker is required to arrange his cards according to a set of fixed rules known as the "house way," the term that refers to the strategy used by all dealers in a casino when playing their hands.

Inside: Used with straights and straight flushes, it means there are one or more gaps in the sequence.

Jackpot: Usually the top pay of any video-poker game. However, some video-poker games have several very large pays that are also sometimes called "jackpots."

Kicker: Select fifth cards that, when combined with select four-of-a-kind hands, pay a bonus. In Double Double Bonus Poker, four aces with a kicker of 2, 3, or 4 pays 400-for-1.

Kings or Better: Video-poker games where a pair of kings or higher is required before winning anything.

Joker: In Pai Gow Poker this is an unranked card that can be used to make a straight or flush in the five-card hand. If not used to make up a straight or a flush, it is ranked as an ace. Five Aces (four aces and the joker) is the highest possible five-card hand.

Lop-Lop: Literally means "nothing-nothing." Refers to a poor hand in Pai Gow Poker that has nothing in the two-card hand and nothing in the five-card hand.

Low Card: Any card that, when combined with a card of the same rank, will not win anything. In Jacks or Better Poker, 2s through 10s are low cards.

Low Pair: Any pair that does not win any money. In Jacks or Better, pairs of 2s through 10s are low pairs.

Muck: The pile of discarded and folded hands along with the burn cards. To muck your hand means to fold.

Multidenomination: A video-poker game that can be played at different money levels. Common denominations for multidenomination games are 5¢/10¢/25¢, 25¢/50¢/$1, and $1/$2/$5.

Multi-Game: A video-poker game where the player can select one of several different games to play. Some multi-game machines even include non-video poker games such as keno, blackjack, or slot-type games.

Natural: Any hand that is made without the help of a wild card. A natural royal flush would contain a suited ace, king, queen, jack, and 10.

n-for-1: A method of representing the return of a winning hand in video poker. A high pair normally pays 1-for-1, meaning you win whatever you bet—you get your money back. Most table games display the odds at *n*-**to**-1. A winning 1-**to**-1 bet would return twice the player's bet—the original bet plus an amount equal to the original bet. By displaying returns in the *n*-for-1 format, it appears the player is getting more than actually happens.

Nines or Better: A video-poker game where the lowest winning hand is a pair of nines or higher.

Not So Ugly Deuces (NSUD): A short-pay variation of Deuces Wild Poker with a return of 99.73 percent. The original full-pay version returns 100.76 percent, so the 99.73 percent return is not as good but also "not so ugly."

Not So Ugly Ducks (NSUD): The same as Not So Ugly Deuces. It just sounds cooler.

Nuts: The "nuts" is the best hand that can be made from the cards on the board and the cards in a player's hand. If you had an ace-high flush, you would have the nut flush.

Open: Used with straights and straight flushes, it means there are no gaps in the sequence and a sequence of five cards can be completed by adding cards on either or both ends of the sequence. Examples of open straights are: 2, 3, 4, 5; 8, 9, 10, J; 3, 4, 5. There are certain sequences that might be thought of as open straights when, in reality, they are inside straights. Consider the sequence A, K, Q, J. There are four cards in sequence, but the five-card sequence can only be completed with a 10. If the sequence were K, Q, J, 10, it would be an open straight because the five-card sequence can be completed with an ace or a 9. What about the sequence K, Q, J? Is this an open or an inside straight? In order to be considered a fully open straight, the five-card sequence *must* be able to be completed with cards on either or both ends of the initial sequence. Since there is room for only one card on the high side of this three-card sequence (the ace), this is an inside straight with one gap. This is an important concept to master when using strategy charts, as the odds of completing an inside straight or inside straight flush are much less than the odds of completing an open straight or open straight flush. Interpreting your dealt hand improperly will cause errors in play and ultimately cost you money.

Optimum: Generally used when describing strategy. Optimum strategy balances the complexity (and therefore difficulty in playing) of the exact strategy with the amount that is lost by playing something different to generate a strategy that is extremely close to perfect but is still playable.

Overcard: One or both of your pocket cards that are higher than any of the cards on the board.

Overpair: A pocket pair that is higher than any of the cards on the board.

Pai Gow: The name of an ancient Chinese gambling game that is played with a set of Chinese dominoes referred to as "tiles." *Gow* means "nine" in Chinese, and "pai gow" loosely translates to "make nine" or "high nine." In the tile game a hand that scores nine is very good and almost unbeatable. Since a nine-high hand is the worst possible hand in Pai Gow Poker, players often refer to a poor hand as a "pai gow." They will often root for the dealer to get a "pai gow" because they want the dealer's hand to "make nine."

Pai Gow Poker: A poker game that's loosely based on the Chinese game Pai Gow. But unlike the Chinese game, it is played with cards instead of dominos, using poker combinations. The ranking in Pai Gow Poker varies from the rankings in standard five-card casino poker only in the fact that A, 2, 3, 4, 5 is the second-highest straight behind the highest straight of A, K, Q, J, 10.

Pair: Two cards of the same rank. For example, the king of spades and the king of diamonds, or the 3 of hearts and the 3 of clubs are pairs.

Paint Cards: Kings, queens, and jacks, which are also called "face cards." You can easily spot a face card by the amount of colors and distinguish it from the other cards.

PAR Data Sheet: Contains all the information required to determine the return of reel-type and video-slot machines. This information is not for the general public and is closely guarded, making it impossible for the normal casino player to know the return of slot machines.

Payback: The amount the player is "paid back" for his play at a machine. *Payback* and *return* are synonymous.

Penalty: A penalty makes a hand less valuable. There can be straight, flush, or high-card penalties. A straight penalty is when one of the cards you are discarding would help make a straight. A flush penalty is when one of the cards you are throwing away would help make a flush. It is sometimes advantageous to throw away a card that would help make a straight or a flush in the hopes of making a more profitable hand. If the term "penalty" is used without specifying whether it is a straight, flush, or high-card penalty, then any type of penalty counts.

Pick-a-Pair Poker: A variety of video-poker game where the original deal produces two cards faceup and two card piles of three each with the top card faceup. The player must select one of the two piles of three cards.

Pick 'Em Poker: The same as Pick-a-Pair poker.

Player: The player is up against the banker and no one else at the table.

Player Edge: The amount expressed as a percentage of total money played that the player wins after playing a game over the long term. Certain video-poker games with the proper pay schedules are among the very few games that have a positive player edge.

Pocket Cards: Your two personal cards that are dealt to you facedown. Also known as "hole cards."

Pot Odds: The relationship between the money in the pot versus the amount of money it will cost you to continue in the hand.

Push: When the banker wins one hand and the player wins the other hand in Pai Gow Poker. It results in a tie with no exchange of money on the hand.

Quad: Colloquial term for a four of a kind.

Quartered: When two players split the low half of the pot, we refer to it as getting "quartered," as you will only win a quarter of the pot.

Raise: To make a bet that is double the size of the bet made by the previous bettor.

River: The fifth and last community card turned over on the board.

Royal Flush: An ace-high straight flush such as the ace, king, queen, jack, and 10 of hearts.

Runner-Runner: When the turn and river card make a winning hand for a player that would have been a loser otherwise. See *Backdoor*.

Set: Three of a kind when you have a pair in the pocket.

Showdown: At the end of the final round when all players remaining in the hand turn over their cards to determine the winner.

Side Pot: A pot that is formed after a player goes all in. This pot cannot be won by the all-in player.

Slow Play: To weakly play a strong hand by calling or checking instead of raising. This is done to conceal the strength of your hand.

Smooth Call: To call a bet rather than raise the pot.

Straight: Cards in sequence—for example, 4, 5, 6, 7, and 8. The cards can be of mixed suits and can be in any sequence as long as they could be arranged from low to high without any gaps. In most cases the ace can be counted as the lowest card in a sequence (A, 2, 3, 4, 5) or the highest card in a sequence (10, J, Q, K, A).

Straight Flush: This is a hand of the same suit where the cards are in sequence. An example would be the 5, 6, 7, 8, and 9 of clubs.

Strategy: When referring to playing video poker, it is the list of cards to save from the originally dealt hand. It is used to maximize the player's return when playing video poker.

Suited: All of the cards mentioned are of the same suit—hearts, diamonds, clubs, or spades.

Three of a Kind: Three cards of the same rank, such as three kings or three 3s.

Trip: As used in this book, a trip is leaving home base, visiting one or more casinos, and returning to home base. It can be a few hours or several days or weeks.

Trips: Three of a kind where a pair is on the board and the third card is one of your pocket cards.

Turn: The fourth community card turned over on the board.

Two Pairs: Any hand that contains two separate pairs, such as 3388, 5522, KKJJ.

Ugly Deuces: A short-pay version of Deuces Wild Poker that returns 98.98 percent of money played. The original full-pay version of Deuces Wild pays 100.76 percent, and the Not So Ugly short-pay version returns 99.76 percent, so 98.98 percent is much lower.

Ugly Ducks: Same as Ugly Deuces—just sounds better.

Undercard: A card in your hand smaller than the highest card on the board.

Underpair: A pocket pair smaller that the lowest card on the board.

Variance: A mathematical number that is used as an indication of how large swings (both up and down) in the bankroll will be. It is the square of something called a "standard deviation," which, for the purposes of this book, need not be explained. All you need to know is that the higher the variation, the wilder the bankroll swings.

Volatility: A nonmathematical way of expressing the up-and-down swings in bankroll. Higher volatility means higher variance, which means large swings in bankroll.

Wild Card: A card that can be used as any other card. In Deuces Wild, the deuce is a wild card. In Joker Poker, the joker is a wild card.

Wild Royal Flush: A royal flush that is made with the help of a wild card. It pays much less than a natural royal flush because it is much easier to make.

About My Books

First come visit my web site at www.frankscoblete.com.

This will seem self-defeating, but some of the information in some of my early books has become outdated, and that information has been updated in my current books. I would not recommend, for example, *Victory at Video Poker* as many, if not most, of the machines are long gone. *Everything Casino Poker: Get the Edge at Video Poker, Texas Hold'em, Omaha Hi-Lo, and Pai Gow Poker!* has all the new video poker games that players can actually get an edge on.

Beat the Craps Out of the Casinos and *Golden Touch Dice Control Revolution* have been totally surpassed by *Casino Craps: Shoot to Win!* (the most comprehensive book ever written about craps) and *Cutting Edge Craps: Advanced Strategies for Serious Players!* The *Golden Touch Blackjack Revolution* has also been surpassed by *Beat Blackjack Now!* So why do such things happen? Because I learn as I go. I know more about the games now than I did way-back-when and/or I have decided to make some books far more comprehensive. New things have happened in gambling—for example the amazing speed count in blackjack.

So I have taken the liberty of saying what I think of some books—and why I recommend that you buy them only as collector's items. As much as I love having people read all of my works, I want my readers to know what's what. (One exception: my wife, the Beautiful A.P., must read all my works.)

If I say that some games can actually be beaten, that means players *literally* can get an edge over the house. The books that teach you how to get a real edge have ***

If you want to order by phone, call 1-800-944-0406.

Current Books by Frank Scoblete

The Virgin Kiss
(A lifetime of my great adventures—non-gambling book.)

***Everything Casino Poker: Get the Edge at Video Poker, Texas Hold'em, Omaha Hi-Lo, and Pai Gow Poker!*

***Casino Craps: Shoot to Win!*

***Slots Conquest: How to Beat the Slot Machines!*
(Yes, some slot machines can actually give the player the edge.)

***Beat Blackjack Now: The Easiest Way to Get the Edge!*

***Casino Conquest: How to Beat the Casinos at Their Own Games!*

***Cutting Edge Craps: Advanced Strategies for Serious Players!*

Earlier works

***Forever Craps: The Five-Step Advantage-Play Method!*
(Has the full biography of the late Captain of Craps, the greatest craps player who ever lived and my mentor.)

***Best Blackjack!*
(Surpassed by *Beat Blackjack Now: The Easiest Way to Get the Edge!*)

Beat the Craps Out of the Casinos: How to Play Craps and Win!
(A true collector's item and my first book—all about the Captain and his methods. Not the best strategy book anymore.)

Break the One-Armed Bandits
(Still a good book but surpassed by *Slots Conquest: How to Beat the Slot Machines!*)

Spin Roulette Gold
(I have this information in *Casino Conquest: How to Beat the Casinos at Their Own Games!*)

***Guerrilla Gambling*
(Still a great book, but I think *Casino Conquest: How to Beat the Casinos at Their Own Games!* is somewhat better.)

Baccarat Battle Book
(Hard to find, but this information is in *Casino Conquest: How to Beat the Casinos at Their Own Games!*)

***The Captain's Craps Revolution*

The Craps Underground

Casino Gambling: Play Like a Pro in 10 Minutes or Less!
(Completely surpassed by *Casino Conquest: How to Beat the Casinos at Their Own Games!*)

***Golden Touch Blackjack Revolution
(All this information, plus an amazing amount more, is in *Beat Blackjack Now: The Easiest Way to Get the Edge!*)

Armada Strategies for Spanish 21
(Out of date. Much better strategies for game in *Beat Blackjack Now: The Easiest Way to Get the Edge!*)

The Morons of Blackjack
(Extremely short work during the dawn of my career.)

***Golden Touch Dice Control Revolution
(Surpassed by *Casino Craps: Shoot to Win!* and *Cutting Edge Craps: Advanced Strategies for Serious Players!*)

Bold Card Play: Caribbean Stud, Let It Ride, and Three-Card Poker
Victory at Video Poker
(Totally outdated.)

DVD
***Golden Touch: Beat Craps by Controlling the Dice with Frank Scoblete, Dominator, Jerry "Stickman," and Bill "Ace-10 Burton"

Frank Scoblete's Get the Edge Guides
I commissioned some of the best gambling writers in the country to produce books on the various games for my "Get the Edge Guides" series.

***77 Ways to Get the Edge at Casino Poker by Fred Renzey

***Get the Edge at Craps by Sharpshooter

Get the Edge at Roulette by Christopher Pawlicki

How to Win Millions Playing Slot Machines!...or Lose Trying by Frank Legato

***Get the Edge at Blackjack by John May

Thrifty Gambling by John Brokopp

(Surpassed by *Casino Conquest: How to Beat the Casinos at Their Own Games!*)

Internet Gambling Guide by John Brokopp
(Totally outdated.)

***Get the Edge at Low-Limit Texas Hold'em* by Bill Burton
(All this information and much more is in *Everything Casino Poker: Get the Edge at Video Poker, Texas Hold'em, Omaha Hi-Lo, and Pai Gow Poker!*)

The Lottery Book: The Truth Behind the Numbers by Don Catlin

The Experts' Guide to Casino Games by Walter Thomason
(Surpassed by *Casino Conquest: Beat the Casinos at Their Own Games!*)

Please note: If you are interested in reading my columns in various magazines, check out my "About Scobe" area of my web site at www.frankscoblete.com. Many of these columns do appear on my site. "About Scobe" will also give you more information about me.

EXPERIENCING
the ENNEAGRAM